WHO AM I?

WHAT AM I?

Searching for Meaning in Your Work

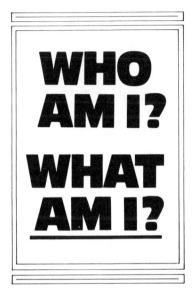

WHO
AM I?

WHAT
AM I?

CALVIN REDEKOP
URIE A. BENDER

**Academie
Books** Grand Rapids,
Michigan
Zondervan Publishing House

Who Am I? What Am I?: Searching for Meaning in Your Work
Copyright © 1988 by Calvin Redekop and Urie A. Bender

Academie Books is an imprint of Zondervan Publishing House,
1415 Lake Drive, S.E., Grand Rapids, Michigan 49506.

Library of Congress Cataloging in Publication Data

Redekop, Calvin Wall, 1925–
    Who am I? what am I? : Searching for Meaning in Your Work / Calvin
Redekop and Urie A. Bender.
        p.   cm.
    Bibliography: p.
    Includes index.
    ISBN 0-310-35581-8
    1. Work (Theology)   2. Vocation.   I. Bender, Urie A.   Title.
BT738.5.R43 1988
261.8'5—dc 19   88-14768
                                                                    CIP

Edited by Ruth Schenk
Designed by Jan M. Ortiz

Printed in the United States of America

88   89   90   91   92   93 / PP / 10   9   8   7   6   5   4   3   2   1

CONTENTS

Prologue:
A Parable of Life and Work

No man is born into the world whose work
Is not born with him: there is always work.
And tools to work withal, for those who will;
And blessed are the horny hands of toil!

(James Russell Lowell,
A Glance Behind the Curtain)

Yorgy died at University Medical Center, at the University of Minnesota, on July 20, 1980. "He was a model patient," said his specialist who, six weeks earlier, had done some complex heart surgery on "George." "A mellow man," the heart surgeon reflected further; "he appeared to me to have come to terms with life, but his heart had simply worn out."

Hard physical labor was the daily agenda during most of his life. His work companions remembered the way he would lead in tackling a job, whether it was excavating a basement for a church building in the Montana prairies or years later, leading a group of volunteers in cleaning up after a flood disaster in Minnesota. His feeble attempts at writing his own life story in broken English were laden with events such as his wedding, his move to Oregon from Montana to escape the depression and droughts, and the births of his children and grandchildren; but they were pathetically spare in reflections of how his mind worked.

In some sense, Yorgy is "every man"; an account of his life is the story of all of us. He took his turn "on stage" with a script which he tried to follow even though he didn't always understand it. Nor could he understand why all his efforts to follow the script yielded only failure. Of course, as is also true of us, Yorgy's script was written not only within and by himself—by his genes and by his choices; it was shaped just as powerfully by environment and events, particularly by a subculture which did not encourage self-conscious introspection, rather a dogged slogging along a track predetermined by tradition. From a general perspective, therefore, Yorgy's life is universal and instructive for all of us.

Yorgy was born July 2, 1900, in Petrowka, Ukraine, to God-fearing parents of Dutch descent. Generations of his ancestors had been farmers and his family followed the tradition. Yorgy had plowed with oxen from the time he was twelve years old. But when poor crops and bands of roving anarchists made the struggle to earn a living almost impossible—and life in general became precarious in Russia—Yorgy's father, an aggressive and stern head of the home, took his penniless family to the New World.

After three years of futile toiling in Saskatchewan, Yorgy's family trekked to Montana where they homesteaded on a section of prairie. Yorgy worked for his father until he was twenty-one, then married and started his own homestead a few "steppes" away. The dust-bowl depression pushed his young family mercilessly into desperate straits so, in 1937, he took his brood to the west coast to work in the fruit orchards in authentic OKIE style. With Yorgy in the lead, he and his family picked fruit during the day. At night the family was able to rest but, to survive, Yorgy also worked a night shift at a fruit drying plant nearby.

This diversion helped to provide some income but it seemed "working the land" was what everyone did, or should be doing. Somehow Yorgy managed to find an old used truck and transported his family back to southern Minnesota in the year of the big war (1940). They settled on a farm so run-down that no other farmer had even cared to bid on it. Single-mindedly, Yorgy and his faithful and hardworking wife struggled to meet each year's dread March 15 deadline for the annual mortgage payment to the insurance company in faraway New York City. Poor prices for oats and unproductive land as well as natural disasters—including a 1943 hail storm which appeared tragically to hit only his farm—seemed to have conspired against Yorgy's hard work for a better life.

At twenty-one, his oldest daughter married into one of the most "established" farm famlies in the area. For the first time in years, Yorgy's family felt a slight twinge of hope that at last things would get better. That hope was buried a year later when this daughter died in childbirth. Then the oldest son, whom Yorgy dreamt would help pay for the farm by becoming a partner, left to shape a "better life" by heading off to college. Yorgy and his wife never complained about this big disappointment. But soon after the son left, the family doctor told Yorgy he would have to leave the farm because of the growing pain in his back and recurring undulant fever.

At that point, it seemed that Yorgy's only option was to return to Oregon, where he could renew some connections made earlier. They returned, but by then deteriorating health would not allow employment of any kind. For some still unexplained reason, a friend encouraged him to enroll in a Dale Carnegie course being offered in the area. He did and the son in college began to notice a difference in the tone of his father's letters.

Within a year (1948), Yorgy took his wife and the remaining three children back to Minnesota—the scene of his earlier defeats. There, in the old community, he secured a job as a salesman for a local machinery dealership. Although he liked talking to people, he quickly became disillusioned with the deceptions the owner of the business tried to force on him. Consequently, he walked away from his first decent source of income in many years. Some of his farmer friends urged him to buy the dealer out, but Yorgy never seriously considered the possibility, for after all, "that would take a lot of money." Furthermore, he seemed to think that neither his mind nor his experience were equal to the demands of managing a business.

He was then offered a job as an area representative for a mutual insurance company. He accepted; he worked hard and conscientiously. By 1952 he had become the president and general manager of the entire organization. By 1972 when he retired, Yorgy had shaped this business into one of the most successful companies of its type.

There were other achievements in Yorgy's life. During this twenty-year period, the town and community was shaken with malfeasance in its government. A local group of citizens including a strong representation from the "coffee buddies" who met at Lola's every morning at 10:00 sponsored Yorgy as the write-in candidate for mayor. He won by a landslide without making a single speech. His humorous, candid, "back-home" style seemed to inspire the community, for he was reelected to office for three subsequent terms without campaigns or initiatives on his part. In fact, before each of the elections, local community supporters would have to take Yorgy to city hall to sign his name to the city clerk's roster of mayoral candidates.

During these years, Yorgy the mayor—as he became known—assumed a bit of a "father image" in this southwestern Minnesota town. Before long, he was thrust onto the public lecture circuit to make speeches on good government, community action and disaster responses—the latter, an activity for which he became the state coordinator. With his quaint Ukranian accent and his ready, colorful and sardonic wit, Yorgy became the delight of many more sophisticated people. They learned to love this uneducated (three grades in the Ukraine) philosopher-citizen. Even the local newspaper seemed to lapse into a strangely uncritical phase, in spite of some of his civic initiatives which challenged much of the hardened crust of tradition.

Yorgy's biography is not a typical success story. He rarely talked about achievement or personal triumph. For him, farming had been the criterion of success and there he had failed. Neither business nor community politics had ever "figured" in his imagination. He never fully understood why his children wanted to go to college; he only reluctantly agreed with his wife's dogged concern that her children get a college education so "they will not have to work as hard as we have." But when she died from leukemia at age 56, her death seemed to whisper to Yorgy's subconscious that the inner self must grow, that it must have a chance to take root and expand beyond itself.

Yorgy always left the vague impression that he had failed. According to his actions, he found it hard to believe his own children who insisted, "Dad, you are a gifted man. Break out of your mold and let yourself go." His response was always silence. Although he seemed unable to admit it, possibly not even to himself, he must have enjoyed his nonfarming work, especially in later years after the Dale Carnegie course, which seemed to free him to express his feelings.

The city clerk who worked under Yorgy's administration for four terms and also rode in the ambulance with Yorgy to the hospital just before his death, later told the family, "Since Yorgy is gone, I have often gone to the council chambers alone, sat in my chair at the right of the Mayor's chair, and thought: You know, Yorgy did good work, because he was the right person for the work he was given to do."

Soon after Yorgy died, the city clerk resigned, saying the spark had gone out of his job.

Introduction

The idea of work permeates our lives. From early childhood until late in life, work is a pervasive presence. The early mothering a little girl offers her doll at a tea table set for two includes make-believe baking—the result of work she has seen her mother do. The first pretendings of a young boy with his toy dump truck in a sandbox are modeled on work in the adult world. Older children also, whether through baby-sitting, delivering newspapers, or mowing lawns, seek work to shape a new independence. When cars and clothes lure teenagers, they learn quickly that work becomes a means to an end.

From the dawn of adulthood to the sunset years when muscles no longer respond and even the will to work becomes enfeebled, most men and women in every culture must deal with the issue of work in very real and practical terms. Every person will have work in one form or another, as long as life lasts or until some incapacity forces one to be served.

At one time, in our Western cultures, the work decision was comparatively simple. Indeed, an individual may have had little power to make a choice in the matter. Peasant children grew into peasant adults. A male child followed in his father's footsteps. Generally, a female child had only marriage, along with hard work in home or field, to look forward to or fear.

In some settings, not too many generations ago, a father chose one apprenticeship or another for his son. From that moment on, the die was cast for that child's work experience. We can only guess at the psychological or social burdens such a pattern may have created; however, with the decision made by a parent for a lifetime, choosing a vocation in early adulthood was not one of the burdens. Nor was a midlife crisis likely in those settings, forced by unemployment or caused by mind-numbing repetition, ethics, or simply new insights about the real meaning of life.

In some sense Yorgy, in our Prologue parable, was ahead of his time. He was assaulted by forces which blocked the fulfillment of his expected lifetime vocational pattern. Financial failure, poor health, even the times in which he lived demanded change. Yorgy changed but the changes and new settings for work were so foreign to the script he held in his hand that he never seemed quite able to believe that he was anything but a failure.

Actually, Yorgy's experiences prefigured the very elements many people today are facing. Suddenly, the scenario of work expectations has been altered drastically. Within a generation or two, the easy slide into one of several likely vocations has given way to a bewildering array of options. Within several decades, full employment for an expanded work force—including many women working outside the home for the first time—has been shattered by stubborn unemployment statistics, uncertain prospects, and breadlines in lands of plenty. In even less time, the beautiful dream of a satisfying lifetime spent in the career of one's choice has evaporated. It has been replaced by the threatening cloud of uncertainty or the dread specter of years of preparation wasted in a dead-end job tolerated only because it provides a regular paycheck.

Yorgy faced the shredding of his life's work script in the only way he knew how—making the best of what life offered. It is not clear that he ever understood the social forces at work or how correct were his responses or how awesomely his personal experiences became a microcosm of an era that would demand the same kind of flexibility in response from entire generations. Yet, along with the apparent lack of comprehension, Yorgy exhibited fundamental characteristics essential to the individual who faces change in the work setting:

1. a basic commitment to life even when the work script was confusing and discouraging;
2. a seemingly gut-level responsiveness to opportunity;
3. a contract of conscience to devote all his energies to the task at hand.

Reluctantly, it seemed almost against his will, Yorgy allowed himself to be drawn into opportunities that uncovered a range of potential never dreamed of simply because his overt gaze never strayed from the scripted agricultural expectations. In these opportunities Yorgy literally discovered a new life, new work settings, unexpected fulfillments and ever-widening fields of service.

Yorgy's life illustrates the two foci we are projecting in this book:

1. The search for meaningful work is personal, existential and deeply interwoven with the cultural and social elements of human existence.
2. The search for meaningful work starts early in life and will likely continue for most persons through an entire lifetime, perhaps never culminating in a fully satisfactory resolution.

However, in the same breath as it were, Yorgy's life also

illustrates that finding meaningful work is possible, even probable, and that it can happen almost in spite of oneself, or of awareness and conscious effort. Of course, Yorgy persisted in his dialogue with life and with opportunity, moving from one to another as his experiences broadened and prepared him for new challenges.

Like Yorgy, many individuals are faced with frightening changes in employment prospects in the workplace and in their personal lives through different kinds of dislocation. Understandably these people are looking at the issue of work with a new seriousness, varied degrees of anxiety, even with a sense of foreboding and urgency—as if understanding the meaning of work could dull the sharp edge of a nagging concern.

It is to these that the message of this book is addressed:

— the young adult still in a quandary about a first major career choice;
— the worker who is "fed up" with meaningless work, or a poor work setting, or ethical discomfort, and is searching for a solid foundation or principles on which to base new vocational decisions;
— the career person who was confident that a certain type of work or a particular position or a vocational track was secure; instead, economic uncertainties, environmental problems, labor unrest, or unemployment are forcing changes or at least demanding a new look at the workplace or the work experience;
— the individual facing a mid-life crisis; one who is asking questions about the meaning one should expect to find in work, even about life itself; or about work objectives and personal fulfillment; or about how work fits into the Christian scheme of things.

This book is also an attempt to look at the questions these groups are asking from a Christian perspective, using insights the social sciences offer. Our treatment of work, therefore, is rooted in two kinds of soil: the soil of a spiritual realm that identifies our partnership with God in his continuing work; also the soil of the earthy, human and cultural realm in which we live and work and where we seek to carry out divine purpose in a self-seeking world. We acknowledge that this task is not easy; indeed, attempting a view of work that embraces these two realms runs the huge risk of misunderstanding from all those whose strong focus is either one or the other.

A second risk relates simply to the incredible scope of a discussion about work. To tackle one of the most pervasive experiences of life as well as one of the most taken for granted topics and propose to create something helpful and interesting out of it may border on either foolhardiness or arrogance. Were it not for our strong desire to see both understanding and change, this risk alone would dissuade us. For throughout our work together on this subject, there have been multiple reminders that humility is the only stance for writers dealing with a subject so vast and pervasive.

A third risk increases our vulnerability greatly. That is the paradoxical need to ground our propositions in principles respected by the sociological community on the one hand and, on the other hand, to express those concepts through approaches and in language that is attractive and readily accessible to persons whose search is sincere but who have limited background in the scholarly discipline of sociology. Only the reader can judge whether either of these intentions has been realized.

Last, the seeming finality of a printed statement somehow appears to leapfrog dialogue which is so basic to community and common understandings. In other words we risk the appearance of an attempt at some kind of last word.

Nothing is farther from the truth. In fact, given the general paucity of Christian statements about work, along with the significance of work in the life of entire nations, we view these pages more in the nature of a first word. We will be highly gratified if our perceptions invite dialogue and, together with the responses from many readers and scholars, contribute to the redemption of work.

In our view, that is a most urgent concern. And we believe that the redemption of work will take place only as a moral reform develops which understands the nature of the crisis, and can motivate people to begin to make a change in their own situations and, subsequently, in the larger social context.

*   *   *

Several things remain to be said by way of introduction. The first has to do with the nature of the collaboration between Redekop, the professor, and Bender, the writer. Much of the material was researched and formulated originally for use in university classrooms. This final product reflects that initial effort along with the result of many discussions, some new writing, rewriting and editing. Successive drafts generated more discussion which led to more revisions. We bring our insights jointly, the product of many strenuous days made challenging, fulfilling and joyful by the opportunity to work together.

This format of collaboration was extended further through the willingness of a number of persons to share their personal experiences and personal viewpoints with our readers. These excursuses or diversions have become an integral part of the authors' effort to illuminate common understandings about work. Indeed, these varied perspectives have added incredible richness to the book and contributed greatly to its original purpose.

In the third place, as authors we must gratefully acknowledge the fine work of Rosemary Smith. With patience, an ever-ready smile and competence she has dealt with the idiosyncrasies of two authors through many changes and a number of versions. Her willing and winsome collaboration has helped to make this volume possible and has added to our own delight in working with each other during the course of shaping ideas into jointly expressed form.

Finally, our thanks to Conrad Grebel College. The administration has been most supportive of Dr. Redekop, a member of the faculty, during his work on this manuscript. They have accorded every courtesy to both authors, including technical assistance, the work of Pauline Bauman on early drafts, the facility provided by computer services and the contribution of a skilled operator.

Perhaps this theme of collaboration, so evident in the development of this manuscript on work, is the most eloquent testimony of the meaning and importance of community in carrying out a task.

BOOK ONE

A LAYMAN'S PRIMER ON WORK

1

Paradox and Dilemma

The bible legend tells us that the absence of labor—idle-ness—was a condition of the first man's blessedness before the Fall. Fallen man has retained a love of idleness but the curse weighs on the race not only because we have to seek our bread in the sweat of our brow, but because our moral nature is such that we cannot be both idle and at ease. An inner voice tells us we are in the wrong if we are idle. If man could find a state in which he felt that though idle he was fulfilling his duty, he would have found one of the conditions of man's primitive blessedness. (Tolstoy, *War and Peace:* 275.)

The definition of work is in a state of flux. While dictionary outlines remain essentially the same—*work*: noun, adjective, verb intransitive, verb transitive—the experience of work is undergoing vast transformations.

Trusted foundations in national economies have turned to quicksand. The plains of tradition in the workplace are overshad-owed, if not threatened, by peaks of new technology. Long-term expectations have tumbled into the abyss of obsolete products and redundant positions. The predictability of a career path has disappeared under an avalanche of new opportunities. The high-ways of customary preparation for clearly defined responsibilities suddenly lead nowhere. The usual certainties have been displaced by anxieties which gnaw at self-confidence, motivation, and pride in one's work.

The experienced worker halts, hesitatingly, at unfamiliar crossroads. Beside him, bewildered, stands the would-be worker fresh from the promise of completed training. Out of the drifting fog another figure gropes his way toward the signposts without arrows—the mid-life casualty torn from a secure position.

Any society includes those who are customarily thoughtful. Today, such are being joined by persons who have been forced into reflection through an unprecedented shifting in work definitions, norms and experience. The chapters that follow are addressed to those thoughtful ones who from personal necessity or out of deep concern for their fellows wish to join the authors in dialogue and search for ways to face the changes that engulf us.

Of course, these changes are not all external. Workers themselves have experienced changes as drastic as the workplace. Satisfaction in a job well-done is often replaced by sterile delight in the paycheck. *Punching out* at the end of a shift has become more important to many than *punching in*. More attention is focused on the length and frequency of coffee breaks, how soon one becomes eligible for four weeks of vacation and the quality of retirement benefits than on the work experience itself. That these facts are becoming increasingly pervasive points of paradox that must be addressed—paradox that is both intriguing and disquieting; paradox that, to some degree, has mired western society in its current dilemma with respect to work, employment and cultural well-being.

The Paradox

The paradox can be stated simply, although it has several different faces:

1. We find many kinds of work onerous so we applaud the new technologies which reduce or eliminate drudgery in work. At the same time we harbor a desperate fear of unemployment seemingly brought on by computers and robots—those children of technology.
2. We either suspect or are convinced that work is at the heart of meaningful human experience. At the same time, we support or participate in the massive institutional forces that exert every effort toward making work undesirable and unavoidable.
3. We acknowledge the need to work in order to make a living. At the same time, we hate the work forced upon us

by our desire for what has come to be known as the "good life."

These facets of the paradox are laden with pathos and irony. To stand on the threshold of a vaunted freedom from the onerous nature of work is one thing. To discover that the new day before us may well eliminate the necessary experience of work for many people is quite another. If this dawning reality has done nothing else, it has certainly laid starkly bare our strikingly inconsistent expectations: delighted with freedom from work but panic-stricken by the absence of work possibilities; wanting to be able to work but not wanting to work; searching urgently for meaning in life but turning away from one of the fundamental experiences through which meaning is found.

Responses to the growing sense of paradox and problem have been varied—ranging from indifference to militant concern about unsettling questions. For some, the end product of a substantial paycheck with which to purchase the good life justifies the means. The real costs of this prosperity, either to oneself or others, are simply ignored. As long as these real costs, in the form of unemployment, for example, do not affect one personally, indifference allows for comfort and self-satisfaction in the midst of revolution in the workplace.

The voices of militant concern tend to focus one's attention, but too often they become only voices crying in a wilderness of inattention and inertia. Many times also they focus on a symptom without dealing with the real malaise. During and following the recession of the early '80s, an obsession with creating jobs began to develop to the point in Canada where Canadian Catholic bishops recently defined the lack of employment as the greatest moral issue of our time.[1] While, in some circles, this concern has reached fever pitch, the drive toward replacing, deleting and robotizing work-places continues apace; not only that, it is considered to be the prerequisite for a recovery of our "march toward the great post-industrial civilization." Obviously, a major discontinuity is developing in our society between values and practice, between what we dread and what we experience. What has gone wrong?

Sociologists have characterized this paradox as having our cake but not wanting to eat it. Why complain about the lack of work, when that is what the dream was all about? According to the experts, we now have the reality of the dream, but we don't like it.[2] Our unthinking paths have led us into the frightening canyons of dilemma (See Table 1).

Table 1. Trends in the Labor Force: 1950 to 1984

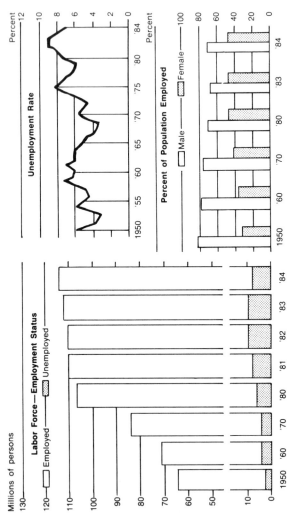

Source: Chart prepared by U.S. Bureau of the Census

Statistical Abstract of the United States, 1986: U.S. Dept. of Commerce.

Dilemma, Irony and the Real Problem

Paradox in the world of work has shaped, at least within the West, a human dilemma of profound proportions: needing work in order to live but often unable to find work one is able to live with!

Although one may approach the obvious malaise in contemporary society from various perspectives, there are few more fundamental than this incredible irony: that an activity so central to human life and well-being is abhorred. Until this underlying discontinuity is addressed, work in our Western world cannot become more meaningful and gratifying to men or women. As long as meaning is missing from work, our society will continue to experience more and more unhappiness.

Technology's increasingly sophisticated attempts to solve the problem by deleting more and more tasks because they seem meaningless will not succeed. These endeavors will only mire us deeper in the morass of misunderstanding as to what is truly significant about work. On the other hand, the scientific efforts to humanize work—as they have largely been developed in recent years—are also doomed to failure because their cures deal more with symptoms than the basic malaise; indeed, rather than providing cures, their faulty diagnoses and prescriptions tend to exacerbate the problem.

The absence of a clear definition of the problem not only allows for these unfortunate results; it also tends to cast employer and employee in confrontational roles. The long and distressing history of conflict between capital (managers) and labor (employees) derives from two basic facts: first, that the laboring person has not been happy about the work he or she was doing; secondly, and at the same time, the manager/owner has been trying to seduce or coerce the laborer to work as hard as possible. In all of this, they appear to be enemies of each other.

In fact, we believe that the enemy has been misidentified. It is our theory that in the massive ideological conflict brewing on a global scale, the enemy is not just oppressive capital. It is rather, or at least very significantly, the loss of meaning in work. This creates the fundamental ideological conflict and therefore creates enemies. In other words, it is not the communist ideology which is the source of the present ennui; the real enemy is the increased deterioration of the family-community-tribal context of work due to modernization.

Premised therefore on the way work is misused, we see emerging within Western culture a colossial alienation. With the coming of industrial technology and the bureaucratic revolution, work has become separated from its productive role in the community and thus has become hated and meaningless.[3] Because of the job holder's distaste for work, it has been further separated from the community. This vicious circle has unleashed a momentum which is best expressed in the unbelievable ambiguity we are witnessing today—*aggressive drives to make ever fewer jobs necessary in the face of massive unemployment.*

Millions of workers are being seduced into pursuing the benefits of work—dollars earned to buy the goodies that make for "a happy life"—but hating every minute of the work itself. It is this separation of work for a living, or work to earn money, from the broader and more generic sense of work as a human experience in the community that has created the alienation from work.

Even the casual observer of life witnesses this alienation. Anyone who has seen people streaming from a factory at the sound of the whistle knows how eager these workers are to exit the workplace. Added to this observation are the mountains of statistics which document the absenteeism, sabotage, low productivity and poor quality of contemporary economic life.[4]

As a result of this alienation, work (human labor) and capital (including technology and bureaucracy) are in mortal combat. Ultimately, one will be swallowed up by the other. Stephen Gaskin, one social prophet who has launched a major alternative lifestyle movement says,

> So now we have the phenomenon of the multinational corporation . . . The only thing that governs what they're doing is profit . . . A corporation is a soul-less entity which grows, reproduces, protects itself and makes policy, even though it isn't anybody . . . And so this is a time when there are demons and monsters loose upon the world. And their names are Exxon and General Motors and Phillips and Mobil and Ford and ITT and Anaconda . . . We can't fight those things . . . What we have to do is massively build an alternative culture. (Gaskin in Laurence: 304)[5]

This intriguing analysis points to another irony of incredible proportions: that working men and working women are looking for their salvation to the very gods that are bringing damnation upon them. The post-industrial order which includes the technological revolution, the multinational conglomerate, the super corporations and the robotization of production will not bring us to the golden age. Indeed, these powerful, twentieth-century gods are much more likely to visit chaos and destruction upon humankind than they are to bring peace and wholeness.

Can Society Be Redirected?

If it is true that our intended "saviors" have turned on us creating uncertainty and anxiety and chaos and crisis, what can be done? Can society be redirected? Are there prophets of hope? Whose are the voices that can offer some understanding and direction? If direction is provided, can we summon the will to act? Some would say it is too late; that the crisis is of such massive proportions that we are already paralyzed. How can the seemingly inexorable social, political, economic and technical forces be turned around? Is there truly hope that something can be done to shape a process as massive as the total redirection of human society?

Many people have spoken to the fundamental question as to how the direction of a society can be or should be shaped. As a result of energetic dialogue on this question, several basic positions have emerged. The *evolutionary* position is the most prevalent; this view states that the evolutionary process determines the direction of society. With the evolutionary view there are two general stances: the *pragmatic* which assumes that the evolutionary process itself determines what is right, and the *ethical* which states that with evolving intelligence, humanity is obligated to give direction to the evolution of society. This latter position implies some objective "truth" by which the force of change should be directed; needless to say, this view has created unending discussion and conflict.

Another position is the *idealist* approach which suggests that society's direction is the result of ideas and their consequences. This also has at least two branches: the *Hegelian idealists,* who maintain that it is ideas which result in social forms; and the *pragmatists* who maintain that material existence creates the ideas which then are rationalized and made to seem reasonable. The Marxist system would be an example of the pragmatic idealists. Conflict sociologists would typify a variant of the former. The works of P. A. Sorokin represent an attempt to indicate the interaction of these two forces in the development of society.

Another view regarding what determines the direction of society is the *moral* one; this assumes that the decisions of people in actual life situations determine what will happen to the direction society takes. This orientation would hold that there is nothing irrevocably predetermined by structures or institutions and that, at every step, it is a human who stands in the gap and must decide. This view is further divided into two camps: the secular wing represented in the *Great Man* theory which places significant persons at pivotal points in history. A religious wing of this view is the *Judeo-Christian tradition* which, though admitting the presence and influence of "principalities and powers," assumes that the moral actions of a person determine faith*ful*ness or faith*less*ness to God.

This position represents the core of our approach to a discussion of work. We believe that the moral approach to our dilemma can yield positive results. Indeed, we would insist that blind adherence to other materialistic and philosophic approaches have brought us to near-bankruptcy.

Of course, it should be emphasized that much has been accomplished through various efforts to humanize society so that work itself can become more redemptive; without a doubt more can still be done. These attempts to reform our societal institutions are commendable and should be supported wherever and whenever possible.

However, it is the thesis of this book that, ultimately, these efforts alone are inadequate, that society's direction cannot be corrected from within. It is our conclusion and conviction that the moral perspective represents the only approach through which the "principalities and powers" can be directed so that humankind will be honored and nurtured so, in turn, each person fulfills God-given destiny and purpose. The socio-political, economic and technical forces which are imprisoning humans can only be brought into harmony by a moral view of history and by a moral response to the general "lostness" of human society. It is this position, we believe, that offers the hints of hope which do exist.

Hints of Hope

At the risk of appearing both glib and arrogant, we suggest that what is so urgently needed can be accomplished by the rediscovery of the meaning of work and its reintegration into the family, neighborhood and community context.

That is not an easy task; it is clear that much dialogue and joint action is required to make possible the redemption of work. Indeed, the road back to certain basics is long and torturous, exceedingly difficult and painful. How difficult and painful will be reflected more fully in the chapters that follow. But in spite of the realisms which must be acknowledged—and the unsettling questions which must be faced—we believe that at the least in our own workplaces *it is possible to begin the necessary process of redeeming work* and *restoring it to its rightful place in our lives.*

Earlier we referred to unsettling questions as one kind of response to the paradox and dilemma in which we find ourselves. It may well be that such questions hold the most promise for change. Obviously there are many more than these several which follow:

1. How can one speak about the humanization of work when
   people are simply being declared redundant?
2. Has man's prowess, creativity and technological discoveries
   brought into being and set in motion forces that will
   destroy his humanness?[26]
3. Is Western civilization now beginning to discover the price
   tag for its commitment to materialism?

We think that questions such as these should be followed by
others which, while still stark in their implications, do open the
door somewhat to hints of hope. Questions like: Is meaningful
work obsolete or can it be redeemed? Is the workplace only a
graveyard of ideals and creativity or can it become one man's
opportunity for personal fulfillment? Are men and women only
victims or can they act upon their work environment in ways that
restore their gift of choice from God?

It is the hints of hope present in these latter questions that
foreshadow the central message of our book. However, before we
reach that "break in the clouds" it seems essential to lay certain
foundation stones and to explore with great care and somewhat
focused vision the "lay of the land" in which we live during this
short eve of the twenty-first century.

That "lay of the land" perception is realized in several ways.
The first chapters comprising Book 1 represent an attempt to erect
certain signposts, particularly for the reader who may be less
familiar with the breadth of the problem, with the methods of
sociological analysis and with the jargon of a discipline that has
worked seriously and quite successfully to understand how our
societies function and why they break down. We are convinced that
the clarities which the scholarly discipline of sociology has to offer
deserve to be brought to a wider audience—especially in an area of
concern so pervasive as work. We are also convinced that workers
have much to offer from their own experience toward further
understandings about work and, therefore, deserve to participate in
the dialogue. We trust that Book 1, "A Layman's Primer on
Work," will be seen as an encouragement to that end, rather than as
a condescending nod to a popular audience.

Admittedly, this quick scanning of the past and essential
glimpses into the field of sociology is limited. But it will hopefully
provide a window into Book 2—"The World of Work." Here, in
the heart of the book, we have tried to outline some of the more
urgent issues confronting workers today.

A unique feature of this book is the *excursuses* found throughout Book 2. In this setting, each excursus* is a digression from the
ongoing processes of description and argument—a digresssion

*literally, *outside the course*

which takes the form of a personal testimony about each writer's experiences of work. They reflect highly personalized, honest attempts to deal with work and life in as integrated a fashion as possible. In some cases, these excursuses are tightly linked to, and illustrative of, the chapters they follow. In other cases, they are less particular but still very significant to the entire discourse on work.

Book 3 focuses particularly on work and the kingdom of God; a concern that we believe should engage the attention and commitment of every disciple of Christ. In Book 4 we present a poetic collage from one who has worked hard with heart, soul and body. We believe it is a fitting capstone to a volume on work.

Finally, the authors emphasize their desire that the reader will view these pages as the initiation of dialogue with a wide variety of readers—an initiation of dialogue to which response is most welcome.

2

The Evolution of Work in Society

> The quality of work, rather, is determined by and in turn determines the nature of society. Thus, for any society, if we understand the essential quality of its work, we will better understand the essential nature and purposes of its social organization, and if we understand the essential nature and purposes of its social organization, we will better understand the essential quality of its work. (Pfeffer: 2)

A focus on paradox and dilemma, by itself, could hobble our search for answers with frustration and despair. And yet facing and understanding something about the current workplace realities becomes a foundation from which to view possible change; indeed, acknowledging both paradox and dilemma, as well as frustration and despair, becomes the first step in the movement toward a coherent Christian position on work.

Of course, other understandings are also important—among them those which may be gained through a quick sketch of religious history relating to work and a few beginning glimpses of the sociological perspective. Perhaps the best way to view these glimpses of introductory background is through a series of windows; like motion picture frames following each other in sequence. In history there has been a progressive formulation or evolution of perceptions about work in society.

Historically, work was undifferentiated.

As Durkheim, Toennies, and others informed us a half century ago, earlier societies reflected *Gemeinschaft*, a communal definition of the good society. Of course, there were obvious variations but, except for the functions clearly determined by sex in certain cultures, a person worked in a family setting—a clear example of the simplest form of *Gemeinschaft*—contributing generally as a hunter, wood gather, weaver, food preparer and the like, or in other roles that contributed to the well-being of the family. In the average community, work roles were simply extensions of the family system, with the added specializations of protection of the community, tribe or clan, and its survival, such as the search for new hunting grounds.

In all of this, however, there existed a central, inescapable fact: the work that individuals did for the physical, social and spiritual survival of the community was *undifferentiated work*. Work was not segregated on the basis of whether it was necessary for the social maintenance of a family, or whether it was a spiritual activity for the benefit of the individual or community. In other words, there were no specific "jobs," only work in general. In addition, the sharp distinction between work and leisure was largely absent.

An example from New Guinea provides an excellent picture of the *Gemeinschaft* type of society:

> It is important for us to understand from the outset that family ties, wider obligations to kinsfolk and to neighbors, loyalty to chiefs and elders, respect for clan taboos and beliefs in control of food and other things by spirits, ancestors, and gods can all play their part in this (work and wealth) system . . . When the work itself calls for industry, or even haste, they respond, but this response is always within the sphere of the needs of the task; again they frequently find other occupations for their spare time. *But a general responsibility to be busy does not lie on them* (Firth: 73–74).

Work must always be seen in the larger context, not the least being the economic organization. Where an economic organization is underdeveloped and dominated by traditional and spirit forces, as this one was, work is rather undifferentiated from community activities (Neff: 52).

Primitive societies are worthy of note, particularly during this time when consciousness is being raised regarding sexism in the workplace. In most traditional societies, work was somewhat different for each sex. In spite of that, however, a crucial characteristic is always present: that is, the integration of work roles within the family, community and tribal setting, whether male or female. *Women's and men's work roles—however they may have been specialized sexually—were not separated socially, geographically or relationally from the larger community.* Accordingly, both were *valued equally* in the workplace, and that not least because value was then not being determined by monetary returns.

Work has now become differentiated from the family, kinship and community.

Traditionally, as has been shown, work was closely related to family and community life, both spatially and otherwise. This was true even when variations between cultures and situations are taken into account. However, for twentieth-century people living in North America, work has become drastically differentiated, specialized and separated from family and community. Furthermore, female work has become segregated from male work in specialization, location and space, and with relation to the community and tribe (See Table 2).[1]

Generally women have remained within the home carrying out most of the work necessary to keep the family functioning, whether it is on the farm or in suburbia. Urbanization has meant that woman's work has become separated from the larger extended family and the community but, in spite of the recent movement of women into the labor force, it is still less specialized and "job related."[2]

Work for the male has undergone an almost total revolution since early times. His work is spatially separated from his family and from his kinship or tribal unit, and from the neighborhood in which he lives. It is frequently so specialized that his children, extended family, community and kinship group do not understand exactly what he does. Work is typically seen as a specialty. Specialization means simply that one's away-from-home subcommunity is composed of persons who do the same work, have the same training and skills and share the same orientations and values.

The social connections of work have also been changed through the intervention of technology and automation. Service workers and production workers relate more to machines than to people: hence these workers often feel the need to increase the "extra-job" settings or times when they can interact with people. Even managerial positions demand large amounts of time working with telephones, dictaphones, computers and papers or sitting in conferences where the people involved play roles representing interests rather than themselves. All of this makes them less susceptible to normal relationships and usual forms of social interaction. In all this, work has been separated from its family,

Table 2. Civilian Labor Force and Participation Rates, by Race, Sex, and Age, 1970 to 1984, and Projections, 1990 and 1995

[Persons 16 years old and over. Labor force data are annual averages of monthly figures. Rates are based on annual average civilian noninstitutional population of each specified group and represent proportion of each specified group in the civilian labor force. See also Historical Statistics. Colonial Times to 1970, series D 42–48]

Race, Sex, and Age	Civilian Labor Force (millions)							Participation Rate (percent)						
	1970	1975	1980	1983	1984	1990	1995	1970	1975	1980	1983	1984	1990	1995
Total[1]	82.8	93.8	106.9	111.6	113.5	125.0	131.4	60.4	61.2	63.8	64.0	64.4	66.9	67.8
White	73.6	82.8	93.6	97.0	98.5	107.7	112.4	60.2	61.2	64.1	64.3	64.6	67.3	68.1
Male	46.0	50.3	54.5	55.5	56.1	59.2	60.8	80.0	78.7	78.2	77.1	77.1	77.4	77.0
Female	27.5	32.5	39.1	41.5	42.4	48.5	51.6	42.6	45.9	51.2	52.7	53.3	58.1	60.0
Black[2]	9.2	9.3	10.9	11.6	12.0	13.6	14.8	61.8	58.8	61.5	61.5	62.2	64.5	65.4
Male	5.2	5.0	5.6	6.0	6.1	6.7	7.3	76.5	71.0	70.6	70.6	70.8	70.4	70.5
Female	4.0	4.2	5.3	5.7	5.9	6.9	7.6	49.5	48.9	53.2	54.2	55.2	59.0	61.2
Male	51.2	56.3	61.5	63.0	63.8	67.7	70.0	79.7	77.9	77.4	76.4	76.4	76.5	76.1
16–19 years	4.0	4.8	5.0	4.3	4.1	4.1	4.0	56.1	59.1	60.5	56.2	56.0	62.3	62.9
16 and 17 years	1.8	2.1	2.1	1.6	1.6	1.7	1.8	47.0	48.6	50.1	43.2	43.5	51.0	52.7
18 and 19 years	2.2	2.7	2.9	2.7	2.5	2.5	2.3	66.7	70.6	71.3	68.6	68.1	73.2	74.4
20–24 years	5.7	7.6	8.6	8.6	8.6	7.2	6.5	83.3	84.5	85.9	84.8	85.0	84.4	84.1
25–34 years	11.3	14.2	17.0	18.0	18.5	19.6	18.1	96.4	95.2	95.2	94.2	94.4	93.7	93.1
35–44 years	10.5	10.4	11.8	13.4	14.0	17.5	19.4	96.9	95.6	95.5	95.2	95.4	95.6	95.3
45–54 years	10.4	10.4	9.9	9.7	9.8	11.1	13.8	94.3	92.1	91.2	91.2	91.2	91.3	91.1
55–64 years	7.1	7.0	7.2	7.1	7.1	6.4	6.3	83.0	75.6	72.1	69.4	68.5	65.5	64.5
65 years and older	2.2	1.9	1.9	1.8	1.8	1.8	1.7	26.8	21.6	19.0	17.4	16.3	14.9	13.3

Table 2 (continued)

Race, Sex, and Age	Civilian Labor Force (millions)							Participation Rate (percent)						
	1970	1975	1980	1983	1984	1990	1995	1970	1975	1980	1983	1984	1990	1995
Female	31.5	37.5	45.5	48.5	49.7	57.3	61.4	43.3	46.3	51.5	52.9	53.6	58.3	60.3
16–19 years	3.2	4.1	4.4	3.9	3.8	3.8	3.8	44.0	49.1	52.9	50.8	51.8	56.8	58.2
16 and 17 years	1.3	1.7	1.8	1.5	1.5	1.5	1.6	34.9	40.2	43.6	39.9	41.2	46.2	48.0
18 and 19 years	1.9	2.4	2.6	2.4	2.4	2.3	2.2	53.5	58.1	61.9	60.7	61.8	66.5	68.9
20–24 years	4.9	6.2	7.3	7.5	7.5	7.0	6.8	57.7	64.1	68.9	69.9	70.4	78.1	82.0
25–34 years	5.7	8.7	12.3	13.8	14.2	16.8	16.3	45.0	54.9	65.5	69.0	69.8	78.1	81.7
35–44 years	6.0	6.5	8.6	10.2	10.9	15.0	17.4	51.1	55.8	65.5	68.7	70.1	78.6	82.8
45–54 years	6.5	6.7	7.0	7.1	7.2	8.7	11.1	54.4	54.6	59.9	61.9	62.9	67.1	69.5
55–64 years	4.2	4.3	4.7	4.9	4.9	4.6	4.7	43.0	40.9	41.3	41.5	41.7	41.5	42.5
65 years and over	1.1	1.0	1.2	1.2	1.2	1.3	1.3	9.7	8.2	8.1	7.8	7.5	7.4	7.0

[1]Beginning 1975, includes other races not shown separately.
[2]For 1970, Black and other.

Source: U.S. Bureau of Labor Statistics Employment and Earnings monthly: and Monthly Labor Review, November 1983.

tribal and community context. *Work has become specialized and abstracted to become that which one does in a job.* The job or position defines the type of work that is to be done and how, where, when, and with whom the work is to be done.

The nonremunerative, spontaneous, casual, relaxed and indefinite aspects of work have been exchanged for an abstracted entity which becomes a means to some other end such as remuneration or status. Work has become the job; when one is not on the job, one is "doing leisure." This division and distinction has become so clearly drawn that the dimension or experience of pleasure has been withdrawn totally from work and associated exclusively with leisure. At the same time, hobbies have emerged with a vengeance as "enjoyable work." To increase the confusion, hobbies are classed as leisure because one is *not forced to do* leisure, while one *must do* the work related to a job.

There is another significant sense in which work has become separated from the person doing it. Work has become objectified as something outside of and different from the person performing it. There is no merit in repeating what has already been elaborated in every conceivable way by Marx. The essence of Marx's viewpoint is simply that the human ability to work has become abstracted from the person to become something he can barter or sell to a buyer.

Hence the family, community and kinship have no direct claim on, interest in, or benefit from the work the individual is doing—other than the paycheck. This is in stark contrast to the traditional context where there was no distinction between the worker and work, and where the idea of unemployment (a person being unable to work even if wanting to) was not even present in the vocabulary.

The job has become the means to status and security.

Today, there are only a very few communities where the job is not a ticket into family, neighborhood or community status. In the Lengua society in Paraguay, for example, a person will eat even if he does not sell his labor (within our terms of reference his labor often is not saleable). He will retain an acceptable position in the family, in the extended tribe and in the community on the basis of other criteria.

In most of contemporary society, by contrast, a person's basic status, security, prestige and self-esteem are determined by his job—that is, by how valuable his work is perceived to be. Ibn Kaldun said that "the differences between different people arise out of differences in their occupations" (Anderson: 29). Another leading sociologist of work states, "A man's work is as good a clue as any to the course of his life, and thus his social being and identity" (Hughes: 7). These approaches tend to ignore other aspects of human worth, placing too much importance on the job itself.

With reference to identity then, a person *is* what he *does*. Almost invariably, in new situations, a person is introduced as a banker, student, preacher, or is given some other vocationally flavored tag. "What do you do?" is the question presumed to provide the most pertinent information about a stranger.

Hannah Arendt suggests that social structure hinges on the way human societies have evaluated the work that humans do and on how humans have been placed in the various sectors of societal work. Certain work became degraded when the powerful classes forced slaves and captured groups to do these tasks. That is, work inherently did not have differential status value; it rather became evaluated on the basis of who voluntarily or by force did which kind of work (Neff: 61).

Typically, a member of a traditional society was given status based on how well he learned the secrets of the warrior, or on how well he could repeat the rituals and magic incantations of the medicine man. There is no record that the amount of corn a tribal chief produced defined his status or prestige. However, in the contemporary United States, according to Neff, the meaning of work stands in sharpest contrast to its negative evaluation during the classical era in Greece and Rome.

Work has become a commodity.

At one time, work and the person were natural extensions of each other—inseparable and not quantifiable. When the barter economy gave way to a trade economy, a specialization began to develop which introduced the fatal separation of the person from his work.

In the traditional contexts we sketched above, work was a natural outworking of family, kin, and community membership. Today, Western industrialization and units of labor have changed work into something defined by contract. This quantifiable, contractually-defined activity we now call work is unitized so *it can be bought and sold to the highest bidder*. And the bidding is controlled by a law of the marketplace. According to Marx, the sum paid for work has been the replacement costs of labor—that is, what is required to keep the worker alive and able to perform his work.[3] Thus, work has changed from a natural and vital part of individual and community life to a commodity traded in the marketplace of a society (See Table 3).

Table 3. Labor Force, Employment, and Earnings

Occupations of the Work-Experienced Civilian Labor Force, by Sex: 1970 and 1980

[In thousands, except percent. As of April 1. Based on sample data from the census of population, subsample of 1970 data reclassified into the 1980 occupation classification system. The experienced civilian labor force includes the employed and the unemployed who have worked any time in the past. See text p. 388 and source, for details]

Occupation	Total		Male		Female		Female as a Percent of Total	
	1970	1980	1970	1980	1970	1980	1970	1980
Experienced civilian labor force, total	**79,802**	**104,058**	**49,455**	**59,754**	**30,347**	**44,304**	**38.0**	**42.6**
Managerial and professional	14,770	22,653	9,765	13,457	5,004	9,196	33.9	40.6
Executive, administrative, managerial[1]	5,970	10,379	4,868	7,210	1,102	3,169	18.5	30.5
Administrators and officials[2]	495	710	380	460	115	250	23.3	35.2
Managers Financial	220	410	178	281	43	129	19.4	31.4
Personnel and labor relations	65	220	51	141	14	79	21.2	36.0
Marketing, advertising, and public relations	433	689	399	567	34	122	7.9	17.6
Medicine and health	58	111	23	55	35	56	60.6	50.8
Properties and real estate	115	200	78	118	37	82	32.1	41.1
Managers and administrators, not elsewhere classified	2,762	5,233	2,340	3,825	422	1,408	15.3	26.9
Management-related occupations	1,693	2,617	1,310	1,618	384	999	22.7	38.2
Accountants and auditors	646	1,013	487	627	159	386	24.6	38.1
Professional specialty[1]	8,800	12,275	4,898	6,248	3,902	6,027	44.3	49.1
Architects	54	108	52	99	2	9	4.1	8.3
Engineers	1,249	1,401	1,228	1,336	21	65	1.7	4.6

Table 3 (continued)

Occupation	Total		Male		Female		Female as a Percent of Total	
	1970	1980	1970	1980	1970	1980	1970	1980
Mathematical and computer scientists	210	330	175	244	35	86	16.7	26.1
Computer systems analysts and scientists ...	108	203	93	158	15	46	13.6	22.5
Natural scientists	228	314	197	252	31	63	13.6	19.9
Health diagnosing[1]	452	647	416	571	36	76	8.0	11.8
Physicians	297	433	268	375	29	58	9.7	13.4
Teachers, postsecondary	511	637	362	404	148	233	29.1	36.6
Teachers, exc. postsecondary	2,956	3,722	872	1,087	2,084	2,635	70.5	70.8
Elementary school	1,510	2,319	243	570	1,267	1,750	83.9	75.4
Social scientists and urban planners	109	218	85	136	25	82	22.5	37.5
Lawyers	273	502	260	433	13	69	4.9	13.8
Technical, sales, and administrative support	23,048	30,884	9,450	11,002	13,598	19,882	59.0	64.4
Technicians and related support[1]	1,821	3,063	1,194	1,722	627	1,341	34.4	43.8
Health technologists and technicians	543	989	96	162	447	827	82.4	83.6
Engineering and related technologists and technicians ...	760	947	692	789	68	158	8.9	16.7
Science technicians	136	193	105	132	30	60	22.4	31.4
Computer programmers	163	318	124	219	39	99	24.2	31.2
Sales[1]	8,021	10,257	4,711	5,262	3,310	4,995	41.3	48.7
Supervisors and proprietors[3]	1,259	1,583	1,045	1,137	215	445	17.0	28.2
Sales representatives[4]	1,112	1,846	918	1,193	193	654	17.4	35.4
Sales workers, retail and personal services	4,534	5,499	1,719	1,807	2,814	3,693	62.1	67.1
Administrative support[1]	13,207	17,564	3,545	4,018	9,661	13,545	73.2	77.1
Supervisors	409	1,078	181	570	228	509	55.8	47.2
Computer equipment operators	169	421	99	172	70	249	41.5	59.2

Table 3 (continued)

Occupation	Total 1970	Total 1980	Male 1970	Male 1980	Female 1970	Female 1980	Female as a Percent of Total 1970	Female as a Percent of Total 1980
Adjusters and investigators[1]	354	531	215	200	139	332	39.3	62.4
Insurance adjusters, examiners, investigators	102	167	71	67	30	101	29.6	60.2
Investigators, adjustors, exc. insurance	189	251	106	94	82	157	43.6	62.6
Service occupations	10,186	13,606	4,102	5,585	6,084	8,021	59.7	58.9
Private household	1,211	627	45	29	1,166	597	96.3	95.3
Protective service	1,058	1,542	988	1,360	70	182	6.6	11.8
Service exc. protective and household	7,917	11,437	3,069	4,196	4,848	7,241	61.2	63.3
Food preparation[1]	3,314	4,830	1,042	1,645	2,272	3,185	68.5	65.9
Bartenders	216	318	170	177	46	141	21.2	44.3
Cooks, exc. short order	689	1,351	226	578	463	772	67.2	57.2
Health services	1,185	1,828	147	217	1,038	1,611	87.6	88.1
Cleaning and building, except private household	2,197	2,980	1,493	1,931	704	1,049	32.0	35.2
Personal service	1,221	1,799	386	403	835	1,395	68.4	77.6
Farming, forestry, and fishing[1]	3,034	3,032	2,757	2,581	277	451	9.1	14.9
Farm operators and managers	1,433	1,315	1,361	1,185	72	130	5.0	9.9
Farm occupations exc. managerial	1,002	976	841	758	161	218	16.1	22.3
Precision production, craft, and repair	11,269	13,555	10,445	12,499	824	1,056	7.3	7.8
Mechanics and repairers	3,275	3,983	3,195	3,848	80	135	2.5	3.4
Construction, trades	3,615	4,814	3,554	4,712	61	102	1.7	2.1
Extractive	177	314	173	306	4	7	2.4	2.3
Precision production	4,201	4,444	3,523	3,632	679	812	16.2	18.3
Woodworking	110	118	102	102	8	17	7.5	14.2

Table 3 (continued)

Occupation	Total		Male		Female		Female as a Percent of Total	
	1970	1980	1970	1980	1970	1980	1970	1980
Operators, fabricators, and laborers	17,385	19,988	12,887	14,501	4,498	5,486	25.9	27.4
Machine operators, assemblers, and inspectors	8,938	10,082	5,391	5,980	3,547	4,102	39.7	40.7
Machine operators and tenders, except precision[1]	6,495	6,544	3,879	3,862	2,616	2,682	40.3	41.0
Printing machine operators	393	442	340	323	53	119	13.5	27.0
Textile, apparel, and furnishings	1,986	1,632	418	303	1,568	1,329	79.0	81.4
Transportation and material moving[1]	3,932	4,820	3,769	4,445	163	375	4.1	7.8
Motor vehicle operators[1]	2,725	32,280	2,593	2,980	133	299	4.9	9.1
Truck drivers, heavy and light trucks	1,949	2,447	1,906	2,365	43	82	2.2	3.3
Bus drivers	258	386	185	209	73	177	28.3	45.8
Taxicab drivers and chauffeurs	170	189	160	167	10	22	5.7	11.5
Handlers, equipment cleaners, helpers, and laborers	4,515	5,086	3,727	4,077	788	1,009	17.4	19.8
Experienced unemployed[5]	110	340	49	128	62	212	55.8	62.4

[1] Includes occupations not shown separately
[2] In public administration protective services and related fields
[3] Salaried and self-employed
[4] Includes finance and business
[5] Unemployed persons who have worked anytime in the past

Source U.S. Bureau of the Census, *1980 Census of Population,* Supplementary Reports (PC80–S1–15)

Work has become the job.

For most of us, work and the job have become synonymous. The idea that work provides a service or a contribution to the larger society, or even that it is done for the glory of God, is played down in the modern positions and activities identified by the term *job*.

With the passing of more natural family or community settings for work, economic forces have become the engine of contemporary labor. We work, if we must, at positions which pay the most and which are the most accessible with the least amount of effort expended in training. We literally sell our labor and offer not one gram more effort than what is required or purchased with the paycheck.

However, we are discovering that monetary reward alone is not enough to feel good about our work. Furthermore, social scientists find no strong causal connection between liking one's job and the traditional perks found in industry and business: work enhancement, enhancement of social relations at work, bonuses, pay increases, to name a few. Perks have mushroomed, yet there are fewer happy workers around.[4]

Some months ago, one of the authors attended the seventy-fifth birthday celebration of a rare happy worker. His wife was asked what had made her husband such a productive and happy person. She replied quickly, "He was so fortunate; his work was his hobby." This rare man found in his job truly satisfying work.

This is exactly what is missing in the lives of many people, except perhaps for the so-called workaholic. It is just possible that not all workaholics are compulsive or feel driven by some social or psychological or economic motivation. Some of them may well enjoy their work so much that they will do nothing to avoid it, indeed, they will look for ways to increase their involvement. For such persons, the job is only a setting and work has retained or regained some of its original value: an expenditure of energy that has real meaning either intrinsic in terms of a task well-done, or having relevance to the good of the larger community.

3

Understandings About Work From Religious History

> The distinction between temporal and eternal happiness is a distinction between a life of work on earth and the activity of contemplation in Heaven. This does not mean the elimination of leisure and enjoyment from earthly life, but it does make labor their antecedent and indispensible condition. It also means that even in his highest activities—in the development of his arts and sciences—man must be perpetually at work. His achievement of truth or beauty is never so perfect and lasting that he can rest in it. (Adler, *Syntopicon:* 922)

We have just completed a brief scanning of how work has evolved in society—*From* community settings for work where work roles were meaningful extensions of the family system *to* the extreme marketplace of settings where the worker sells his labor like any other commodity and *where neither process nor result has any significance to the worker* other than the fact that the job provides a paycheck. In this chapter, we will look at a limited selection of understandings about work taken largely from religious history where documentation is more accessible.

The study of philosophical or practical definitions of work, drawn from the past, is sharply restricted by the fact that much of human history has not been written. Where written records do exist, they may well be devoid of references to work even though the *evidences* of work in many civilizations do exist.

The Egyptian civilization is a case in point. Even though statements about work are not available, we may deduce a great deal about the Egyptian experience of work from the range of evidence still extant. Like the Egyptians, a number of other societies offer a significant record of attitudes toward work—in art, artifact and architecture—if not also considerable information about the actual work experience.

Greek history affords easier access to a study of work in the past. Greek attitudes toward work were very pronounced and the documentation of such attitudes is surprisingly broad; naturally, the availability of these documents adds significant dimensions to our understandings. And even though Greek views on work are not normally thought of as part of a religious history sequence, they are instructive since they provide important stepping-stones toward an understanding of Judeo-Christian thought and practice.

Greek Attitudes Toward Work

Although there were exceptions, most Greeks disparaged physical (mechanical) labor. Xenophon, for example, said that the "mechanical arts bear the mark of social decay and bring dishonor to Greek cities."[1] Aristotle regarded work as a lower form of human activity. He felt it was better for man to relate to his true essence by the life of thought and thus participate in the work of God. For Aristotle, thinking (*theoria*) was the way to blessedness.

This view of work affected the nature of the social structure. It explains in part why Greek society was composed of social classes divided by unequivocal designations: philosophers, freedmen, indentured servants and slaves. The Sophists, however, insisted that there was virtue in work; they maintained that work gives dignity to the life of man. It is possible that every society, in order to survive, must have somewhere in its social fabric a positive attitude toward work. In any case, the Sophists played this role in ancient Greece.

The great importance in Greek society of the life of the mind is significantly different from our present age where high value is placed on activity directed toward achieving measurable goals. In light of the contemporary plundering of our planet, it may be well for us to listen again to what the Greeks can tell us about the good life.

Significantly Greek civilization along with the strong flavor of Roman influence provided the cultural setting in which much of early Christianity took root. Obviously this cultural setting with its crosscurrents of thought helped to shape both early and later

Christian views of work, whether by incorporating or reacting against the attitudes toward work and mores of that era.

The Judeo-Christian Perspective on Work

The Judeo-Christian view of work is complex. It derives from sources that not only span centuries but are also rooted in cultures and perspectives as diverse as those represented by primitive nomads wandering in the Near East and concerned theologians confronting the religio-politico status quo during the Reformation era in Europe. It grows out of ancient traditions that looked for a Messiah. And it flowered in the teachings of that Messiah—as announced and proclaimed in the New Testament Scriptures—and in the interpretations of those teachings by his followers.

In general terms, we are able to deduce a beginning Judeo-Christian perspective on work from two distinct strands present in the Old and New Testaments: what the reader understands God to be saying about work and what the Jewish people, as described in both Testaments, understood about work. For example, the Judaic view of the future, or Shalom, envisioned a world without drudgery, free of hard labor, a place where milk and honey would flow. In that prospective Shalom, nature would produce in abundance with each person sitting under his vine and fig tree with plenty on every hand.

However, these documents from Jewish society also reflected the hard and unrewarding side of work, based no doubt on their bondage first to the Pharaohs and later to the Babylonians. The patriarch Jacob, who worked a total of fourteen years for the hand of his beloved wife, demonstrates the importance of work in the Jewish tradition.[2] The six days of work and one day of rest prescribed in the Mosaic Law seemed to indicate the need and desire for a balance of work with nonwork. As the record indicates, this reflected God's own personality and the acts of God evident in the creation of the world. Also, as time passed, work slowly took on a form of worship to God, a sure provision for sustenance and a discipline toward the growth of human virtue.

Jesus' View of Work

Jesus experienced work in the Jewish tradition in a positive manner. He was born the son of a carpenter/builder, and apparently carried on that occupation in a rather successful fashion. It is said that he supported a large family. He worked in this occupation for many more years than he preached, and it seems that throughout his life he moved easily among people of both the working and merchant classes. He taught and preached using the idioms of work and the marketplace: his parables have to do with farming, trading, building. His closest disciples were fishermen, tradesmen and a tax collector.[3] And in terms of his own life, he ultimately identified his mission as doing *the work* of his Father.

There is much that we can learn about Jesus' understanding of work when we listen to his teaching. He downgraded undue obsession with work for accumulation, saying, "Do not store up for yourselves treasures on earth . . . " (Matt. 6:19ff). He also promoted the idea that working for physical security is a misplaced objective, for God takes care of all his creatures, including the birds. He stressed rather that one should work for heavenly riches, which pointed toward doing good to others.

On the other hand, he was concerned about the physical, social and spiritual needs of the people. Mingling with the people, he often saw those with sicknesses and diseases. What pity he felt for the crowds that came, because their problems were so great and they didn't know what to do or where to go for help. They were like sheep without a shepherd. "The harvest is so great, and the workers are so few," he told his disciples. "So pray to the one in charge of the harvesting, and ask him to recruit more workers for his harvest fields" (Matt. 9:36ff TLB). Working to help the needy was high on his agenda.

Jesus also recognized the naturalness and dignity of work. His disciples, being human, often were hungry. On one occasion they stopped in a field on the Sabbath to thresh wheat and eat. When the Pharisees condemned them for working on Saturday, Jesus told them it was not ritual that pleased God, but kindness. "I desire mercy, not sacrifice" (Matt. 12:7).

On several occasions Jesus discussed the importance of faithfulness and industry. In one situation the workers in the vineyard had worked varying hours but received the same pay. Jesus taught that a person's word and commitment was primary, and should not be determined by the pay received (Matt. 20:12–14). In another setting, two sons were asked to go to work in the vineyard. One said he would go but didn't, while the other, not sure he could fulfill the requirement, finally decided to go to work. Again the faithfulness and obedience of the worker was rewarded (Matt. 21:28–32). The same theme is echoed in Matthew 24:46–51 where the idea of a faithful servant is discussed.

The overwhelming impression one receives from reviewing Jesus' life during the three years of his formal ministry is that his work was to preach the good news of spiritual, social and physical release. When he felt his disciples were ready to understand, he called them together and "gave them power and authority to drive out all demons and to cure diseases, and he sent them out to preach the kingdom of God and to heal the sick." (Luke 9:1–2). We are told that the disciples "set out and went from village to village, preaching the gospel and healing people everywhere" (v. 6).

Other New Testament Voices

Many non-Christians and Christians are aware of the apostle Paul's strong affirmation of the dignity of work. His teaching has been called the Magna Charta of labor. He taught that work was necessary to provide the needs of life, to avoid idleness and evil, and to make almsgiving possible. Work was also service to Christ. To those who were anticipating the early coming of Christ and therefore stopped working, Paul said, "We hear that some among you are idle. They are not busy; they are busybodies. Such people we command and urge in the Lord Jesus Christ to settle down and earn the bread they eat" (2 Thess. 3:11–12).

The authors of the other New Testament Epistles reflect the same assumptions regarding work. John preached that action including work was the fulfilling of the love commandment. "Dear children, let us not love with words or tongue but with actions and in truth" (1 John 3:18).

The Church Fathers and Work

The Christian church had a deep respect for work from its early years until the Middle Ages. This view was based on the belief that work was performed and enjoyed in Paradise before the Fall, even as God had enjoyed *His* work.[4] Augustine and John Chrysostom developed theologies of work which were applied in the monastic orders. The monks valued work not only because it provided for the necessities of life, but also because it served as a spiritual exercise and discipline, as an expression of humility and as a channel for the achievement of a Christian order—*laborare est orare*—to work is to pray.[5]

The scholastics of the twelfth century recognized the role that work played in developing community and the common good. The concept of the order of creation in which each person had an assigned position to fulfill accompanied the theology and philosophy of Thomas Aquinas. In this view, all persons in the social fabric were combined into a harmonic order which was ultimately capped by God himself. This rationale was very useful to the hierarchy for it allied the church and the state in a mutually supportive system, and *placed the individual's responsibility to work at the disposal of either or both of these overpowering institutions.*[6] This kind of obligation for the individual to work, however, seems to diverge from the real intentions of the biblical message. In fact it could be argued that Martin Luther's emphasis on the "freedom of the Christian man" was a direct response to the way this concept of work had forced the enslavement of the laborer; Luther's bold statement became the mainstay of Reformation theology.

Work in the Reformation

It was Luther who literally changed the definition of work with relation to Christian salvation. He had become impressed by the great ambivalence inherent in human existence (man as sinner *and* child of God). From that perspective he also began to see work as two-sided: as a means for revealing God while at the same time hiding God.

Work for Luther had three elements: (1) Every act in life can be an act of worship if it is directed toward God; therefore, work can be considered as the position or setting in which God has placed man so he can glorify God. In other words, everyone has been placed in a particular work as his or her "calling" or little niche in the household of God. (2) Love of God and love of neighbor are the same and inseparable. If work is seen as an act of devotion to God, it must also be seen as an act of love for one's neighbor. (3) Human work tends to lead toward two consequences for man: first, work may become a temptation and a snare to serve personal ambition and egotism. But, second, since it is also burdensome, work serves to humble people and lead them to repentance.

Max Weber maintains that Luther was basically traditional in his view of work and that it was really John Calvin who became responsible for a dramatic shift in the understanding of work. However, Luther and Calvin did not differ in theological fundamentals. Calvin believed as strongly as Luther in the depravity of man and in his inability to save himself. It was in the practical application of this view that Calvin separated from Luther and developed a view of work which has helped to shape the so-called and well-known "protestant work ethic."

According to Calvinist perspective, work is an expression of brotherly love and not at all a service of the self (Weber, 1958:108). It is a fulfillment of the natural law and the highest expression of glory to God. In other words, work is one fulfillment of God's will or purpose that we glorify him. As a fulfillment of the natural law, work provided the basis for the ongoing life of society. Seen as an act of obedience to God, one avoids the temptation to understand work as a means of salvation.

John Calvin went beyond Luther in placing great stress on predestination and divine election. He also believed that success in work or vocation was indicative of election, although working itself was irrelevant for election. He thereby avoided the "salvation by works" theology attributed to the Roman Catholic Church. Calvin believed that "The world exists to serve the glorification of God and for that purpose alone. The elected Christian is in the world only to increase this glory of God by fulfilling his commandments to the best of his ability" (Weber, 1958:108).

For the Christian, therefore, work became the calling by which he glorified God, whether he was sure of his election or not. Work was thus not a means to an end (salvation) but rather an act of appreciation for having been given salvation. Work became the channel through which the social order was served by God's providence, even though individual Christians may not have received any direct personal benefit from it. Reformed theology expressed in religious language what was already happening in the marketplace, namely, what John Wesley said in such classic form regarding the Christian calling—"Christians cannot help but get rich, for the harder they work, the more they save. . . . " (Weber, 1958:175, paraphrased).

Beyond the Reformation

No *major* revisions of the Christian work ethic have appeared since the Reformation! With the coming of the Enlightenment, work became almost deified, especially among the idealists such as Fichte, Hegel, and Marx.[7] In their view, work was defined as one of the basic elements of life while, at the same time, the state was becoming one of the transcendent institutions—a result of the integration of the efforts contributed by all the various segments of society. Karl Marx, particularly, made work (labor) the basic human fact. From this cornerstone he developed his interpretation of history on the way in which human labor—which is all that most humans have to offer—is exploited by others. Marx said that the basic human fact of work made possible a massive oppression of those who had no way of defending themselves against exploitation.

Marx was not wrong in his diatribes against exploitation. However, in our view, neither he nor other leaders in world thought have offered adequate responses to the human dilemmas related to work experience. In the same critical vein, it is our conviction that, in general, Christian perspectives have not gone far enough to meet the need for a fundamental understanding of work that is authentic, biblically based and sociologically respectable. Hopefully, this volume will make a contribution to the dialogue that we consider so essential to change.

4

Glimpses of the Sociological Perspective

> This most universally performed activity has received scant attention directed at the examination of its surrounding beliefs and its fundamental values. Perhaps it is *because* work is so general and common place that we believe it to be a matter of common sense and general agreement our assumptions about it are so basic that we do not even recognize them as assumptions . . . what we are asking here is why it should be done . . . what is work for? (Anthony: 3–5)

This entire book is shaped by a sociological perspective. In addition, chapter 12 deals specifically with a sociological analysis of work. However, to provide some background for readers without training in sociology, it may be helpful to sketch several rather fundamental understandings about work developed by a variety of scholars within this discipline.

Contributions from the discipline of sociology toward an understanding of work range across a broad spectrum of concepts. They include significant clarifications with respect to division of labor, social roles and status questions. They have provided us with classic discussions on the interrelationship of elements in the economic order. Among the more noteworthy of these are Emile Durkheim's *The Division of Labor* and Max Weber's *The Protestant*

Ethic and the Spirit of Capitalism. They have highlighted problems and defined issues which must be faced.

Some analysts suggest that in its later development, sociology has narrowed its purview; that it has paid more attention to the objective and observable aspects of work such as the analysis and description of the occupational structure, occupational mobility, organizational theory and management/union relations. At the same time, it is clear that many sociologists have continued to think more holistically about work. Within the sociological tradition, work has been seen as central to the ordering of major aspects of a social structure.

The Social Structure

One of the earliest sociological concepts was the idea of social positions within a society. These social positions referred to the assignment of duties *and* rights to certain persons with specific qualifications and included positions such as parent, child, priest, prince, soldier, peasant. Common understandings of the duties and rights assigned to each position were fundamental to maintaining the society. When they were questioned or when deviations were tolerated, the entire social structure was at risk.

Of course, the family positions—parents, children; husband, father; wife, mother; son, daughter—constituted the basis for the entire social order. The duties and rights of each (or lack of rights) were understood. For example, the specific obligations of persons in the "father" position would include the paramount duty of providing a livelihood for their children; the rights of a father would include the obedience and respect he could expect from them. In the family setting, such parental duties and rights would be defined specifically also with reference to the age of both parents and children.

This approach to duties and rights was typical in the case of other positions within a given society—whether priest or prince, soldier or peasant. Obviously, such detail in defining each position in the societal structure highlights the primary importance of the whole; indeed, the compliance of individuals filling each position formed the warp and woof from which a strong social fabric was woven.

Exactly the same was true in the case of *rites of passage*. This term identifies and explains the norms pertaining to a change from one position to another and the ceremonies which accompanied and marked such change. A typical example would be the rites of passage from the position of daughter to the position of wife. Just as willing submission to the responsibilities of a position was understood to contribute to a strong society, so the faithful performance of passage rituals helped to confirm the significant primacy of the social order over individual desires or interests. Understandably, all of this affected the evolution of norms regarding work. In fact, certain types of work were expected of persons in each of the social positions. If the person in a particular position did not perform the work expected, he could expect the censure of the society in some form. In the case of a priest, he could be relieved of his position, ceremoniously or otherwise. A soldier who refused to fight would be dismissed summarily or even killed. Those positions which pertained to essential provision for the *important* needs in society have always been carefully monitored by the whole.

In the case of parents or surrogate parents, for example, dismissal was out of the question. However, in almost all societies, the care of children has been an important matter. Parents or surrogate parents who failed to properly care for the children under their jurisdiction generally faced serious sanctions. In some societies, the same would be true of children who failed to fulfill their obligations to parents or other elders in family or tribe.

Contemporary social science theory has increasingly come to recognize the central importance of work in social structure. That is to say, work is being recognized as a system of social norms relating to the time, place, type of activity and remuneration for the performance of countless duties: norms relating to what shall be produced and norms relating to who shall be in positions of superordination and subordination. One might venture to suggest that the structure of every society is shaped significantly by the impact of work.

In addition to societal structure, it is clear also that basic societal values are expressed through the kind of work that is done in a society. When a society focuses on military hardware, or when presidents of automobile companies receive annual salaries greater than the lifelong income of an assembly-line worker in the same factory, the values regarding work stand out in bold relief.[1]

The Individual

Of course, it is obvious that society as a whole is not the only beneficiary of work as a common activity. Work is also of signal importance for the *individual* and for his or her relationship to the group or society.

Work fulfills a great many important functions for the individual: (1) Work provides a means of making a living for the members of a society (excluding the ones unable to work or those whose wealth allows them to avoid work). (2) work has become the single most important source of social identity and status for the

individual. Research in different disciplines corroborates the importance of the type of work one does relative to the individual's social
status and prestige. (3) Work is one of the most important sources
of personal meaning and, therefore, self-acceptance. Research on
the unemployed underscores this conclusion emphatically. Furthermore, the same research insists that the degree of self-depreciation
felt by a person out of work can only be realized by experience.[2]
(4) Work provides a setting for the expression of different forms of
creativity for the individual, thus enhancing purpose for living.
(5) Work is the means by which most individuals achieve their life
goals, whether it be retiring with a million dollars in the bank,
being the best author in America, or rearing a large family.

Sociological study has contributed greatly to our current
understandings about how closely and intricately work and the self
are intertwined. When the WAY test (*Who Are You?*) is given to
most people, they will respond by saying, "I am a teacher," or "I
am a housewife" or "I am a business executive." Many of us have
known persons whose lives became almost meaningless when they
were retired or through misfortune became unable to work. In
addition, many persons have experienced the bitter paradox
inherent in Western values—values which emphasize the importance of becoming wealthy and independent so work will become
unnecessary only to discover at that point that work seemed to
provide a meaning to life which neither wealth nor independence,
by themselves, can offer.

Sociologically speaking, work is the means that human beings
in society have at their disposal to achieve all the ends of which they
are capable: (1) Work is the means of providing the necessities for
physical survival, including propagation of the human race.
(2) Work provides the surplus goods which allow societies to
hedge against inclement economic weather and other unforeseen
contingencies. (3) Work provides the additional surplus goods
needed to free humans for activities unrelated to sheer physical
survival: to play, to dance, to contemplate, to paint, to write
books—to name only a few of the many experiences deemed
imperative for a fulfilling human existence. (4) Work thus contributes to the aesthetic, spiritual and intellectual growth and experience of individuals. (5) work is the medium for the development of
all the social and cultural artifacts and systems which provide for
the ongoing social structure and which most of us take for
granted—such as political, economic, and educational institutions.
(6) Work is required whenever humanity, individually or collec-
tively, purposes to achieve any of the hopes, ideals, objectives or
goals of which they are capable.

It is clear, of course, that not all work has been directed
toward the ideal purposes outlined above. For Christian and non-

Christian, work has often been misapplied. The potential and opportunities inherent in work have often been abused, exploited, squandered, and wasted. Instead of producing fulfillment, work for many has become futile and meaningless; instead of emphasizing and nurturing creaturely humanity, work has turned into a dehumanizing experience. The following chapters will deal with these problems in greater detail.

BOOK TWO
THE WORLD OF WORK

5

The Critical Search for Meaningful Work

All things are full of labour, man cannot utter it: the eye is not satisfied with seeing, nor the ear filled with hearing. (Eccl 1:8 KJV)

After all, it is work which occupies most of the energies of the human race, and what people actually do is normally more important, for understanding them, than what they say, or what they spend their money on, or what they own, or how they vote (Schumacher: 3).

God gives every bird its food, but he does not throw it into the nest (attributed to Josiah Gilbert Holland).

Entering the world of work can be one of the most anxious and stressful periods in the life of an individual. Unless the person taking that step has some particularly vital skill in short supply or an exceptional record in academia—or is superficial and thoughtless—both the search for and the choice of work are seen to be critical. How one should pursue the search and also make the right decision produces an anxiety that is dissipated only after the career choice begins to be affirmed through actual work experience that brings a sense of meaning and fulfillment.

Certainly, the questions revolving around work constitute one of the leading issues of our time. Unquestionably, work is existential for the great majority of citizens in many cultures. Few, if any, are excluded from some form of work experience. Some achieve this existential involvement with work only when they reach adult years; multitudes of others around the world have experienced work while still children.

Where primitive societal patterns still exist, the child moves into adulthood experiencing work situations in a more or less natural progression—fully subject to long-established family and tribal or community norms and usually without the prerogatives of individual choice. In societies where apprenticing traditions remain the norm, the young worker may also have little choice.* There are also autocratic settings in which governments dictate the nature and the place of work experience. But for a great majority of workers in the industrialized free world, the choice of occupation or job or work setting is not only an option; it has become a requirement, indeed, a heavy responsibility.

This responsibility for selecting one's work is present whether an individual is plunged into the world of work by early family or personal necessity or enters that world through a more systematic career training door. It is precisely at this point of choice where the thoughtful potential worker confronts the important questions about meaning in work—questions that range all the way from work for survival to work which brings emotional and spiritual fulfillment.

It is also at this point of decision where historical knowledge is seen to be just that, where the abstractions of sociological and theological discussions give way to hard reality, where fantasy collapses and theory is tested. To enter the world of work is to enter a labyrinthian maze where the first choice may well affect every future turning in the path. This is why the search for meaningful work becomes critical.

The Objective

More than nineteen hundred years ago, a certain man spoke to a crowd gathered around him on a Galilean mountainside. Highly charged with an awareness of the universal yearning for happiness, he offered an answer to the unspoken question every human heart is asking: How can I be happy?

His beginning words, "Happy are those who . . . " became a litany of suggestions to still the yearning in the human heart and fill

---

*However, it should be noted here that communication with, and information about, other cultures has brought confusion, if not turbulence to a growing number of these formerly orderly enclaves.

life with meaning. For he knew that the real question had to do with meaning in life and until that was seeded in experience, happiness would elude the seeker like a butterfly flutters always beyond a child's eager grasp.

Then, very significantly, he ended his litany with a strong affirmation and a wonderful signpost: You who discover this road to happiness "are the light of the world. A city on a hill cannot be hidden . . . Let your light shine before men, that they may see your good deeds and praise your Father in heaven" (Matt. 5:14–16). For Jesus, happiness was the result of response, of decision, of *action*—a decision to heed God's call; to discover God's purpose and thus find meaning in life; to *do* God's will and enjoy fulfillment.

Interestingly, Aristotle had reached a similar conclusion three centuries earlier. "The happy life is thought to be virtuous; now a virtuous life requires exertion, and does not consist in amusement."[1] He summarized his thoughts in this way: "If happiness is activity . . . it is reasonable that it should be in accordance with the highest virtue."[2]

Aristotle had a definite idea about what was the most virtuous activity and hence most likely to make one happy—the life and thought work of a philosopher. Even though we may disagree with his philosophy, we must be aware of a central understanding in Aristotle's ideas of happiness and those of Jesus: *happiness is the result of satisfying and important human activity; happiness derives literally from what we do.*

There is no way to escape this principle. It holds true for those who are alive now and those who lived two millennia ago; whether they live in North America or the Amazon basin in South America or Asia; whether they believe in one god or none; whether or not they believe in the transcendent spiritual realities Jesus represented in his life and teachings.

Of course, Aristotle went beyond this fundamental relationship between activity and happiness; he believed that happiness was the highest good and goal of human life. He said, "For in a word, everything that we choose we choose for the sake of something else—except happiness, which is (the) end (or goal)."[3]

At this point Aristotle and Jesus part company sharply. While Aristotle concluded that happiness was the end or goal, Jesus saw it as result: do this, or that, and happiness follows. Furthermore, although Jesus clearly related action to happiness, his ideas offered a spiritual dimension as well—the dimension of obedience to God's call.

We dare not conclude this brief discussion about the meaning in life and fulfillment in work that bring happiness without acknowledging the enormous amount of unhappiness in human history, including this present time. In a gripping "History of

Western Civilization" film series, Kenneth Clark, a dean of Western history, says that the seventeenth and eighteenth centuries produced millions of very unhappy people. He includes the black African victims of the "Middle Passage"—slaves who were captured and shipped to America, being treated worse than cattle both enroute and after arrival—as well as the new slum dwellers of London and Birmingham, to name only two of the scores of cities that could be mentioned.

Many of these unhappy people have had choice wrested from them and have been unable to change their condition. Toward such who have no choice we have but a single word: a prayer to God that he will forgive us for our complicity in allowing and even promoting human misery, many times through our own demands for the good life.

This sad state of affairs, however, does not undercut our basic thesis: that many of us are free to make choices and must therefore assume responsibility for our own happiness. We are free to choose to be active, to do those things which are more virtuous, to reflect the call of God in the choices we make so that happiness may be brought to others and ourselves. Only by choosing and acting responsibly can we expect to find the meaning in work that results in happiness.

That many have not done this is obvious. That each such personal decision *not taken* has contributed greatly to the current crisis in the world of work may not be as clear. In some sense, this book is dedicated to that purpose—accepting responsibility for "the critical choice" so our lives and our expenditure of energy can fit into the purposes of God and at the same time bring the fulfillment that makes life a joy.

The Current Crisis

Choices related to work have always been important, yet the current crisis (outlined in detail in the chapters that follow) makes choice of career track more critical than ever before. However, perhaps even more urgent than the choice we make are the understandings we achieve about work and the attitudes and objectives we bring to the decision-making process.

Of course, each person's crisis relative to work is unique simply because each individual relates to work in a singular, personal way. At the same time, there are general perspectives that may be useful as we search for meaningful work.

This crisis is no respecter of age, experience, training, or longevity in a job. It affects the first-time job seeker and the person nearing retirement. It threatens to overwhelm those who have been summarily dismissed because of turbulence and reductions in some part of the work force and the individual who has come to realize that he or she is in the wrong place. It touches the man who works with his hands, the woman at a computer and the professor with three degrees and credibility within a scholarly discipline.

Simply stated, the crisis has two parts:

1. Finding work that is virtuous (according to Aristotle), work with meaning, work that is responsive to Jesus' call.
2. Finding that "right work" in a contemporary setting filled with complex, confusing and contradictory forces which have unhinged the reasonably stable workplace patterns of the past and the usual worker expectations.

Adding to the sense of crisis may also be an enhanced awareness that "my work should be serving God and my fellow creatures in ways that the present job does not make possible!" This new awareness among thoughtful persons helps to create discomfort with some types of work and a desire to be in a job that really makes a contribution.

It is true, of course, that there are other crises which also deserve our attention—injustices of many kinds around the world, the environmental destructiveness of certain types of activity, and the threat of nuclear destruction. Certainly, these problems are urgent; they may well affect our survival in the world as we know it.

However, if we focus on all the people of the world who are in the workplace and if we ask whether or not their work experience is contributing to their fulfillment and happiness as persons, then the crisis of finding "virtuous" (meaningful) work is the most pressing and urgent by any measure! For no segment of the human family is exempt from the results of what happens in the workplace. There are clear grounds for Marx's unrelenting critique of the alienation of modern man from his work, for that alienation has produced one of the greatest social upheavals in human history. Human beings have experienced and continue to experience massive unhappiness in their work.

Before going on, we should make note of two kinds of potential reader response. Some from among those with a Christian heritage or viewpoint may well say: "You have already made reference to Jesus and his teachings. Why don't you just come out and say boldly that men and women must accept Christ as Saviour? Then all these work problems will be solved."

Others who may not have espoused a Christian perspective or made a Christian commitment could say: "Look, I'm ready to listen to your comments on the current crisis and to your sociological analysis. I'll even think about your proposals as long as they follow some form of logic. Just don't give me that 'Jesus stuff' as an easy answer!"

We'd like to remind both groups of an underlying assumption throughout this book—that both the human scientific orientation and the perspective of Christian principles have something to contribute to a discussion about work and a resolution of the crisis. Even though we make no apology for our Christian commitment and the conclusions that issue from this commitment, we also hold firmly to the conviction that sociological principles and understandings are just as essential to many of the changes necessary in our approach to work.

Where Are the Booby Traps?

Undoubtedly, few would deny that a crisis in the world of work exists, that to choose one's work rightly brings significant satisfactions. It is precisely these two elements—right choice in the midst of crisis—that create the quandary facing most job seekers.

At one time it was possible to move confidently from adolescence into adulthood—from dependence on parents into the independence of one's own work and paycheck—expecting to find a satisfying and meaningful life of work. This is no longer true. Instead, most of us are now facing a veritable no-man's-land of booby traps which threaten every unsuspecting traveler. Walking into such a trap can seriously maim one's sense of self-worth and self-understanding, can literally destroy the motivation to search for happiness and fulfillment in work and may well shatter one's faith in the ability of the world to provide a life worth living.

The first booby trap is hidden in the social and cultural pressures that shrilly call for our allegiances and commitments. Many of us have had parents who expected great things from us and practically lived their lives through our achievements. Many of us have had strong ethnic backgrounds that caused us to become substitute achievers for parents who had barely survived many hardships. Either the depression years or bad fortune caused such serious setbacks and disappointments that parents often compensated by saying, "I hope my children don't have to struggle like this." For still others of us, the hope that our own son and daughter would "make the grade" compensated for our own personal failures or missing the high goals our mothers and fathers set for us. Freud was not far from the truth when he wrote about the pride of progeny being an extension of personal ego.

Of course, family and friends were not the only source of such external social pressures that trap us unwittingly in wrong choices. The community also has always monitored success and achievements very carefully, although subtly. The family which was financially successful would show it by buying a new car or building a bigger house. Everybody knew by way of the grapevine that the Peters' son had been admitted to medical school and was headed for a prestigious and comfortable existence in some big city. The community newspaper carried notices about the promotion of a local high school graduate of 1956 to the presidency of a leading drug firm in Pittsburgh. Achievements, success and promotions made good copy. Why? Because *we,* as the consumers of information, react so positively to success and achievement.

It should be noted, however, that our positive reaction is not only an innate and almost instinctual reverence toward achievement, excellence, and power—a reflection of our own inner drives. It is also the result of the value our society and culture places on certain definitions of success. From *Fortune* magazine to the annual Emmy awards, we are nurtured on the high stakes of prestige, power and wealth. The winners in the struggle for wealth, position and fame are held before us as models to be emulated. Almost every town has its Carnegie Library; every college has a host of scholarships "in memory of Mr. and Mrs. Hugh Johnson"; and many cemeteries have an almost instantly observable pecking order of those who carry prominence.

Our culture has shaped a definition of happiness and offers a formula to achieve it. Work hard, get ahead of the pack, climb an organizational ladder to the top, achieve or create a power base. Then one can take the time for the finer things in life, upgrade home and furnishings, travel to exotic places. The ability to purchase things, to manipulate resources and events, to be known as successful—all of this appears to lead to the epitome of happiness. What we may not realize is that we have been seduced into following a path made treacherous by a hidden booby trap.

Suddenly, in the midst of our pursuit of happiness, all the success and achievements and material rewards blow up in our faces. We discover that prestige, power and wealth leave us empty. Almost as devastating—for some even more so—is to spend a lifetime on that path with very little to show for the years and energy expended and, near the end, to trip on the same trap. In either case, the realization that one has walked the wrong path can shatter self-esteem, motivation and what little courage remains to risk a new road toward fulfillment.

Without a doubt, external factors are important in determining self- awareness and providing a context for choice. Just as certainly, some of these societal elements exert pressures which affect our choices. These pressures are subtle, seductive and persuasive. We are conceived and nurtured, and we mature in the midst of the norms and expectations established by, or evolved within, our culture. This means we must walk carefully and deliberately.

However, just as significant as this booby trap outside ourselves is the *internal* booby trap most of us must deal with. Simply stated, this trap is the misreading of who I am, what I can do and what will result in fulfillment and happiness for me. All of us have certain abilities and potential. But discovering these is not always easy. In grade school, perhaps, we may think the whole world is open to us; but very few of those early dreams become real options simply because we haven't the opportunity to try them out. A little later some achieve a bit of sophistication and realize that aptitudes and interests play a part in revealing which choices may be better. Still, how can I tell in advance that verbal skills should lead me into information technology, creative writing or a legal career in criminal defense? Or is there a way to determine that, had I chosen differently, I might have become an outstanding orthopedic surgeon?

Beyond personal abilities, how can we know what our needs are, or might be, and how best to fulfill them? Who will tell us when we are fifteen or twenty what work activity will be most satisfying and meaningful to us when we are forty-five? How do we know which will be the most fulfilling goals toward which to strive, particularly while we are in the formative years, a time when everything seems possible and even desirable? But most important of all, how will we know which hopes and goals *should be* most important for us, especially when we have so little experience to draw on? Ironically, the trauma is much worse if we are still asking the question when we are forty-five and beyond—quite possibly because we have had so much experience and the question still remains unanswered. This trauma will be addressed briefly in chapter 11.

This second booby trap includes the frustrating paradox that we should live our life backwards, but can't. That is, we should have all the experiences of life first so we could explore our opportunities accordingly. This reflects our strong desire for the wisdom of hindsight. In retrospect, we can see much more clearly what was worth striving for, or what our ambitions, hopes, and dreams should have been.

We seem to learn much too late to be useful which abilities are the strongest, simply because abilities are realized only as they are utilized. It is difficult to know which fulfillment is the most important because awareness of need intensifies after a time of starving or denial; which hopes should be clung to and nurtured because this knowledge comes only after we understand where these hopes will lead; which ultimate goals are worthy of our lives and energy because this becomes apparent only when we have tested potential with lesser goals. All of this highlights and aggravates the frustration we feel and makes this booby trap more deadly. For, driven by our frustration, we may simply throw up our hands, assuming it is impossible to integrate these elements in a way that makes sense and forms a coherent goal. When this happens we give up choice and yield to happenstance.

The third booby trap, which can be even more shattering, but which also can turn out to be our salvation, is the explosive power of the discovery of the third dimension in our lives—that spiritual realm of experience which is beyond the physical and mental.

For many of us—whether we are religious, Christian, or agnostic—the shattering blow comes when we are finally forced to ask the question, "Is that all there is?" In that moment of truth, we sense a gnawing emptiness in our inner being and we know that there must be more to life than the programmed struggle for the "good life." Something like a casual remark from a friend, "May you have a rewarding summer" lingers in our subconscious and slowly comes to the surface as serious doubt that we are really doing anything worthwhile.

There are many solutions offered in the marketplace for this question about the nature and quality of our third dimension—ranging from the self-acceptance theories of "I'm OK, You're OK" to the strong affirmations present in "the power of positive thinking." This is not to disparage the effectiveness of these approaches nor the help they may have to offer. Many have been helped by the Dale Carnegie course, or seminars on personal effectiveness. But the real "third dimension" questions cannot be answered in seminars. They cry out for more than a course outline or a mechanical "how-to" approach. The ultimate question is "What am I here for?" or in Christian language, "For what purpose did God create me?"

This question brings us back to the idea that both Jesus and Aristotle put forward: happiness is somehow related to doing. Of course, even acknowledgement that this idea is correct and fundamental does not resolve the problems with which we are faced:

1. How should we respond in light of the booby traps? What are the criteria to be recognized while making a decision? Which pressures, factors, values or issues are relevant? Which are important? Which are totally extraneous, useless or even misleading? How can one know when one knows?
2. How should we respond when suddenly we are informed that our entire career track is becoming redundant? Or when we have been over-trained for available work and are unsuited for other work?
3. What response is "correct" when we discover we are preparing for work that no longer exists or work which has

changed so drastically that it no longer seems suitable. Or—assuming we know all about work and its meaning and our own personal needs and goals—how should we prepare for work which is changing, appearing and disappearing? Or prepare for a world which is constantly slipping beneath our feet? Or how can one prepare for a world of work which is not yet on the horizon?

These may seem like discouraging notations. On the other hand, they can be viewed as challenging and exciting. Indeed, the uncertainties in the world of work may not be much different than those in marriage. Actually, no one knows what will happen in a marriage. But with the right intentions and commitment along with a great deal of energy applied to the joint venture, marriage can be an extremely rewarding part of life.

So it can be with work—unless we choose an avoidance approach, an ultimately subtle and most problematic response to the crisis we have outlined. To look the other way and "just let it happen" is to succumb blandly to the society around us.

The Third Dimension

We've mentioned the third dimension as a booby trap area— the dimension of life that is transcendent. That potential transcendence for our approach to the world of work deserves a somewhat sharper focus.

Whether or not we wish to acknowledge the fact, all of us are confronted with God's "holy call." Adam and Eve seemed startled by the call. Against great odds, Noah heard the call and, in his response, defied the ridicule of his relatives and community. Abraham responded likewise with an incredible display of faith, as did Moses; the list could go on. What is this call? Does it come to people today? What does it include? At the baptism of Jesus, a dove came down and alighted on Jesus' head; then a voice said, "This is my Son, whom I love; . . . Listen to him" (Matt. 17:5). The call then was to listen to Jesus. Against the background of this message, Jesus called men and women to follow him, to find life and happiness.

This third dimension recognizes and takes us into another realm of experience beyond the material, the physical and the mental. Within this realm we perceive ourselves as significant beings, loved of God, called by him to participate in his work, worthy of respect regardless of the particular cultural view of a given activity in which we may be engaged, knowing that our self-worth is intrinsic and wishing, naturally then, to do work that honors the God who has so graciously given us status and meaning to our lives. Within this frame of reference, we achieve a good and proper self-image and are thus able to love ourselves, to grow in self-understanding and, out of these feelings of essential self-worth, become able to contribute with joy our unique gifts to the benefit of others.

In the authors' view, this perspective of ourselves affords the setting within which meaning to life and the fulfillment of our potential can take place. Happiness is then a result, first of serving God through our work and then—indirectly although not insignificantly—serving God's creatures, fellow human beings. Indeed, one can reverse the equation and say that helping others to realize the intention of God for their lives is the best way to serve them and thus to serve God!

Without question, God's desire for us is to be happy or blessed. The doorway to this happy state is outlined very simply: to do the will of God. Jesus said, "Now that you know these things, you will be blessed (happy) if you do them" (John 13:17). Against the backdrop of knowledge, the doing comes by choice. Choice is a gift from God. Because choice is a gift and because choice can unlock the door to meaning, fulfillment and joy, it is irresponsible not to choose what to do with our lives.

The World of Work

Finally, we want to focus on the world within which all of us must live and to which we must relate. Sometimes we talk to our children or students about the "real world out there." The world of work is one such real world out there—away from home; outside the protective walls of parental responsibility and guidance; beyond the campus where the young adult is plunged directly and sometimes reluctantly into a sea of opportunity and a maelstrom of changes in the workplace.

This is the world in which all of us face the critical choice of job and workplace. These are the settings where we encounter the "real world out there" and where we must find meaning and fulfillment if indeed we expect that to be part of our work experience.

Working in an organization is one of the realities faced by many people. Although increasing numbers take the frightening road of entrepreneurial risk, many more workers find themselves engaged in corporate, industrial and organizational settings. Even professionals in a variety of fields and disciplines are beholden to some form of organization, association or control. While the organization performs many useful functions—in a certain sense representing some of the elements of community—it has also evolved into something "other." From this "other" perspective, the organization often engenders hostility, creates stress and anxiety and somehow becomes a power to be feared and confronted. In any case, the organization is part of the real world of work.

Another part of experience in the real world is *alienation from work*—a sense that one's work and one's self are distanced from each other, that the work activity is not only foreign to the self but is also actually destroying the self and what one may become. Certainly, other issues are significant but, without doubt, none is more fundamental. Profound psychological and spiritual dislocations and great distress accompany this growing malaise in our society. How to deal with this is one of our concerns.

Many workers are also subject to the stresses of *professionalism*. This is another form of alienation insofar as it represents "a tendency for those norms and values within a particular occupation or profession to determine the values and behavior in the work position rather than one's own inner purpose and a given moral perspective."[4] Subtle, insidious and seductive, the perils of professionalism infect the workplace and threaten the well-being, even the survival, of many. On the one hand, professionalism is a liability; on the other hand, it is a basic need of society as it has evolved to this point. It is, at any rate, a pervasive reality.

The world of work is marked and shaped by another reality: a great upheaval in *male/female roles, responsibilities and relationships*. For many centuries, gender restrictions and discriminations have existed and become institutionalized. Attitudes of males and females in the workplace, community, home, and church have often reflected these discriminations. Patterns of conditioning have become imbedded so deeply in our cultural consciousness that superior/inferior thinking has become accepted as the norm. This is beginning to change; actually the workplace has become one of the settings for change in the way males and females perceive one another and themselves. This is the real world.

A fifth area of exploration into the real world of work relates to change itself—particularly *the changing nature of work*. It is likely that workers today face no more frightening reality than the very obvious fact that norms are dissolving, long-held expectations are being shattered, lifetime career plans are being shifted into neutral or suddenly made redundant, and comfortable retirement hopes are becoming a fantasy reminiscent of the way childhood dreams created a never-never land. Everywhere in the world of work, change is present, in greater or lesser proportions.

Of course, there are more dimensions to the world of work than these we have mentioned. But for our purposes in this particular exploration on work, these five significant realities constitute a large part of that world and call for more than brief notice in passing; they demand our attention and serious consideration. The next five chapters provide this opportunity. The final chapter in Book 2 highlights another agonizing reality of our decade: when an individual's world of work, apparently organized and stable, suddenly "falls apart."

Excursus 1
Some Reflections on Sculpting as Work

by Margaret Lorraine Hudson

I was forty when I discovered clay. Gil and I, with our four young sons, had just returned from Korea where we had lived and taught for ten years. My sculpting began as a compulsive means of communicating who I was and what life meant to me. It flowed out of a deep struggle, a sense of release from guilt, along with acceptance by God. In a fresh awareness of being loved and of natural skills and talents being validated, images were freed and the inner flow of reflection/imaging/work began. I was concerned only with stating authentically and clearly the images that formed in my mind. This became supremely important to me. Public approval or monetary reward meant nothing. My art was a deeply personal act, outside the ordinary structures and routine patterns of my life. No permission was needed or sought from anyone. From the inner core of a freed spirit flowed its unique view of nature, of life, of the universe, and of God.

*   *   *

What more can I say? I wish Cal and Urie had asked me to sculpt something instead of write an essay! Words are so difficult . . .

*   *   *

I find it confusing to write about work! Am I not rather writing about life? About the things I love to do? About the challenges that occupy my mind and spirit in all my waking hours? Or perhaps I am writing about my faith? Or should I write instead about how our family needs were met through the gift of little clay animals? Since this essay is to be part of a serious statement about work, maybe I should write about how deep and complex issues are resolved in the sculpting process. I wonder if business persons will read this book. They might prefer to read how the studio—its development and our methods of management—has opened the door to a tremendous challenge in Christian discipleship and the economics of caring.

I try to sort through the piles of jottings gathered around me on the table. Ideas pop out at me, then race toward each other and commingle. I rearrange the piles. Finally, four foci emerge: thoughts related to my inner work as an artist, the relationship of the artist to the church, of men and women's work, and the external organization—Earth Arts—which has emerged as a full-fledged testing ground for new ways of being in business. (I think now there is a fifth: women as artists.)

The thoughts that follow are simply reflections on my experience as a sculptor, the work in which I find an integration of all aspects of life—making it a whole lived in celebration of God's goodness and love as well as in relatedness to humanity.

*   *   *

The cat sits perched atop one pile, so I shall begin with another.

*   *   *

Sculpting is an incredibly delightful form of work, for it totally engages my mind, spirit, and body. All dimensions of life converge to bring into being its object!

I love to take in my hands a soft lump of clay, squeeze it into a fantastic shape, and remind myself (and anyone watching) that no one else on earth can bring into being the same object I have created: for I am unique, as is every other person. To bring that uniqueness into play in life, to discern and develop the talents and gifts one possesses, is a major work in life. At forty, I accepted this insight for myself and began to live that way.

However, for one who had grown up in the church, out of this exuberant mid-life burst of freedom was born a tension, both creative and anguished. New questions tumbled over each other. How does serious discipleship relate to the deeply personal inner compulsion to create? How does commitment to Christian community affect the individual freedom so essential to an artist? Can one, in the practice of caring economics, choose, seemingly selfishly, to pursue a "nonessential" career in art rather than a "useful" service occupation or religious vocation and still be a serious follower of Jesus? I struggled mightily with the issue of my integrity as a follower of Christ and my integrity as an artist. Finally, I concluded that—whether art is a reflection on life's meaning and struggles and hopes, or a celebration of the wonder of life and of all creation, or pure delightful playing with concept, medium, color, form and line—when one is sharing freely a unique vision of reality, to create that art becomes one's highest service to God and to humanity. It is in this process that objects of beauty and the symbols of hope and inspiration come into being, meeting very real human needs. Sometimes, the church will share in that affirmation and sometimes the artist will stand alone.

Earlier I said that to discern and develop the talents and gifts one possesses—to bring them to reality in my life—is a major work. In one sense, that is a work primarily of the individual; in another sense, for the Christian, it is also a work of the community, of the church. Therein lie other searchings and discoveries.

Generally today, in our society, it seems that an artist's most meaningful work is individual, springing from an inner vision, or synthesis. What then is the role of the church as a community in such a life? I have reflected much on this and feel that the church is uniquely equipped to serve as a valuable resource and support for the creative person, artist or otherwise.

The church can nourish a free, transparent spirit, authentic and without pretense. The church discerns and affirms gifts, encouraging an attitude of self-confidence by placing value on natural talents and gifts. It also offers opportunity for their development.

More than that, however, the church can encourage the free flow of ideas, exploring the relevance of faith to all areas of life. And within a loving fellowship, one may test ideas and concepts without fear. The church stimulates the development of a framework of values to give stability to life. It encourages families and individuals to take time for reflection on nature and beauty, for creative thinking about life, its meaning, its joys and sorrows, its responsibilities. The church can also encourage the open, caring expression of each person's uniqueness and thus encourage the development of whole persons. It points the way to entering into the kind of relationship with God where one finds the load of guilt lifted, the creative flow unblocked.

Within a world of conformity, the church affirms the validity of the individual search to know truth. Within a profession of extreme individualism, it offers loving, stimulating community. Within a world of competition, the church affirms the possibility of living in cooperation and harmony.

> There is a strange thing:
>> this letting go of life . . .
>>> the awareness that we are not our own—
>>>> we are called to be part of a community,
>>>> we are called to be loving, giving, and caring,
>>>> we are called to surrender all and follow!
>
> . . . and at the same time
>> there is the dawning realization
>>> that we must each—alone—
>>>> assume responsibility for our lives:
>>>> to cease drifting along,
>>>> to stop allowing circumstances
>>>>> to stifle us or
>>>>> to push us into the common fault of
>>>>> blaming others for our weaknesses.
>
> We must choose to do the work
>> to which we are called:
>>> the work for which God has
>>> prepared us—
>>> gifted us.

*   *   *

The cat has moved again.

*   *   *

One of the most serious problems we women face is the tendency to devalue ourselves. Taking the biblical injunctions seriously, we tend to accept endless responsibilities exercised towards others without adequate recognition of our responsibility to personal vocation and professional growth. While the church strengthens its understanding of the meaning of community in decision-making and in carrying out God's purposes in the world, we women—just beginning to emerge from our self-effacing "good-little-girl-always-ready-to-help" role—may find inner tensions and guilt emerging while at the same time savoring the newly won freedom and making commitments to our own growth and development.

Childbearing and the nurture of the young are extremely demanding occupations. They will continue to appropriate the very best in creative energy and imagination for both men and women during a substantial period of their lives. Sensitivity to the needs of one's family, maintaining caring, nurturing relationships when the fierce drive to create calls one back to the studio is not always easy. Yet it is precisely this sensitivity, this awareness of people, this entering into their joys and sorrows that become one of the artist's treasured resources.

Artist Suzanne Sloan Lewis finds that the preparation of food, the maintaining of a lovely, loving home, volunteer work with the Hmong craftspeople, and time spent at the drawing board create a stimulating and satisfying rhythm for her that results in both a sense of harmony with life and superb art.

Those who have found the perfect synchronization of skills, gifts, and tasks report work and play merging in deep satisfaction and delight. Jan Habbegger of Mennonite Voluntary Service, and director of a local Boys' Club, finds a joyous sense of play in her work, ideas flowing freely at almost any time or place. "Work" for her is merely the time slot during which those dreams and ideas are translated into reality, an activity filled with exhilaration (and frustration). Natural skills and strong interests, well developed, exercised and coupled with love cannot but result in genuine fulfillment.

Then, as families mature, many of us enter a new stage in life, highly productive in other areas. In addition to maintaining the home as a center for the expanding or dispersing family, new skills are discovered and developed, old ones revived. The death of a spouse, separation, divorce, or loss of a job may require the rebuilding of marketable skills. Sometimes it is the pressure of traumatic events that forces the insecure person to plot new directions. One of the great challenges facing the church today is to encourage persons at these critical turning points to explore thoroughly God-given gifts and talents. To enter or re-enter the job market at mid-life without exposing ourselves to the call of God to be instruments of peace and grace in the world through the exercise of our unique abilities is to betray ourselves, society, and the church.

Pearl Janzen, after her husband's death and the sale of their hardware store, entered voluntary service to become the prime mover in a vigorous support program for an alcoholic rehabilitation project on the Hopi Indian reservation.

Of course, finding the work one loves to do does not automatically assure an easy life. Often creative individuals struggle against great odds to be true to their calling, even though they may enjoy the support and encouragement of church or other close friends. Violin maker Tom Metzler and wife, violinist Barbara Don—each meeting strenuous and diverse demands in their beloved world of music—find their life as newlyweds taking varied and interesting forms. "I have yet to cook an evening meal for Tom," Barbara reports. Violin lessons are most in demand after school and after work. "But our breakfasts have taken on a whole new significance," she says. Ron and Roxanne Claassen, while pioneering the development of a Victim Offender Reconciliation Program on the West Coast, have experienced the discomfort of uncertainty and dependence on others. Yet as the program grows and flourishes, satisfactions increase.

Cal Redekop cites the need for freeing work from monetary imprisonment. Sometimes the church, sometimes the family, and sometimes close friends form the group to provide support and the economic base for creative initiative. It is important to recognize that all we have and all we are is a gift from God and that—as individuals and groups—we and our resources can become instruments of God for freeing persons to live a life of exuberant and creative service. Women, especially at mid-life, may need to return to school to train for imaginative and creative tasks where skills and gifts blend in work to the glory of God. Often they will need moral and financial help in taking this step.

This chapter would be incomplete without sharing a few thoughts on men and women in art. It seems to me that underlying the whole artistic process is a passion to communicate to others an inner vision of reality: who I am and what the world is about.)

When this passion is present, so-called "men's work" and "women's work" are actually one; it is a force which cannot be limited. Men may choose to work in heavy materials, strong styles, or great massive forms, but sometimes they also work in the most subtle variations of color and form. Women may choose gentler substances and styles, yet Polly Victor, nearing retirement, re-entered graduate school for a Master's program in art and delighted us with massive, dynamic steel forms. All aspects of our being—bigness, smallness, gentleness, drivenness, inwardness, outwardness, reverence, sacrilege, relatedness, aloneness—make up our individuality and character. It is these as well as gender that, joined with the whole body of one's experience, define the style and content of our art. But for men and women the work is the same that of translating concept of experience into image and image into visual form. Ours is the task of being authentic, whatever the medium, whichever the sex!

*   *   *

The cat is sleeping now, obviously bored with black marks on flat white paper in contrast with the excitement of a new clay form taking shape. (I hope Cal and Urie aren't bored.)

*   *   *

Finally, my personal involvement in art has opened up a wholly unexpected world—that of business. During the early years of working in clay, a series of birds and animals emerged: they were a kind of celebration of God's goodness and my love for his creation. I saw them as a gift from God to meet the needs of our family during Gil's long illness. Popular demand in the marketplace led to the establishment of a studio that now employs seven persons. Earth Arts has become a major challenge: trying to build a caring community for all who work in it. Feeling the need to pursue my own personal art, I have chosen to avoid a hierarchical structure for the organization. In fact, the idea of such a structure was abhorrent. With the encouragement of Ron Claassen, I set out to embody basic Christian and humanitarian principles in a statement of goals and policies. Following is the preamble to that statement:

All that we have
And all that we are
Ultimately is the gift of God.

In response
we offer our energies and resources
to be a positive, creative organism in the world
modeling caring community relationships
bringing into being
both popular and serious art forms
that celebrate the wonders of nature
the goodness and mystery of life
aspiring to goodness, integrity and high
quality in craftsmanship as a way of life
serving the interests of community, customers,
employees and owners—each not at the
expense
of the other
sharing with the needy of the world.

To carry out our goals, we formed a managerial committee of three with one person each from production, sales, and engineering. This committee handles the day-to-day affairs of the business; the staff is directly involved in most decision-making. Relatively open-time scheduling encourages personal growth opportunities. A policy of an across-the-board bonus and salary increases is practiced to lessen the "seniority gap." Bonuses based on two percent of gross sales rather than profit have proved to be more stable and allow greater freedom in investment and contributions. Also, the work of the staff at the studio has given me the economic base for engaging in serious personal art that does not depend on public approval.

Earth Arts sponsors a part-time crafts person at a local Boys' Club. It also makes major contributions to the Hopi Alcoholism Rehabilitation program and to other agencies. At least two months of personal worktime are devoted each year to school children on field trips who visit our "backyard studio." Here "hands on" experience in clay is provided for over 2000 children each year. We are currently experimenting with providing part-time on-the-job experience for two young people with multiple handicaps.

The business provides constant opportunities for creative problem-solving and the application of one's faith to the work world. The continued growth of the business and the obvious fact that its increased earnings are due to the hard work of the whole staff is leading in the direction of creating an organization in which employees hold real ownership and participate completely in major decision-making. How to accomplish this and still maintain the unique character of Earth Arts—its highly personal sense of a celebration of God's creation—is a challenge. In order to stimulate the personal growth and development of the entire staff, perhaps a second studio housing a staff art cooperative will become the answer.

Meanwhile I struggle personally with the problem of how to maintain credibility as an artist having become so involved in business, in teaching, in sharing life with many people in many places. At this point, in terms of importance, discipleship seems to outweigh credibility. In any case, I celebrate the work which has helped me to define who I am and to test what I believe in practical ways—the work that has given me opportunity to grow, to struggle, to rejoice in the fact of my uniqueness as a child of God.

*   *   *

The cat is standing, stretching long, with high arched back. What beautiful form! I wonder . . . No, I haven't sculpted her waking up. I must leave these words and get back to my studio . . .

*   *   *

. . . to work.

6

Work in the Organization: The Angry Octopus

The understandings of the greater part of men are necessarily formed by their ordinary employments. The man whose whole life is spent in performing a few simple operations . . . has no occasion to exert his understanding . . . He naturally loses therefore, the habit of such exertion and generally becomes as stupid and ignorant as it is possible for a human creature to become . . . (Adam Smith in Schumacher:42).

Most of us, like the assembly line worker, have jobs that are too small for our spirit. Jobs are not big enough for people. (Pfeffer:255).

One of the most haunting songs we have ever heard is entitled "Sixteen Tons." Listen to the words of the second stanza:

I was born one morning when the sun didn't shine,
I picked up my shovel and I walked to the mine.
I loaded sixteen tons of number nine coal
And the straw boss hollered, "Well, bless my soul."

Sixteen tons and what do you get?
You get another day older and deeper in debt.
Saint Peter, don't you call me cause I can't go;
I owe my soul to the company store.

In commenting on its popularity, the editor of *Songs of Work and Protest* suggests "Some attributed its success to the fine driving beat achieved in Ford's record; others say the song strikes home because so many of us live on credit and owe our souls to some sort of company store" (Fowke and Glazer:53).

It is not just *Songs of Work and Protest* which points out that humans have worked within one organizational framework or another; other evidence also points to this unavoidable fact. The older master-servant relationship, the more contemporary boss-employee relationships—along with many other images and scenarios—have etched deeply into our consciousness the reality of working in organizations. And though not all work situations have exploited and oppressed people as these lines from "Sixteen Tons" intimate, most people who work have had to adjust to organizational demands.

It is almost impossible to think of work without considering its social organizational context. Without a doubt, when we talk about the "work position" or, in more common parlance, "a job," we are talking about a phenomenon which is woven into a web of norms, human relations, and social structures. It is possible that in the distant misty past, work did not involve similar social structures or some organization. Today, however, all of us, with only a few exceptions, work in an organization.

Many ask an understandable question: "Why is it necessary for work to be located within organizations?" The answer is simple: almost invariably, work is created and ordered by organizations. "In the study of formal organizations, work tasks must be the starting point. Formal organization of management arises as a response to the problems posed in the organization of work tasks" (Miller and Form:108). In ordinary terms, work in modern economic systems means performing interrelated tasks to produce products, services or values which are demanded by society. This fact is so important because the organization is not only the source of the work itself; the organization usually has the power to make a task meaningful and rewarding. On the other hand, the organization can also become a key factor in making work the most debilitating and dehumanizing aspect of life.

In this chapter, we deal with the way a Christian confronts the organizational aspects of work. What stance should a Christian take toward work in organizations? What are the basic problems and issues in the organizational dimensions of work? What does working in a modern organization do to the individual? Is there in fact anything anyone can do about the organizational impact of work on the individual? Much has been written on this subject, mainly from a theoretical and scientific perspective. Here we want to deal with the issue from the perspective of the person who is either choosing a work position, or who needs help in making the organization in which he works conducive to the achievement of his own personal commitments.

Work and the "Company"

There is considerable variation in the particular settings in which we work. However, a large number of us work within an organization which, in work-a-day language, is called the company. Others of us work for organizations with other names, such as hospitals, clinics, schools, universities, service organizations, corporations, or voluntary organizations. But all of these are organizations of people brought together—or who have brought themselves together—to achieve specific ends.

According to national statistics, most of us do not work in large companies or organizations; rather we work in settings that are relatively small in size. With reference to the manufacturing establishment in Canada, one statistic indicates that 64.9 percent of all employees work in organizations with less than 200 employees. Another statistic—this one pertaining to retail employment in Canada—indicates that 59.6 percent are employed by establishments of less than two employees (Peterson:76–77). However, even though the majority of us work in small organizations, organizational problems still confront us. We will take a more detailed look at four:

1. *One of the most common observations about work relations in organizations is that they tend to become impersonal, rigid, routine, inhumane and restrictive.* In other words, organizations tend to become bureaucracies.

The bureaucratic malaise is not restricted to large organizations. Small ones can become infected as well, even though less acutely. All organizations—regardless of their size or nature—have the tendency to bureaucratize, which includes, among other things, the following characteristics:

1. continuous organization of official functions bound by rules;
2. each member of the bureaucracy has a specific scope of competence;
3. the organization of offices or positions follows the principle of hierarchy;
4. organizational affairs are normally placed in writing.

The entire bureaucratic effort is motivated by the desire to rationalize the objectives of the organization. By rationalizing is meant "the methodical attainment of a definitely given and practical end by means of an increasingly precise calculation of adequate means" (Weber, 1946:293). There is general agreement that modern capitalist organizations are highly rational because of the interest in optimizing profits and wealth.

The human tendency to bureaucratize does not necessarily flow from an evil motive. In fact, at least some of the bureaucratizing develops from a desire to establish fair policies that are stated precisely so misunderstandings are diminished. Also there is a strong desire for equality, consistency and continuity and for efficient use of human resources. Many of the evils that appear within bureaucracies seem to develop in spite of the goodwill of people who are responsible for the organization. Many presidents, managers, deans, and others have tried desperately hard to keep their organizations from becoming impersonal and dehumanizing, but few succeed. The reasons for bureaucratizing are many but, according to Max Weber, one of the most important is the fact that our general religious orientation has created a rational orientation toward economic life. He states:

> When fully developed, religious associations and com-
> munities belong to a type of corporate authority. They
> represent "hierocratic" association, that is, their power to
> rule is supported by their monopoly in the bestowal or denial
> of sacred values (Weber, 1946:294).

If religion itself has become rational and if we assume that religion has an influence on social institutions, then it is easy to see that other social institutions will tend to take the same general orientation and position. In any case, Weber says that all modern associations have an authority which is premised on the right of the "powerholder to give commands (resting) upon rules that are rationally established by enactment, by agreements, or by imposition" (Weber, 1946:294).

As we have noted above, there is nothing intrinsically evil about a bureaucracy, wherever it appears—whether in business or so-called secular organizations, or within religious organizations. The fundamental and overriding reason is always the same: the human need for a rational ordering of institutional objectives and organizational process. However, in spite of the fact that bureaucracy is not in itself evil, the term is immediately suspect. Indeed, terms like bureaucracy, bureaucrat and bureaucratic red tape are spoken almost invariably with a sour flavor—a certain signal that bureaucracy tends to strike us negatively. Apparently all of us like to be treated as individuals—not only as particular persons, but also special in some way—rather than as examples of a category or classification. It is this latter depersonalizing result that we associate with bureaucracy and which we decry so vigorously.

But our criticisms of bureaucracy often have a hollow ring, particularly when they are made by those of us who are within and benefit the system. For in the same breath, the spoken criticism is often followed by a kind of fatalistic and smug self-justification: it is simply not possible to be human in a bureaucratic setting.

That is unadulterated nonsense. More likely than not, when this argument is voiced, the complainant reflects his or her own personal lack of concern and compassion rather than a problem with the system. Bureaucratic structures can be humanized, and it is the first obligation of all employees to put a human face on every company policy and on standard procedures.

We use the term *employees* advisedly and we emphasize *all* with deliberate intention. In the normal organization, all or almost all members are employees. Even the top boss in an organization is an employee of the stockholders. Bureaucratic structures do allow room for both ethical and compassionate transactions. The unfortunate truth is that bureaucratic regulations often become shelters protecting both employees and management from accepting responsibility for a state of affairs in which dehumanization takes place. Silence eventually corrodes our ethical commitment to the point where we no longer see the opportunities to effect change, nor have the will to act.

For the Christian, retaining a sense of responsibility is particularly pertinent. One cannot stand idly by when the process of dehumanization takes place because of bureaucratic structures. Part of one's response may well be exercising every prerogative within one's power to act and bring about change—either for oneself or others. We certainly do not suggest that changing the stance or style of an organization is easy. On the contrary, it can be extremely difficult; but barring fascist and autocratic extremes, bureaucracies can be changed and improved. Where, after a time, this seems impossible, the Christian should consider the option of terminating his or her position within that organization.

2. *The varied forms and uses of power within a company or corporate structure constitute another area of concern to the worker.* Again—whether employee or boss—power that is usurped or wrongly used can create great difficulty throughout an organization. Unfortunately, such abuses are common, sometimes conscious and deliberate, other times the result of poor organization, administration or neglect.

Almost all organizational scenarios in history have included some unequal distribution of power. Many times, the power in an organization is parallel with the bureaucratic system, but not always. Often there is considerable informal power exercised. This power may inhere in certain individuals such as the owners of the company; or, for example, it may reside in others who, for reasons of tenure, have been able to accumulate power. In any case, the organization normally possesses considerable power; the use or threat of the use of power creates the sociological facts of coercion, opposition, breakdown of communication, hostility, dissent, conflict and negative feelings.

Before going farther, however, we must state clearly that not all the effects of the use of power are necessarily detrimental. The power to set up an organization to produce goods can be good unless the products are intended for a wrong purpose. The power to hire people and give them work for pay represents a positive value and fundamental necessity. Not even all the power used to terminate persons from organizations is necessarily misused power. Sometimes circumstances legitimately require terminations for the life and well-being of the whole organization. But when power is exercised at such times, it is almost always viewed as being harsh, no matter how it is administered.

A friend of ours, a very fine Christian, fair and evenhanded, has had to terminate many people who had been hired earlier to work in his organization. Even though he has tried to be as compassionate and generous as the conditions would allow, he has often said, "No matter how hard I try to be fair, I have never yet fired a person who did not feel very badly toward me." Naturally, it is very difficult to feel good about someone who has done something to us which we do not like or with which we disagree.

But in contrast to this man's sensitive approach, power also can be used callously or unfairly in an organization. We all know persons who have been wounded by the thoughtless or uncaring use of power in an organization. People have been fired without prior notice; they have been shunted around or demoted because of interpersonal conflict or neurotic needs. Other times, although there is no demotion or termination, intolerable work conditions are allowed to continue or worsen simply because people matter less than profit. *Organizations can really hurt people.* And often the person with lesser power, because he or she has little or no recourse, is the one who gets hurt the most. In most situations, the aggrieved employee can only pass quietly from the scene, nursing his deep hurts along with those who cannot do much about rectifying the injustice in the organization which perpetrated the wrong.

Of course, there are many ways in which an employee can "get even" with the unjust use of power: sabotage, theft or malicious gossip. But these are clearly not appropriate for a Christian who believes that Jesus taught His followers to "turn the other cheek" rather than to hate. At the same time, all of us know that it is easier to condemn vindictive feelings than to offer a solution to those who are dealing with such feelings that so naturally follow unfair treatment. Fortunately, there are procedures which may help to mitigate the misuse of power.

One of the most important is increased communication. Whenever there is dislike or distrust toward another, one of the most obvious and natural human responses is to decrease communication. When there is a negative feeling toward someone else, the great temptation is to turn away thus increasing the estrangements. But Jesus said, "If your brother sins against you, go and show him his fault, just between the two of you" (Matt. 18:15). One may grant that Jesus could have been referring to a community of Christian disciples; however that likelihood does not deny that this principle of Christlike behavior can be applied—often with surprising results—in other structures.

Thus, when power is exercised unfairly in the workplace, it is incumbent on us to go directly to the person responsible and discuss the problem. This is not easy; most likely it will require a lot of patience, prayer and support from others. It is possible that the person in power may retaliate in some way. Generally, however, if this approach is taken, the outcome is positive. Often there is an exhilarating reconciliation of persons and a clarification of misperceptions which had been building up over a period of time.

Another response to the misuse of power is to try to rectify the conditions that allow power to be misused. For example, if a boss continues to assume that the women employees in an office should consider making coffee a part of their responsibility, it may be necessary and effective to develop a list of such peripheral tasks, clearly defining what is expected of whom—instead of making assumptions that affect a certain category of employees. This procedure can often help unclarified problems to surface. Or if a foreman expects an employee to do a lot of extra work or threatens an employee by withholding a pay raise, it may become necessary to revise the job description so that the work becomes part of the job for which the pay is given; or the task can be delegated to some other person.

Of course, another technique to deal with the misuse of power is to use the channels which the organization has established to handle problems and tensions. One example is the personnel department's ombudsman. Most organizations and the people who run them are well-intentioned; they want the best for their employees—if for no other reason than their awareness that satisfied employees help to maintain a successful business. Usually they will do what is possible to make necessary changes. In some settings, there is the possibility of recrimination or revenge; but if the conditions are so bad that recrimination is part of the administrative pattern, it may be advisable to think about looking elsewhere for work.

Organizations can contribute to both good and bad behavior patterns in those persons who are part of a particular working community. What is always crucial is the spirit of the people in organizations and the way organizations are structured. Good people can make a bad structure work, bad people can erode a good structure. In the same way, social structure can help people be humane to each other, or a totally adequate social structure can be frustrated by the intentions of the people in it. The fallacy of a one-sided view, such as Marxism—which maintains that it is the institutional elements which corrupt man—is exposed everyday in the Soviet Union's continuing attempts to set up good institutions. Human beings will corrupt institutions and institutions will corrupt human beings. Good people will "redeem" institutions and good institutions will help to "redeem" men and women.

Earlier, we mentioned an employee's option to terminate if the work setting became too difficult. Of course, one may ask whether terminating a job is not a cowardly way out or if it is always the *right* thing to do? Many would suggest the option of "fighting fire with fire" or confronting power with power—usually referring to resorting to union or worker organizations. At this point, however, it is necessary to say that the Christian gospel does not teach that a misuse of power should be confronted or dealt with by power or that force should be met with counterforce.

We do not consider it naive or sentimental to suggest that Christians can and must be the reconciling force in situations where power is misused. The Christian theology of regeneration and reconciliation means that peace is and should be declared between human beings. Throughout this book, we maintain that the work position is the most important arena for human relations and the interaction of persons. If the Christian gospel cannot contribute to making peace in the workplace, it has no relevance at all. The gospel does not take Christians out of the world into some utopian fantasy land; it leaves them precisely in the middle of this world; for most of them, that is the work situation. But while they live in that work world, the gospel of Christ provides a viewpoint and resources and suggests approaches and attitudes so they can not only survive but also contribute to change that will benefit their work partners and themselves. In a society that is often called Christian, how irresponsible it is to assume that changes cannot be made within a system or that the factory is not the place where the misuse of power can be confronted and rectified. Changing the system will not accomplish this objective because of the reasons given above, but making changes within the system is possible!

3. *A third area of stress for the worker in the organization arises out of peer group and informal group pressures.* One of the most impressive discoveries of social science with reference to organizations is the reality of informal pressure groups and their power. Informal pressure groups exist at all levels of an organization and in every setting where organizations exist—secular, religious, business or social.

The pressure group often performs a very positive function by mediating between the individual and the organization. Thus when a person is newly employed or lacks self-confidence and experience, the informal group can explain, support, encourage or run interference. But if, instead, the informal group has developed patterns of slowing production, destructive attitudes toward management and the company, cynical views of their own role in the business (many of which may well be justified), the individual is normally helpless and may have to capitulate. For if the lone individual does not yield to the group, that employee will be punished until he or she relents or is forced to resign.[1]

Furthermore, a negative informal group spirit is not limited to the shop floor; it can permeate all levels and sections of most organizations including church mission board offices and Christian colleges. How does the Christian respond? A person's response may be determined by many factors. If one is totally isolated in a work setting one may have a difficult time, but even there, an individual can take some action. One person with a positive, wholesome and honest attitude can transform a department and even help redirect an entire organization. It is vital that the intentions of such a person be genuine. If not, or if a person is inordinately ambitious to move up in the organization, then clearly the informal group will apply pressures which cannot so easily be dealt with and which will likely also inhibit the climb.

The Christian's role, therefore—much the same could be said for any reasonable person—is to initiate or contribute to the changing of those conditions that make individual survival in the workplace difficult. If survival is in question, even with the support of the informal group, then again termination might be the only course of action. The same would be true if the objectives or methods of the informal group are radically different than those of the individual and do not seem susceptible to change.

In the analysis of problems in organizations, however, one principle must always be kept in mind: no one ultimately responsible for an organization's well-being and success is interested in intentionally creating or perpetuating dysfunction through discontent, tension, conflict or other forms of counterproductive activity. To believe otherwise would require the absolute suspension of normal patterns of logic with respect to an organization's goals. A better explanation of tension and malaise in an organization is that the structure somehow inhibits or even blocks the best intentions of people from emerging, or that the structure inhibits serving the needs of people within the organization.

Of course, when informal pressure-group dissonance exists, the most crucial key in its resolution is the "informal manager" of the pressure group. Also, tension often can be resolved through a sensitive boss or foreman in the department. Respect for the other person, coupled with personal integrity, tends to be very effective in bringing about improvement. If the boss is not sensitive, is incompetent in human relations, or is retained because of personal or political connections, the prognosis for change may seem dim but is seldom impossible.

Since one cannot avoid the informal group phenomenon, there are several options. One can simply join with little ethical concern about the group functions. In some cases, fighting it may be an option, but one must be prepared for possible adverse reactions arising from direct confrontation. For the Christian, the most effective challenge to the group may be to "work from within" as Christians were accused of doing in the Roman Empire. To illustrate, let us take a very small but important example: cursing and swearing. Usually, swearing is almost entirely the offspring of informal group pressure. Outright condemnation may well create counteractions. Consistent modeling by resisting personal use of curse words and at the same time casually but firmly showing how the use of expletives and hyperbolism is self-defeating and indicative of a lack of integrity, will often convince even the most cynical.

Many scholars are becoming thoroughly convinced of the importance of the informal group in individual experience. Christians also, as they wrestle with how best to share their faith, discover that the informal group is one of the most effective settings for communicating the gospel. Many of us will never find a better place within which to witness and live out our faith than our "work group"; for it is precisely the dynamics of the informal group which provide the context and the occasions for dialogue and exchange on the basic issues of faith and life. Thus, for the Christian—instead of the informal group becoming only an occasion for stress—the informal group can provide a challenge and an opportunity.

4. *A final "organizational" problem which needs to be analyzed is the issue of organizational goals versus goals of the individual.* One of the central elements of organizational theory is the fact that most organizations have goals—if not explicit, then certainly implicit. The term "organizational legitimacy" refers to the right of the

organization to expect individual subordination to these organizational goals.

We need not spend much time discussing any work situation where the goals of the organization (company in our discussion) are totally opposite to the goals of the employees, for if this should ever be the case, there is only one option for the Christian—to absent himself or herself from that workplace as soon as possible. The Christian need not and should not wrestle long with the issue of incompatibility between personal goals and company goals. For example, if Christian principles are primary, the employee working in a liquor plant should resign forthwith. The same judgment could apply also to the manufacture of munitions or armaments or tobacco. A Christian cannot work in some types of organizations because their ultimate goals represent a contradiction to the principles and commitment he or she holds dear.

However, when there is not an unreasonable incompatibility between company and individual goals, the employee should make a supportive contribution toward company goals. Since the individual has accepted employment, the company has legitimate rights and expectations. The Christian, or any other reasonable and honorable person, will recognize and honor these legitimate expectations. At the same time, in at least some organizations, there is a very wide but hazy middle ground where the individual's goals and perceptions may be subtly different from those of the organization. Finding the right answer in these hazy areas is difficult—particularly when an overall compatibility exists but there are still specific divergencies.

A few examples of such divergencies are: 1) amount of time expected by the company; 2) amount of energy and effort demanded at work; 3) amount of time spent away from the family; 4) type of work demanded which may not be included in the job description; 5) work required in areas for which a person is not qualified; 6) expectations regarding promotion, pay increases, and working conditions which may be different for both parties.

It is clear that no standard criteria can be established by which all the nuances can be recognized or all of the questions answered. Each individual faces a unique situation; each must commit to basic principles and make his or her own application. In some sense, millions of people are making daily entries in private double entry bookkeeping systems, tallying the costs and trying to balance these costs with their rewards for working for the organization. Of course, the entries are never the same for any two individuals. For example, how much can a "Christmas turkey" offset the nagging feeling that "My work is not really challenging me"? Or does a major promotion, achieved ultimately through travel away from home, balance adequately with the time spent away from family?

Several principles will provide significant beginning points for process, even though they will not resolve all the problems.

1. When organizational expectations are unreasonable, reflecting unfair demand or exploitation, good reasons exists to initiate proceedings to rectify the situation. Most reputable companies or organizations provide procedures to handle internal grievances of many kinds. Where these exist, the employee has a responsibility to utilize them to their fullest extent and purpose. If adequate procedures for the settling of such grievances do not exist, the employee has an obligation to initiate corrective actions to help the company get "up-to-date."

This latter point may very well apply even more to church institutions than it does to organizations and companies in the commercial or industrial sectors. Some of the bitterest employees we have known or counseled have worked for church institutions. Some of the poorest employee benefits are found in church offices and organizations. Many church institutional workers have given the best years of their lives only to discover, upon retirement or termination, that the future is financially bleak because of the total absence of retirement, disability, and health benefits.

The best contribution an employee can make in such situations is to work for the resolution of such inadequacies. One person may very well help to create improvement in attitudes and general employee "climate" to the point where the organization operates as it should. Even though each organization will be unique, there are enough general standards in existence to offer guidance; from these the employee and the company will be able to decide upon a fair set of expectations for employment within a particular workplace.

2. When company expectations are not unreasonable but operating dynamics still create difficulties, employees and employers are obligated to ferret out the difficulties and resolve them. Many experts in the field have noted that we are living in a period of newly enlightened policies regarding *quality of work life* for employees, and that most progressive organizations have such policies in existence. When differences of opinion about the legitimacy of company demands on the employee do surface, it is the employee's duty to utilize any available procedures to the fullest.[2]

But most statements of enlightened organizational philosophy overlook one element: the fact that there are often individuals in the management or supervisory structure who have psychological, social or even faith problems which may impinge upon the subordinate in very direct ways. There is no practical way in which individual neuroses and the psychological needs of managers and supervisors can be contained so they don't intrude on subordinates. Obviously, this kind of problem almost always impinges most directly on subordinates. It is very hard for a beleaguered subordinate to confront a neurotic superior, for the boss normally has the power to fire him.

If the superior's demands are not the result of serious personal problems but rather are structural in nature, or the result of personal problems of peers or subordinates, there are grounds to believe that a reasonable and loving approach can solve the issues. This approach then becomes a matter of developing effective strategies to work at the problem. But, of course, if the ultimate superior is dominated by personal problems of his own, the situation becomes much more complex. If the organization is structured on the traditional bureaucratic-corporate model, the line of authority runs from the superior down to the inferior so that the "man on top" is always the boss. And, neurotic or not, the boss usually has the last word.

One of the responses to employee needs—established and maintained by enlightened organizations—is the role of ombudsman. This position assumes the hierarchy of bureaucracy but allows some bypassing of authority in an ordered and responsible way. If such a role exists in a company, it is entirely proper for the employee to use this channel, thus allowing and even assisting the organizational structure to rectify its own problems.

However, wherever there are no mechanisms available to alleviate the static in employee relations, the problem can be serious and sometimes insoluble. In numerous such cases with which we have had personal acquaintance, there was practically nothing a subordinate could do. In such circumstances, the only possible counsel has been to change jobs. It is futile to assume that the boss's neurotic behavior will lead to his early dismissal. The inevitable happens, sooner or later, but it can take years.

When the problem is serious and the real locus of the problem is at the top, then "hanging on" in hopes of improvement usually represents a dead-end street. In such situations, it would seem much better to seek new employment. The benefits of finding new employment along with the resultant release from the former debilitating tension—to say nothing of its impact on the family— far outweigh any possible advantage gained by waiting for a change that is a long time coming. Also, changing to a new job or position often brings about an expanded vista and a far greater opportunity. The "leap of faith" into an unknown situation may be the most creative thing a person can do.

In conclusion, it may be stated that the Christian employee enjoys certain assets and advantages in dealing with peers who have problems, especially when the problems are based in spiritual needs. But a balancing factor must also be recognized: It is easy to be too hopeful that the Christian witness itself can change a situation where there are deeply buried structural problems or organizational power difficulties. Where the needs of the boss constitute a major part of the problem, a subordinate can sometimes help the boss resolve personal problems, but that kind of effort is delicate at best. It may be successful, but change in such a relational setting depends to some degree on how open the boss is, and on how he chooses to respond to the Spirit of God and the possibility of healing and new life.

Work and the Labor-Professional Union

The relationship of the worker to the union is a highly complex and ambiguous one, especially for the Christian, and is almost impossible to discuss in a few pages. A few principles, however, may be useful in helping us to orient ourselves to the issue.

1. The *objectives* of the labor union movement insofar as they are concerned with decent wages, hours, working conditions, benefits and respect for labor are thoroughly Christian.

2. The basic means structured to achieve the above goals does not necessarily run counter to Christian teaching. When done in good faith, collective bargaining can be a very good experience and yield an excellent result. But much of the coercion, corruption and violence which some labor unions have used to bring about the bargaining exercise clearly must be rejected as being out of harmony with Christ's teaching and life. (Of course, from a Christian perspective, there is also no way to condone company violence against the employee.)

3. In general, the labor union movement has been so varied, so changeable, so unpredictable and contradictory, that it is difficult to shape a clear response to the labor union phenomena without knowing the specific conditions of a particular case. In the same breath, it must also be said that the shape of the labor union movement in our time has been affected greatly by managements that have acted just as capriciously and greedily.

This third point leads to the question of the Christian worker and organized labor unions. It is important for Christians to develop a stance toward organized labor, for even though the organizing of employees is declining, there are certain expectations in the labor movement which can be very difficult for the faithful Christian.

a) A Christian manager cannot actively and aggressively oppose organized labor's purposes and objectives. He or she may resist the means that labor uses to achieve its objectives; but fair wages, decent working conditions, adequate benefits and respect for work are principles announced in the prophetic calls of the Old

Testament and Christ's proclamations in the New Testament. Christian entrepreneurs in particular, and employers in general, need rather to take Christ's teaching position of the second mile seriously, giving more than labor asks.

To many hardened veterans of the business world, this may sound like irresponsible heresy. Nevertheless, it can work. In numerous companies about which we have knowledge, the labor relations are peaceful because the company has gone beyond the normal demands of labor; still, profits have continued to build. Lincoln Electric of Cleveland, Ohio, is only one of the many leaders and models in this sphere (although an early one). A visit to the company is an eye-opening and invigorating experience to those who insist that the traditional adversarial role is a necessity.

During this time of a massive restructuring of the economic order, some form of partnership between labor and entrepreneuralism will increasingly become a necessity. With decreasing resources and markets, cooperation and partnership, instead of conflict and battle, are the only ways in which the world economy will survive. Profit sharing, employee stock ownership in the company, partnership in management, community audits and many other new approaches—considered "utopian" a few years ago—will be the new frontier in business-labor relations. Those countries that are experimenting with new forms, such as Japan and Germany, are showing that certain new ideas can work and be beneficial for the balance sheet.[3]

b) From the perspective of the employee, the labor/professional union takes on a different face. From this point of view, the individual employee is less able to determine conditions; he or she is either the object of union recruitment or they are the beneficiaries of union activity or both. It is difficult for an employee to be neutral when unions exist in the company structure. In many cases unions have done a great deal for the rank and file laborer. In others, few actual benefits have been achieved.

But from the perspective of the individual conscience, union objectives, methods and results are not an unmitigated good or evil. The Christian cannot support featherbedding, the limiting of production or proliferation of jobs, to name only a few of the many union activities which serve to keep employment numbers up but undermine the viability of a company. As a matter of fact, most Christians would have little trouble deciding which practices and activities of the local union are wrong and/or right. Most problems emerge when the individual conscience stands at odds with the union procedures, but there is no way to refuse to participate.

At this point we are confronted with the fact of union legitimacy in the same way as company legitimacy was discussed earlier. It is interesting that most of the same principles apply here as well. A few of the special difficulties can be dealt with briefly.

1. *Misuse of trust and power.* Though labor unions are probably no more corrupt than any other type of organization, they frequently do provide the setting within which an individual is confronted with a real dilemma wherever the union *modus operandi* and the Christian conscience do not coincide. Sometimes it is possible to help reform the practices and/or change the structures so these kinds of things do not happen; the likelihood is great, however, that this will not always be fully possible.

One of the most prevalent misuses of trust in the labor movement is the exploitation of union resources, power and benefits for the union's officers and friends. Favoritism is not limited to city hall; labor unions are past masters at this game. Where such practices are matters of policy, the obligation to change the policies is clear. But that may not be easy to achieve. And sometimes, the involvement in some attempt to bring about change may result in greater involvement and more compromise on our part than we expect. At the same time, such risks should not keep us from trying to change the union structure. Of course, if corruption is accepted procedure, the option of withdrawing is much more viable and realistic.

2. *Informal group pressures.* The union's general objectives and organization may be relatively honorable, yet the informal implementation may swing wide of the mark. In such a situation, even though the union may have reached a formal agreement with the company for stipulated work performance including quality, the informal group structure in a company shop can effectively diminish or undercut such agreements. In cases like this, a conscientious employee finds himself in a serious dilemma. As indicated in the section above, direct confrontation may not be as effective as consistent modeling. But the need to change the climate of the informal group is strongly present and it may well require the direct confrontation of union leadership if the informal group cannot be made to become more responsible.

3. *Self-preservation rather than service to its membership.* One of the saddest aspects of the labor union movement has been its success and affluence. As with many other institutions—including those of the church—when good times come, the union organization becomes self-satisfied and complacent, less sensitive to members, and works mainly to keep itself in power with a secure future. This attitude can be very devastating to the purposes of the organization and to the relationships among members. The membership can become infected with a deadly cynicism and fatalism. Distrust and mutual exploitation can then begin to take place, making the organization dysfunctional.

If this situation involves the Christian in any form or degree, and if he feels membership in the union is necessary, then he has the opportunity of infusing a spirit of wholeness and integrity which can make a real contribution. Christ's metaphors of light on a hill, or salt to preserve or leaven in a lump of dough are appropriate here. Demoralized organizations can be "redeemed"; only one righteous person may help to start the ship on another course. It is not at all irrational to suggest that one lone voice, one dissenting vote or one remark or one logical question can start the process of change, a retracing of steps that eventually results in a total reorientation.[4]

The issues of union corruption, injustice, oppression and similar problems in the labor movement must be broken down into smaller dimensions. Then the problems will be seen to be no different, essentially, than those that exist in other organizations; for on the institutional level, business organizations are clearly just as corrupt and unjust as unions. Both, along with church institutions and other social structures, perform very useful functions, but they are constantly in need of caring, renewal and criticism.

The human being will never be able to avoid organizational affiliation. Increasingly, work life is life in an oganization. We can be consumed by organizations; but we can also use, manage, and control them. However, self-preservation or personal advantage cannot be the ethic from which one relates to organization, for that attitude and approach is precisely what causes many of our problems. The Christian brings a different approach—that of serving others—along with a sensitive conscience. A Christian conscience, nurtured in the Christian community, is the only way our work in companies and institutions can be redemptive—the only way we can avoid being consumed by any of the organizations within which we are obliged to live and work.

Excursus 2
Why I Went to Work When I Was Already Working

by Katie Funk Wiebe

My eighty-eight-year-old mother sits idle, looking out the window toward the empty street, one hand unconsciously fingering the material of her skirt. Earlier, she had carried her workbasket with her knitting to the bedroom. We ate cornflakes for breakfast instead of the usual cooked cereal. On Sundays neither she nor my father have worked at something ultimately useful. Their unspoken theology of work has always been clearly stated by their actions any day of the week: six days are given by God for work, the seventh for rest; no job, regardless how lowly, lacks dignity if one has to do it; when possible, work should be done with joy and should bring pleasure. Work, for my parents, has seldom been a four-letter word.

I consider my own view of work. In some respects it resembles theirs; in others it differs. I feel free to knit on Sundays, even to prepare for classes I will teach on Monday morning, but I don't do laundry or go shopping. Unlike my father, who never took one lengthy vacation in his lifetime, I readily accept the pleasure of not working. In other areas, I tread more cautiously.

Because I was expected to support myself until I married, I worked as a bookkeeper/stenographer for several years. Then married. Then didn't work. Of course not. At least not at work so defined by social custom. My work became my husband and children. This work was set against "work-as-the-job," and therefore out-of-bounds to the respectable wife and mother. Whereas "wife and children" were considered a state of being for men and "work-as-a-job" expected of them, marriage catapulted me headfirst into the classic wife's confusion of marriage as vocation *versus* work as vocation. Often I stood at my kitchen sink, wondering guiltily why the intellectual stimulation of the adult community of the

96

marketplace attracted me when my conscience said I should be satisfied with where I was in the home.

Years later, I learned that work for men and women was interpreted differently. Men worked in the public sphere, free-roving and unfettered by childcare. Women were expected to remain in the limited domestic sphere, content with its geographic and intellectual limits. Husbands could announce "I'm going to check out a business deal tonight" and expect wives to acquiesce without a murmur because to come and go freely was the husband's right and responsibility just as it was hers to say, "I'm going to can beans all day; don't expect much supper tonight."

My husband's early death precipitated a quicker re-entry into the work-as-job world than I had planned. My main activity for about fifteen years had been the care and feeding of children and husband. I knew how to manage a family; my office skills were rusty. Although I had been convinced that all work for pay should be creative and fulfilling, when I returned to the marketplace, it was primarily for money to pay the grocery bill and the rent.

My experiences since then have led me to accept a number of principles regarding work.

The voluntary or involuntary domestic enclosure of women is not a biblical precept. Both men and women are in charge of God's entire world and responsible to him for what they are and do. No one group (segregated either by sex, race or class) should be coerced by primarily social means to perform what Ivan Ilych classifies as "shadow work," a kind of nonwork which is sentimentalized and glorified to convince the people doing it that the economy cannot exist without it. In Ilych's view, shadow work is not badly paid work, nor unemployment, but unpaid work feeding the industrial economy and unique to it.

He asserts that the amount of shadow work laid on a person today is a much better measure of discrimination than bias on the job. When shadow work is forced on groups of people, in the end it destroys them. Blacks of southern Africa, for example, are asked to accept that their work in the mines is necessary to keep the economy going, yet that very work is their destruction. Women who are persuaded to make consumerism their main work are engaged in their own destruction. When women lost the privilege of being, with their husbands, coproducers of subsistence needs of the family, and instead—during the industrial revolution and thereafter—became "man's beautiful property and faithful

support needing the shelter of home for [their] labor of love,"
they took on shadow work.

The myth of women's necessary enclosure in the home
seemed reasonable to me as I listened to preachers extol the
virtues of the ideal Christian woman, especially from pas-
sages like Proverbs 31. I accepted that my "shadow work"—
not the aspects of my life which contributed to the subsistence of the family but the aspects which society demanded of
me as a consumer—was essential to the welfare of husband
and children and to my personal development, until I studied
Proverbs 31 for myself. What I saw there was not an isolated,
clinging female, but, rather, a mature responsible woman,
making wise business decisions, respected by her husband for
her effective functioning in the world beyond the gates of her
home. Other examples of women in the Bible convinced me
of women's freedom and responsibility to work with God in
bringing all his works of creation to fruition. The Bible did
not restrict the sexes to different spheres.

My first step in developing a useful statement of work was
to allow myself the right to work at something that was a
function of my being an adult member of the human race,
and not primarily a consumer. I rejected cultural forces and
religious messages advising me it was unfeminine to move
out of the stereotypical woman's role. Little by little I gave
myself freedom to buy my own typewriter and briefcase, to
maintain my own office in my home without guilt feelings or
the need to explain. God was going to judge me for my
discipleship before him, rather than for how brightly my
glasses sparkled or my clothing hung static-free.

Sidney Callahan writes in *The Illusion of Eve* that the only
benefit a woman should get from her work in childbearing is
her matured personality and a certain joy in contemplating an
independent developed person. I found I was a better mother
if I lived with my children and allowed them to make their
own mistakes, rather than if I worked on them and made
them my vocation.

Giving myself permission to enter the public sphere did not
end my conflict with the deeply ingrained view that a woman
should be willing to sacrifice her own pursuits and creativity
for the sake of her family; for Christianity teaches submission, self-sacrifice and service for the sake of love. To
contemplate a vocation outside the home while also being a
responsible mother of four children, even if necessary,
seemed wrong. Callahan writes that she struggled to find the
fine line between sacrifice for the Lord and psychological
suicide. I found I had to live with some intellectual stimula-

tion and some systematic nondomestic work in the adult world to survive. I accept that this will vary for different women. Each person should be free to choose. I believe that if I had not returned to remunerative employment, I would still have changed my work patterns while at home in order to meet these needs.

When I re-entered the work force, I accepted a position offered me because it seemed to fit my qualifications: typing, copyediting, proofreading and a little writing. After a few years of this, I woke in the morning hating the day for it often meant eight hours of very routine tasks. I found myself a statistic in that group of workers who are on a payroll they'd rather say goodbye to, but who can't leave because they have to stay on.

Ralph Bugg in *Job Power* writes that people transcend their circumstances in various ways. Some unplug their sensory equipment and put their minds on "idle" while at work, or they view their present situation as a step toward a goal (money, advancement, leisure, retirement, etc.), or they focus on their contribution to the users of their product or service. Others find special meaning in being part of a team, institution or other shared enterprise. Still others survive demeaning situations by asserting their basic dignity and integrity by being true to God's purposes as they understand them.

My thinking was muddy then, but I believe now that *whenever possible, work should be determined by innate talents and spiritual gifts rather than by external circumstances;* yet, even as I write these words, I know that spiritual growth is possible in the most difficult situation. We may feel wasted in a work situation, yet we need not be wasted. Longshoreman-philosopher Eric Hoffer in *The Temper of Our Time* bemoans the fact that our society warns us not to waste our time, yet we are brought up to waste our lives. We tend to choose a job by external criteria rather than intrinsic rewards. He deliberately stayed close to the working-man's role because of the intrinsic benefits he derived from it.

My father-in-law used to tell his son, "If you can do what no one else can, you shouldn't be doing what everyone else can do." Most of us work best if our work is an expression of our gifts, yet a talent or gift may be a long time in revealing itself. We often make many wrong guesses in the process of discovering our vocation. Not everyone's gift and work will coincide nor will everyone need to engage in some service or ministry in addition to work, yet the greatest satisfaction comes from work one enjoys. Further, if one commits oneself to it, it becomes impossible merely to dabble in it thereafter, or to relegate it to the hobby category. Hobby for many people becomes work in the highest sense.

Though many people agree with Dorothy Sayers that "Work is what one lives to do and not what we do to live," work as the sole rationale for life is fragile, for it can be destroyed quickly by sickness, unemployment, retirement, old age and, for some women, by childbearing. It took me several years to come to terms with myself as a person working at a job I was doing mostly to live. What I really needed was work I could live to do, that would meet my basic commitment to Christ and his mission and affirm to me my identity as a worthwhile person, an identity that might then transcend the work.

Thinking of going back to school, I faced the kind of identity crisis most men face early in life, in high school or in college. Our culture expects men to push into the future, pursuing a career image they admire. They choose a trade or profession and move into it gradually, but steadily, with the encouragement of family and friends. I had once chosen marriage and family as my calling and dabbled in writing. Now I had to deliberately choose a career—a frightening proposition. I couldn't go back to only homemaking; that decision was made by my financial situation. I had to face what to do with my life for the next twenty or more years, and I knew I didn't want to spend it in general office work. I had to find an identity in the work world that I could respect and live with for a long time. I feared not being myself, yet I also feared being myself—whoever that was—but then not getting the recognition I cherished from those I respected. What did I want from the years ahead? Money? Power? Love? Fame? Security? What did God want of me? Could I even ask such questions after my teenage years were long past?

Some people work for self-esteem, some to avoid boredom. Others work primarily for an identity: to be able to say, "I am a teacher," or "I am a businessman." Who will deny that a worker gains confidence in self as a person when the worker can act or react more freely to external and internal forces? Anxiety, loneliness and fear rarely upset a person engrossed in an enjoyable task. We consider a person's vocation as the most significant aspect of life—a calling, that which gives meaning to life and possibly also provides cornflakes and milk for breakfast. I wanted to work not only for an identity, but for the joy of creating, if not artifacts in writing, then my own personhood using my particular gifts and abilities.

I soon accepted the fundamental fact that I had to assume personal responsibility for my mental, spiritual and emotional growth until death. To enter into one's work means entering a kind of school and developing there a plan for lifelong learning; it means also not hanging onto concepts that have outlived their usefulness nor becoming defensive and frightened by changes. As a newcomer to the work world, I had enough to be fearful of, so I had to learn to swing with the blows—not an unusual but certainly a trying experience for women entering the work force late in life.

People who know me now don't usually think of me as a fearful person. They are unaware of how I inched my way through a multitude of fears. Sometimes I struggled with myself for hours before making a phone call to do an interview for an article. When I began teaching eventually, I felt so insecure I wrote out every word of every lecture. When I gave a public talk, even a very informal one, I trembled visibly for a long time afterward. The easiest way out would have been to avoid the frustration of making decisions that would direct me to my ultimate goal: to become a thinking, contributing person. I could simply have drifted.

By then I had added another thesis to my statement on work: *I have to live my own life. No one else can live it for me. And I cannot merely think of my life.* I must do my own work. No one else can do it for me. I must live and work in relationship to others, testing, trying, working out my own salvation with fear and trembling. The temptation to hide behind others and let them do the thinking, planning, and deciding while I coast will always be appealing. But just as I can't survive on borrowed ideas or on someone else's work, I can't shift to a holding pattern, hoping for some mammoth sweepstakes or lottery to shower me with the means to make life easy. As I moved further into the work-as-job world, I clung to Dr. Marion Hillyard's words in *Women and Fatigue,* "From the time a woman is born until she dies she is not only a woman but also a person. All persons have basic human needs. The basic need for every woman is to have a central core inside herself, a center and a strength that is entirely her own. Without this she's going to be whatever turns up—whatever the economy asks, or what the men think beautiful, or what the children want to make them happy" (p. 136). That core for me was knowing that I was a valued child of God on a personal pilgrimage with him, and not obligated to a society attempting to funnel everyone through the same mold.

My new life brought me more and more out of the home and into the public sphere to which I had previously sent my husband and children. I now had to question matters I had accepted as natural to the Christian life when I wasn't being forced to test them personally. I learned that I had to accept my children as individuals with the right of free choice. Life became easier when they stopped being the total focus of my life. The neat formulas I gave them so glibly about what to do when they collided with moral and social issues now needed examination and a stronger underpinning.

Yet, as I mentioned, not everyone works at a job which adds immeasurably to the quality of life. I began to enjoy my work of teaching, but working on an assembly line, punching a keyboard, teaching kindergartners, may not be the kind of work which inspires long letters home. Not all persons want to be identified first by their work simply because it doesn't mean much to them. If they return willingly to work on Monday morning, it is because their job calls them into an adult community, where they enjoy the side benefits of being part of a team that enjoys one another's company at coffee breaks and during other activities.

What becomes the center of life when work is boring? What do you write home about or talk about to friends? Obviously it's what you do when you aren't working, leisure-time activities.

According to Robert Lee in *Religion and Leisure in America,* leisure-time activities are moving into the center of life and threatening to replace work as the basis of culture. A goal of many Americans is to own leisure-time goods because they provide a meaning for life. Yet the more of such goods a person acquires, the more time and energy are committed to using them. Families that own a boat or ski equipment want to get their money's worth out of them each season. They feel obligated to use them, but this means that they will have less free time for other activities.

Hoffer makes the point that greater leisure in our society should produce greater creativity. In the church, more free time should mean there are more people visiting the sick, helping the poor, being actively kind to neighbors. But it doesn't work out that way. Our society is simply moving faster in the direction of materialistic pursuits, convinced that leisure is time that the individual owns personally and that the best leisure activity must be bought with money. What gets lost in the exchange are the fine arts, religious values, and family life. Material goods purchased through work are substituted for spiritual and social values. I accept the fact that leisure, including vacations, becomes a stronger revitalizing influence when leisure is considered a necessary part of the pattern of life, rather than as something very different from and separate from the regular routine. The core of leisure is celebration, writes Josef Pieper in *Leisure: The Basis of Culture*. Every feast or holiday in the history of humankind had its origin in divine worship. The Sabbath, Christmas, Easter and other holy days were originally reserved for worship. Vacations, which are nothing more than a number of holidays clustered together, are most meaningful if they are also a time of worship, an affirmation of peace with God and humanity and a celebration of the joy of life. I readily accept creative work and leisure as bringing the most satisfaction if they are cut from the same piece of cloth.

I was ill prepared for my next lesson in the world of work: *Every work situation is also a political situation, which, depending on the people involved and my own attitude can become either a power play or an opportunity for service.* By politics, I mean the way any group of people governs itself or allows itself to be governed or arranges for decisions to be made.

Arriving on the work scene from the isolated perspective of a homemaker, I was not ready for the political aspects of work, operated generally by male rules and principles of power. Some men see women as intruders unless they are content to remain in traditional positions and types of work. Socialized to act out the theme of powerlessness, and never having learned to confront or to deal with market information, many women are at a disadvantage.

Now, as I think through the early years, I chuckle at my naivete and weep over my gross misassumptions. I knew too little about power in the work world and about how decisions are made by persons in control. At first I could not accept that a political system should exist; next that it actually existed; finally, I came to conclude that I should not only be aware of it but that I was responsible to exercise whatever power I had as a servant of Christ. For men, power and politics is an accepted way of life. They expect women to be supportive of them and their structures and hesitate to encourage them to take work risks. So the working woman has to come to some agreement with herself regarding the stand she will take on the need to win versus the building of community, the emphasis on the appearance of success versus genuine success, on learning to stroke the right people; for to fail in the work world often means that one has failed politically, rather than failed due to a lack of skills or a willingness to work hard. I viewed with awe the way some individuals barreled into a political fracas headfirst without regard for others; I felt perplexed and dismayed with others who bowed out of the decision-making process entirely to keep themselves untainted; and I rejoiced when I saw others, servant-like, passing on power and privilege to those without either.

I agree with Sara Maitland in *A Map of the New Country* that the Christian community lacks a theology of institutions and the power related to them, as well as a "spiritual language to discuss power in the context of supertechnology and institutional bureaucracies" (pp. 124–29). She writes that how an institution is run is closely, even intimately, related to what that institution really is and not just symbolically. Power comes from hierarchy, usually made of homogenous-thinking people who tend not to champion little people. They tend to pass power on to people like themselves. And power is seldom, if ever, given up voluntarily.

For me, servanthood in a work situation means I do not need to adopt unacceptable values of existing power structures. I must maintain individual integrity. Yet I must accept the stewardship of accepting risks, of joining in making necessary moral and ethical decisions when this is expected of me, and of seeing each person with whom I work, regardless of his position, as being on a personal spiritual pilgrimage and therefore worthy of respect. I have not yet taken a course in assertiveness training, although such training might be useful to me. Nor have I read many books and articles offering advice on how to dress for success. I recognize, however, that power and politics is an accepted way of American life, and that it is often complicated by sex roles. Yet I consider it important that no person working with or for me should ever feel utter powerlessness.

I conclude. Sidney Callahan defines work as a "conscious attempt to impose order or pattern to meet some internal or external necessity" (p. 179). To be satisfying, work can be either paid or voluntary. As a homemaker, I choose to impose pattern, order and harmony upon our family life. As a teacher I choose now to impose another kind of pattern upon ideas, so that my students can trace that pattern. As I examine my work I celebrate the Creator of every good and perfect gift. Author Richard Llewellyn in *How Green Was My Valley* reveals so sensitively how the Welsh miners celebrated work as an integral part of their lives. Their work in the pits was underpaid, with long hours under hazardous conditions, yet many who left soon returned because the pit work had a mystique worth more to them than greater security and financial advancement elsewhere. They worked at subsistence wage levels in a spirit of community—the men in the mines, the women at home.

Payday was a day of celebration. On Saturday the men came up from the mines, black with dust, laughing, in groups, and the women waited, dressed up specially in their second best with starched stiff aprons. As each man came to his front door, he threw his wages, sovereign by sovereign, into the laps of wives and mothers, fathers first and sons or lodgers in a line behind. "Up and down the street you would hear them singing and laughing and in among it all the pelting jingle of gold. A good day was Saturday, then, indeed" (p. 164). Their common work built family and community as well as provided food for the table.

In Shelley's poem, "Ozymandias of Egypt," the traveler from the "antique land" tells the narrator how he had come upon a shattered sculptured head lying half-buried in the "lone and level" sands beside two vast and trunkless legs of stone. These words appear on the pedestal: "My name is Ozymandias, king of kings: Look on my works, ye Mighty, and despair!" But the works are gone, for they built only himself; all that remains is the boast and the sneer. For me, to work is to build self-identity—yes, but also to celebrate by building a spirit of community.

7

Alienation From Work: Can Work Be a Curse?

> Used to daydream on the job, now I don't. My mind would be a long ways off. I just really was not conscious of what I was doin'. Like I been goin' to work in the mornin', when I go through the light, sometime I know it and sometime I don't. I don't know whether that light is red or green . . . You couldn't guess what I'd like to do. I'd like to farm. But there is no decent living unless you're a big time farmer (Terkel:239).

What does alienation from work mean? Why discuss this issue in a Christian treatment of work? Both questions are important; we will deal here with the first.

Alienation from work simply means that a person does not feel a part of the work that he does; instead he feels hostile—not only toward the work itself but also toward the results of his work. Karl Marx has given us a profound understanding of this concept:

> The alienation of the worker in his product means not only that his labor becomes an object, takes on its own existence, but that it exists outside him, independently, and alien to him, and that it stands opposed to him as an autonomous power. The life which he has given to the object sets itself against him as an alien and hostile force (Bottomore, 1956:170).

107

Instead of being enjoyable, therefore, and a vital, contributing part of the worker's life and experience, work becomes distasteful and the products of work become meaningless and strange.[1]

Of course, Marx is not alone in believing that work can become alien. Many non-Marxists also have come to the conclusion that much work is alien to the worker. One of this century's leading sociologists—Emile Durkheim, a pioneer in the study of the division of labor—concluded that human happiness is not increased with the evolution of labor:

> Assuredly, there is a host of pleasures open to us today (that) more simple natures know nothing about. But, on the other hand, we are exposed to a host of sufferings spared them, and it is not at all certain that the balance is to our advantage (Durkheim:241).

Jacques Ellul also has studied the influences of the technological society; he concludes that work in this civilization does not make people happy, that in fact it tends to dehumanize them. Research studies continue to confirm what Karl Marx and others have maintained, namely, that in modern industrial society the worker is often "separated" from his work, and in fact is psychologically estranged from himself (Pfeffer).

Those who have not experienced work that is alienating are fortunate indeed; they are also rare. Most people have experienced alienation from work at one point or another in their lives, some more than others. Studs Terkel's *Working* represents one of the most heart-rending accounts of people who are caught hopelessly in the alienation of work. Terkel introduces his book by stating:

> This book, being about work is, by its very nature, about violence—to the spirit and to the body. It is about ulcers and accidents, about shouting matches and fist fights, about nervous breakdowns as well as kicking the dog around . . . . To survive the day is triumph enough for the walking wounded among the great many of us (1972:xiii).

Terkel concludes by saying, "Most of us, like the assembly line worker, have jobs that are too small for our spirit. Jobs are not big enough for people" (Terkel, 1972:xi–xxiv).

Before we take a closer look at some of the root causes of alienation, it will be instructive to note one underlying and principal reason that affects almost all instances of worker alienation: the alienation that is present because individuals either have no choice in the type or amount of work they are doing, or they see no way of changing or avoiding the work they consider alienating. Research studies show that persons who can choose the type and amount of work they do are much less alienated from work than others (Champion:196ff). This inability to choose the work one will do in a job, an occupation or a vocation is a serious matter that strikes at the very core of a Christian's understanding of humanity. *God created men and women with the gift of choice; whenever this ability cannot be exercised or is not allowed, a human being is something less than God intended.* This is why a discussion about alienation from work belongs to a Christian treatment of work. And also why we believe that solutions for worker alienation which do not take account of the Christian perspectives are inadequate and likely to fail.

The traditional solution suggested by many thinkers on this topic is a radical social upheaval. This view proposes that the only way work can be made humane is to change the entire social fabric so that the worker will not be forced to do alienating work. There are, however, several historical problems or fallacies inherent in this orientation:

1. Changing the system so that the proletariat becomes the ruling class does not change the nature of work and its alienating tendencies. An assembly line worker at General Motors is just as alienated from his work of inserting bolts and tightening nuts as is the Lada car factory worker in the Soviet Union.

2. Unless our societies become entirely automated, there will always be a massive amount of work which tends to be alienating; this will still have to be done by individual people. To say that no one should be forced to do work which is alienating allows no option: if no one *chooses* to do such work, it means that such work will not be done. That could lead possibly to even more serious disruptions in the social processes.

3. The assumption that improving social systems will automatically improve human motivations and remove human exploitation is dubious, especially for the Christian. That is not to say that improving structures for humane social relationships doesn't make a difference. It does. But it usually helps only in degree, although any degree of improvement is worth striving for.

However, it is clear that the fundamental nature of the problem requires more than an improvement by degrees. For most people, work is alienating because work is not seen as an integral part of their physical, psychological, social and spiritual lives. Such malaise is not superficial. Although the Christian may not choose revolution as a path toward helpful change, the ultimate solution may be nonetheless radical. But before we approach solution, let us attempt a more detailed understanding.

The Monotony of Work

When people speak of undesirable characteristics in their work, one of the most frequent complaints is the monotony of it—doing the same thing over and over, day after day. Monotony is cited as the major cause of alienation in the modern industrial society, since the fundamental principle of mass production requires a monotonous and repetitive production of similar products.[2]

However, it would seem that repetitiveness, in itself, is not the culprit. For all of us, sleep is a very routine experience, yet not many people complain about the monotony of sleeping! Or eating! Even young people, full of vitality and always craving new and exciting experiences, are repetitively and monotonously present at the table whenever it is time to eat.

Repetitiveness is a part of life. By its very nature, much of terrestrial, physical, psychological and sociological reality is repetitive. Actually, repetitiveness is quite attractive since it often provides order and stability for our lives. We can hardly imagine living in a world where the earth's repetitive orbits around the sun were not taking place, or where day was not repeated on a regular basis, or where night was an uncommon occurrence. None of us would like to live in a world where human relations would need to be reordered every day or where the behavior of others was continuously unpredictable and never repetitive.

From the perspective of these fundamentals, it seems clear that, by itself, repetitiveness is not the cause of monotony—that the repetitiveness of an act does not inherently cause alienation; that the sameness of an act or the sameness of a product which results from an act is not primarily to blame for the widespread sense of alienation felt by many persons in their workplace.

As a professor, I have taught certain courses for over twenty-six years. I must confess that boredom was often a threat until I learned to remind myself that this class is one hour of my life (which is getting shorter every day), that this hour will deal with a topic that will never be repeated again, that I am dealing with students whom I will never meet again in quite the same way, and that there is indeed an intrinsic enjoyment in sharing my insights and being part of stimulating interaction.

To deny that boredom is a distinct possibility in all we do is not very useful. However, we can assert that boredom is not always necessary. In fact, we must assess our inner orientation towards repetitiveness. Furthermore, we must search creatively for the intrinsic enjoyments which often do exist but are unacknowledged before we succumb to the glib conclusion that since our work is repetitive it is therefore also monotonous and boring.

Indeed, our attitude toward repetition and our aggressive involvement in the activities of the workplace may well determine whether our work will be alienating or not, rather than only the formulation of repetitiveness.

Repetitiveness need not be alienating if we keep in mind the Christian principles about the meaning of work presented in chapters 13 and 14. If we believe, for example, that work is honorable and believe that it is a method of glorifying God, then repetitive work, even with its potential for boredom, need not be a source of alienation. Endlessly cleaning the barn, feeding the pigs and plowing thousands of acres of furrows—and a host of other types of farm work—can be dreadfully repetitive, but it is not the nature of that repetitiveness that is alienating. Our inner orientation is the key.

The person who has a Christian view of work will certainly not allow work to be alienating simply because it is repetitive. He will of course make his work as creative as possible, but he will not say quickly and superficially that "this work is repetitive, hence boring, and finally alienates me from it and life." As Christians we need to recognize that creaturehood means repetitive events and cycles; we need also to recover the ability to delight in the joys intrinsic in a work activity. Ever since reading *The Practice of the Presence of God* by Brother Lawrence, we have had more respect for the mundane. We find him worshiping more in his kitchen than in his cathedral: he could pray, with another—

> Lord of all pots and pans and things
> Make me a saint by getting meals
> And washing up the plates.
> (Brother Lawrence, 1958:6).

Along with Brother Lawrence, most wives and mothers can tell us more about heroism in the kitchen than assembly line blues!

Work as Commodity

It is often said that our society is built on a monetized economy. This means that many, if not most, of our cultural traits and activities have a monetary value and meaning. Almost every element in our society—including persons—seem to be classified on the basis of money. A banker friend of mine responds half jokingly to questions which involve the possibilities of selling something: "Everything is for sale for the right price, except my wife." Another friend, when describing the behavior of a budding capitalist, quotes an old adage: "He knows the price of everything, and the value of nothing."

In this kind of monetized setting, human labor has also

become a commodity, an entity which has a price, and which can be purchased. The worker attempts to sell his or her labor to the highest bidder. At one time, this was a fairly straightforward transaction. However, in our industrial, technological society, the market for labor is becoming increasingly unpredictable and erratic. Sometimes a person who is dependent upon selling labor for money, cannot find a buyer, in which case the worker becomes unemployed—a terrifying situation. It is terrifying not only because he or she no longer has access to the necessities of life, but because the former worker now feels a total rejection and a pervading sense of uselessness.[3]

Labor has become such a central commodity in our society, that when it cannot be sold, a person has nothing left to offer, hence becomes a nonentity in terms of societal esteem. Since being unable to find work is such a serious issue, all of us need to be concerned to do all we can to create work. This means, incidentally, that the captains of industry who proclaim the creation of jobs as one of their motivations for being in business are doing a good thing, even if other parts of their behavior are exploitative.

The larger and more prevalent problem for those who can find work is that labor or effort is often "stolen" from the laborer. Upon retiring, a wealthy businessman and entrepreneur told a group of Christian businessmen that the issue that had given him the greatest concern in his career was "what to pay his employees." He went on to say that he was relatively certain that he had acted ethically in labor relations, in competition, in terms of quality of product and other similar areas; but he had never been altogether certain he had paid his people adequately. He said the easiest solution was to let the market determine wages, but then he asked, "What is my responsibility to the faithful employee who has a large family, much illness and many expenses?"

The question of what is an adequate return for work done has been argued for centuries. One of the most outspoken critics of labor as commodity was Karl Marx. He maintained that the capitalist economies would pay the replacement price of labor but keep a certain portion of the labor productivity for themselves. Marx wrote, "He (the capitalist) would have no interest in employing the workers unless he expected from the sale of their work something more than necessary to replace the stock advanced by him as wages; . . . The capitalist makes a profit, therefore, first on the wages . . . " (Bottomore, 1963:86).

That leads to a pressing question: Is it right that someone else should make some profit on my labor? If labor is seen totally as a commodity, the answer is *yes;* for within that frame of reference there is nothing wrong with "buying cheap and selling dear." But for the Christian, labor is not just a commodity; it is all the things we describe in chapter 13. An employer who buys an hour of a person's time, along with a certain amount of his energy and creativity, has more than a monetary obligation to his employee. A Christian employer therefore cannot simply pay what the market pays.

If it is true that a man's labor (that is, a part of himself) produces a profit, then the laborer has a right to a portion of the profits of that contribution. Ironically, labor—if it is defined as a commodity, i.e., wealth—has as much right to the return as any amount of capital does. From the perspective of the capitalist ideology, therefore, a laborer has a right to some of the profit generated because of his exertion. But if labor is defined as part of the person himself in relation to God and man, then there is actually no way a monetary value can be put on labor. And that is what was bothering the capitalist friend quoted above, as well as many others.

A Christian employer has no alternative but to engage in profit sharing with his employees. He does this by making it possible for the employees to invest monetary capital in the company. Since they are already investing a form of capital in the company—their labor—it is only logical that this principle be extended into a form from which returns can be realized. Profit sharing and employee ownership are well established and affirmed by successfully proven programs. Above all, they are highly profitable.[4] Christian employers therefore need to commit themselves to a sharing of profits with employees; this can then become a challenge to the capitalist creed that labor can be separated from the one doing the work, that it can be bought, and that it can be exploited and made profitable, but only for the entrepreneur.

But, one may ask, what of the many governmental, service, nonprofit, charitable and other organizations which are not profitable in the strictest sense of the word? Do they also make labor a commodity and hence become guilty of exploitation? The answers here cannot be quite so categorical. Certainly such organizations can be just as susceptible to *viewing* labor as a commodity even though they do not *make* labor a commodity. Indeed, without profit potential, there may be even greater pressure on the worker in some settings. In any case, the exploitation of labor is often present in these organizations, whether or not labor is forced into the commodity definition, or is seen as such. (Of course, where profit sharing is not possible as a means of bringing into balance the labor/commodity factor, some other ethic must be developed.)

The service sector is a good example of labor exploitation even where labor may not be considered a commodity. It may take various forms: financial, physical, even sexual. By virtue of their status and authority, employers and managers are in a position to exploit any or all of the workers under their jurisdiction. Of course, it should be kept in mind that managers themselves are often subject to exploitation; for within the chain of command and lines of responsibility present in most organizational structures, managers are usually subordinate to higher officials.

When any worker is exploited in his or her work position by being underpaid or being expected to work beyond reasonable limits, one has a limited range of responses: (1) resignation, which is often not practical for a variety of reasons; (2) protest and try to have the situation changed, which is not always very easy because of the possibility of recriminations on the part of the superior or the company;[5] (3) try to change things by peaceful means through available mechanisms such as personnel department channels of complaint or management-employee hearings; (4) confront the management through the union's power of numbers and united action.

Employees have done all four for many years. Under appropriate conditions, all four are obviously legitimate. It is a sad commentary on the Christian presence in the marketplace that the violent and bloody confrontation between the captains of industry and labor has involved Christians on both sides. In fact, the secularism of the labor movement is largely a result of the cynicism of many industrialists who have claimed a Christian faith.

Ideally the Christian employee should be able to achieve his or her goals with the third option. It is true that this approach may fragment the issue, thereby allowing management to retain its exploitative position (if that indeed is the situation). On the other hand, if Jesus' teaching on the issue of management exploitation of employees is being followed, a union would not be necessary to bring management to its knees. Instead, both employer and employee would be called to repentance and to follow the golden rule—do to others as you would have them do to you!

Where the worker does have some discretion on whether a questionable act is done or not, the decision should be based on the moral considerations rather than on company biases. But there are often gray areas; these may give a Christian employee the most uneasiness. Where there are questions, the ultimate principle is simply that of justice—doing to your neighbor what you would have done to you. This is a simple, yet basic principle and one that can be applied in practically every situation. Yet even here there can be a problem: that one's understanding or interpretation of what is "just" in a particular case can often be tainted ever so slightly in favor of one's self or the company business. But the questions remain and must be faced! What is a just and fair wage? How many mistakes can the foreman tolerate of an employee? How much does one tell an employee about the profits of the business?

Jesus gives us many unusual insights about relationships in the marketplace. Some of them appear a bit strange to us, such as the parable of the steward who paid all workers the same wage whether they worked one hour or the whole day. But we need to be careful to discern what Jesus was saying in an individual "sermon." In general, Jesus' teachings focus clearly on compassion for the helpless and unfortunate, on truthfulness and honesty in human dealings, and on loving all our neighbors. It may seem to be a bit disconcerting to ask "what would Jesus do" in a corporate boardroom, or on the assembly line, or in the retail store, but we must believe that he could operate there. Jesus did not join the Zealots or any other subversive movement in the Jewish society; he chose rather to work within the system. He worked as a carpenter-builder. There is no record that he created a revolutionary uprising. But he did exemplify the golden rule as he taught it. And that can be revolutionary!

The Lack of Meaning in Work

Meaningless work often alienates. This fact derives from the very substance of work. When human beings work they not only labor physically, but physically, mentally, and socially as well. An engine does not have a problem with the meaning of the work it does. But human beings demand to know what they are doing and why.

A friend told of the frustration he experienced as a conscientious objector in the United States during World War II. Most of the time the work he was required to do had some meaning—digging postholes for fences, or digging holes for trees. But, apparently, on numerous occasions there was no meaningful work available, so the men would go out on location, dig holes, and the next day close them up again. Richard Pfeffer, a university professor turned laborer for one year, describes the great anger he noticed among workers when they were given busy work, or nonsense work. The truth is, human beings want their work to be meaningful, that is, to have a purpose and to make sense.[6]

Work can be meaningless for several reasons. First of all, lack of understanding; the worker often may not understand what he is doing. However, meaninglessness is not necessarily a result of ignorance. Many prescientific peasants derived considerable personal meaning from sowing and cultivating, even though they did not fully understand the nature of germination, metabolism and growth. But in our industrial age, many people perform activities on the job for which they see no overall purpose. An employee in a giant government bureaucracy, who adds figures or processes forms, may have no clue to what he is doing in terms of how his work fits into some larger purpose. The most disturbing work I ever did was statistical computations that were required during my graduate school days; here I arrived at correct solutions (some of the time, at least) but had no understanding of how they should be used. The division of labor and its fragmentation into ever more minute specializations—which is at the core of our contemporary work scene—makes the specific motions or acts less and less meaningful.[7]

But a more significant part of the meaninglessness of work is that the person may have no awareness of how the particular task fits into, or contributes to, the larger social enterprise. A maintenance worker in a large corporation such as the university in which I work, has a right and obligation to know what he is doing and what it means in the ultimate sense; in many cases, probably, he has not the slightest clue. A person may need to sell a part of himself for wages, but he has a right to know—indeed, he has an obligation to discover—what he is selling his labor for.

In the extremely complex society of our day, the average worker has little comprehension of how his labor contributes to the larger picture. Specialization, separation of activities and functions, synchronization of similar and dissimilar functions in higher order structures and many other processes tend to mystify the laborer who is assigned to one work position. Now, with the increasing acceptance of electronic media, many of the cues and bits of information which earlier were communicated personally have now been coded so that the average person at work is in no position to see how his or her labor fits the total picture.

This condition is not limited to big business corporations. It applies to hospitals, universities, recreational institutions, and even to church organizations. I have reluctantly given up trying to understand how various procedures work at the university where I teach—procedures such as registration, course counseling, grade reporting, notification of changes. The student who takes a course from me is a stranger a year later because of the specialized work relationship which was established. In most cases, I have no way of knowing how my teaching affects a student, since our exposure to each other is such a small segment of the final product—the graduate.

The alienation resulting from meaningless work is a serious illness in our society, but that fact alone does not mean that work as such is meaningless. It means that we do not understand the work we are doing either in terms of the immediate specific consequences or in terms of the larger consequences of how that work achieves certain goals or fulfills the purposes of society. For the Christian, most work can and should be meaningful. In the first place, if it is not meaningful, the Christian should not be in it. Secondly, if it is by nature meaningless and the worker cannot choose to leave, he or she should do all possible to make it meaningful, if in no other way than by realizing that work can find its meaning as an act of bringing glory to God.

Work can also have meaning if the *results* of the work are desirable or valued. Hence, as a young man, I felt that cleaning the pig sheds was meaningful because that work contributed toward paying off the mortgage on the farm and helped to produce food for human consumption. Most self-employed people do not have difficulties with the meaninglessness of work from the perspective of results. If the results are not satisfactory, whether in terms of profits, products or services, they will make the necessary changes.[8]

Even though there may be little evidence that my own occupation has made a direct contribution to a better world, I have continued in the teaching profession because I believe in the general power of education to bring about social betterment. As a result of that conviction, I have maintained some positive orientation toward my work. I believe that the greatest source of alienation from work is a person's lack of faith that his work is making a contribution to the larger scheme or purpose of human society. Of course, Marx maintained that the worker was alienated from his work because it enriched his employer and impoverished himself.

But an employee in a government agency or service industry—as well as industry in general—who is not convinced of the significance or legitimacy of the results of his or her work is in a difficult situation. If, for example, a postal service worker does not understand or value the results of the work being done, then that work is meaningless. If being part of a chain of activities that bring letters from the writer to the reader is not desirable or valued from that worker's perspective, then work is meaningless to that worker. Should he or she quit? What action can the worker take?

Before doing anything of course, a person should reflect on the fact that work is necessary to provide the food, shelter, clothing and other amenities needed for an adequate and human existence. Most service jobs, professional work and productive work are necessary for societal well-being, and hence derive meaning from that perspective. If a Christian is doing work which is for the benefit of a full and humane life—his or her own or someone else's—it cannot be meaningless.

A Christian employer should see to it that the work an employee is given to do results in worthwhile consequences. A Christian should never be employing people to achieve results that cannot be respected and considered important to the community or within society. (The principles presented in chapter 12 offer further guidance here.) Most service industries and production industries are intrinsically worthwhile and valued; a worker should select one whose values match his or her own.

The ultimate basis for deciding whether work is meaningful is not the nature of the specific work itself, but what the consequences of that work are for God, the neighbor, and oneself. This opens the question of *the end of the work*. This we believe is the source of the most serious types of alienation. If we believe that what we are doing is for the ultimate benefit of mankind, the alienation of "meaninglessness" is then more a matter of personal position than the inherent nature of the work.

Work and Values

In treating work and the choice of a work position (job) it is a temptation to state specifically which jobs, occupations and professions are best for the Christian. But that temptation must be avoided since each person needs to make a host of decisions based on the principles and issues outlined above. It is necessary, we believe, to try to avoid "politicizing" or "ideologizing" the topic of work; the very necessary discussion about work should not become a vehicle to promote a socio-political philosophy such as capitalism or Marxism; rather, it is important to see work as a reality independent of this kind of "categorization."

One does not need to be a Marxist or an Adam Smith capitalist[9] to understand the nature of work and its role for oneself. These two systems and other historical models, after all, are only human attempts to understand and possibly improve a particular historical period in terms of labor, production, distribution and consumption. The Christian faith actually promotes its own view of all these elements; in the final analysis, one must concede that the Christian blueprint cannot be fully achieved in any system. If one can be free from the constraints of a theoretical system which forces work into a straightjacket, the following remarks will make a great deal of sense.

Since a Christian will not be a slave to the Marxist or Smith capitalist view of human nature and human history, he or she is in a position to redeem work. That is, if work is intrinsically good—as we have proclaimed elsewhere—then the work position, which determines the how, what, when, where and why of work can be managed and molded to fit the Christian view of life. This means that Christian employers will change the nature of work positions to make them conform more closely to the Christian gospel. In more specific terms, if a Christian employer is forced to underpay employees in order to stay in business, that employer has the

Christian freedom and duty to terminate or restructure the business. If a Christian manager seems forced to exploit others in work positions under his or her control, that manager must exercise the Christian freedom to change the work positions of others or to resign from the work position he or she holds.

The same freedom applies to employees in all the levels of work assignments. In most societies, no one is totally bound to any work position; in an ultimate sense, each person is free in Christ to starve rather than to be exploited. The alternative to exploitation is not revolution as Marx would believe, but neither is it passive submission!

As was indicated earlier, working aggressively to change the system is in order; at the same time, the Christian must be aware of the subtle trap of assuming that aggressive change will Christianize the system. More than that, one must avoid falling into the trap of assuming that a system—whether it is Marxist or capitalist—can solve the problems of work. Ideological systems often take lives, but do not solve the problems of justice, hunger or exploitation. Work is such a central and comprehensive reality that no secular system will ever fully comprehend or develop it appropriately.

We are not able to provide an exhaustive answer to the problem of the alienation of work: it is far too complex. But we can suggest an axiom that helps to clarify the issue: *The viability of any solution to the meaninglessness of work is directly proportional to the degree of concern and conviction the individual or group holds.* In other words, the more individuals or groups there are who are concerned about the dehumanizing aspects of work in experience, the better they are able to do something about it. There is nothing revolutionary about this principle; it is pragmatic and eminently functional. "What would happen if everybody would take your advice?" —It would be a better world. Someone may remonstrate: "Most people are not in a position to do anything about the conditions in which they work." If that is true, then we are close to a mechanical society. We do not consider the world to be that hopeless.

If the work a Christian is doing is meaningless, that person is obligated to find work that is meaningful—not only for the sake of his personal interests, but from the perspective of a moral imperative. Can meaningful work always be found? *Yes—if* one is prepared to bear the cost involved—looking for a long time and possibly incurring considerable expense. It may require relocation; it may require changing occupational commitments; it may require retraining or even a reorientation of life's objectives. But it can be done!

For many years, I have counseled people who were facing serious job difficulties to consider changing occupations and professions; many have done so. For most, the change has been a rewarding experience. On the other hand, for the Christian, finding meaningful work may require one to stay in a work position and discover there the ways in which it provides opportunities to fulfill vocation, of which he or she may not have been aware before. Brother Lawrence expressed this many years ago when he said:

> The time of business does not with me differ from the time of prayer; and in the noise and clatter of my kitchen, while several persons are at the same time calling for different things, I possess God in as great tranquility as if I were upon my knees at the blessed sacrament (6).

So the Christian may be called to stay where he or she is. But for many, beginning a new work venture is the right antidote to alienation from one's work. Some years ago a maintenance worker in a rather large institution became bored with his work; (he was probably also a bit unhappy with the low status of his job). He came to me with his concern. After considerable discussion, we decided that our community needed a credit union. We did the necessary research and succeeded in getting one organized. But the most revealing and exciting element in the new adventure was what happened to the ex-janitor. He "hit the deck" running every morning and "lived his work."

One of the most revealing aftereffects of the now-famous "sixties" is the way many young people refused to be "reined in" by institutional requirements and corporate structures. Instead they went to the potter's wheel and kiln; to the lathe; to the press; to the loom. This wave of creative entrepreneurs has developed an infinite number of specialty product businesses. Naturally, living "ain't easy" all the time and many of these noble experiments fail, but the rewards are undeniably present. In this creative sphere the entire gamut of types of alienation of work are absent. Of course, other problems take their place: financing, return on investment, leisure, labor problems, to name only a few. But in spite of the difficulties, few of these "explorers" would be willing to return to the factory.

For the Christian, however, there is an even greater challenge and opportunity. That is to "create" work by innovating in areas which desperately need servicing. In the area of energy conservation and respect for the environment, the Christian should feel an increasing obligation to make a contribution, provided he has the interests and abilities demanded in that area. Of course, many innovations demand cooperative effort, but that fact makes these possibilities all the more probable since Christians are called into communities of faith and action. Thus the area of waste reduction, recycling of wastes, exploration of alternative energy uses and production, and many others are becoming increasingly the domain where Christians should be deeply involved.[10]

Innovations in the material productive world are not the only challenge. The frontier of social services is vast, not only in terms of providing material benefits but in terms of enhancing social, emotional, and spiritual elements. The world of the elderly is one such example. Church institutions are another. It is generaly assumed that there are almost unlimited work positions within church structures. But we must insist that there is still a need for creativity and innovation which will create more meaningful work within church institutions.

There is little reason to be alienated from work if a person is willing to work at that problem. There are too many needs in the world, too many challenges, and too many opportunities to allow any of us to cling to the feeble excuse that the world of work is only or primarily a world of alienation. Jesus talked about the alienation among humans, as well as between humans and the natural environment, but he said in conclusion, "If anyone would come after me, he must deny himself and take up his cross daily and follow me" (Luke 9:23). That cross may well mean joining the struggle to make work meaningful for the sake of self and commmunity as well as for God's sake!

Excursus 3
Lord of the Onions

by Wally Kroeker

The sun hung like a flamethrower in the southern Manitoba sky, frying everything but the onions I was weeding on the family farm. The days seemed endless—seven to seven with an hour for lunch. Eleven hours (at 60 cents per) for the hoe handle to raise blisters, sores and calluses on adolescent hands. Scratching, clawing and cutting weeds; acre after acre of sour-smelling onions; finish one field and move on to another.

Unrelenting drudgery.

Would these onions ever grow to maturity? Does the hour hand never move? It was hard to see my toil as a good work that glorified God.

But grow they did. After weeks and weeks of hoeing, cultivating, spraying and irrigating, the onions finally grew, bigger than baseballs.

Marvellous things happened at harvesttime. Work was more fun. We no longer minded the stink. Oh, the onions still reeked, more than ever, for amputating each top released a gush of juice that flavored hair, clothes, and bone marrow. Noses burned and eyes dripped. We worked harder and longer than ever. But it didn't matter anymore. It wasn't drudgery because, you see, it was harvesttime. The fruits of our labors were being plucked from the soil. The result of our work was there before us—to see, to weigh, to sell. As the bins filled, our sense of worth and joy welled up within us.

The product even looked different during that festive time of year. Behold the noble onion, no longer a delicate sprout to be coaxed and coddled, but now a firm and robust bulb ready for hamburger, omelet or stew. (Not only that, but the medical folk were saying they were good for the heart!)

It was there on the sauna-hot onion field that I gained my first insights about work. I learned about the link between work and harvest, the chain of production that transforms calluses and acid sweat into a product—be it an onion, carrot or potato—to grace a festive table miles and months away.

Even as an adolescent I was conscious of needing a useful purpose for my toil. Farming was a noble, biblical occupation, but it could also become mind-numbing drudgery. Since work would be with me for the rest of my life, couldn't I find a form of it that would be a little more enjoyable? I resolved to seek work that would be useful, would be somewhat enjoyable, would provide opportunities for personal growth and development, and would make possible a "decent" living. Farming, as I saw it, achieved too few of these values.

I put these "work values" to the test several years later in a southern California pizza parlor. Here I climbed another rung on my ladder of four. First, I considered making pizzas to be a useful enterprise. We didn't then think of pizza as junk food. If it was, at least it was the king of junk foods. Hearty dough, low-fat cheese, juicy tomatoes and savory meat and vegetable toppings, not fried in grease but baked on stone as the children of Israel had baked their unleavened bread—who can call that junk food? And don't people need to get out once in a while? Where better to observe a family ritual than over a reasonably priced and protein-rich pizza? Sure it was useful.

But was it enjoyable? Without a doubt! No job before or since has been as much fun. Making dough, 300 pounds at a time, rolling the "skins," grinding cheese, mixing sauce, slicing pepperoni and salami—I loved it all. Add to this the constant flow of friends and visitors, the camaraderie of six bustling chefs working together with fluid precision during the frantic dinner rush, all to the accompaniment of a rollicking ragtime band. To a nineteen-year-old this was real fun.

The job even had some possibilities for growth and development. It was a time for a reticent youth to develop social skills and learn to work under pressure (valuable later in the daily newsroom). One learned forbearance and toleration for the blunders of others. The dinner rush was no time to pin blame or quarrel about individual rights and wrongs in the pressure cooker of the kitchen. One learned to give and take, to calmly compensate for error, with no thought of "who goofed."

Amid all this fun and personal growth, however, the pay was $1.15 an hour, scant even by any standard in the 60s. Survival wages for a single teenager; certainly not enough to build a future.

Meanwhile I entertained dreams of literary greatness. My oregano-stained hands were destined for greater things. From my pen, I fantasized, would come novels that would radically alter the course of events by sensitizing a vast and no doubt spellbound audience to cosmic values of life, death, virtue and eternity.

But along the way must come training and discipline as a wordsmith before I could even attempt to transmit grand thoughts and ideas. I would first serve my time as a journalist.

I would be in good company. I would join a pantheon of great newsmen-turned-novelists. (I was accustomed to good company, after all, in the onion field.) John Steinbeck's toil in the beet and barley fields around Salinas, California, had laid a foundation for *Of Mice and Men,* one of his better works. If the *Kansas City Star* was good enough for Ernest Hemingway, the *Regina Leader-Post* was good enough for me, for a while.

Now, in the news world, my full set of work values was being fulfilled. My work was certainly useful; no one disputed that. Even before Watergate and "Woodstein" ennobled our profession, it was assumed that the work of the journalist was vital to civilized existence. None other than Thomas Jefferson had declared that a society with newspapers but no government was preferable to a society with government but no newspapers. Not every story pushed back the walls of ignorance, of course, but even physicians had their share of hypochondriacs and malingerers, and college professors had sluggards who were along only for the ride.

The work was enjoyable, enriching. The cascade of ideas, events and stories of human failure, progress and triumph (not to mention the ego-inflation of bylines) had its own narcotic rush.

Not much of this rush was derived from my first editorial task of writing obituaries. But there were many things to learn even there. Such as the need for accuracy. "For most people," my avuncular editor told me, "the obit you write will be the last public mention, the last clipping to be placed in the family Bible. Make sure it's right."

Here one learned the niceties of dealing sensitively with newly bereaved people, a skill too many reporters and editors lack. Here one also confronted the ironies of power and prestige, the relative importance of "little people" whose well-spent lives had never before received credit in the public ledger. Here the lopsided scales of public prominence were at least occasionally righted. I remember the immigrant homesteader from Elbow, Saskatchewan, who had quietly tilled the soil for half a century and left the world better fed and better populated with a dozen able progeny (all duly listed, plus spouses) swelling the obit to five column inches. His neighbor, a prominent bachelor banker who'd had his share of public glory, stretched only three. The longer the obit, the larger the headline was our rule of newspaper graphics, so our immigrant homesteader was dispatched with a thirty-point headline while the bachelor banker with no survivors was laid to rest with twenty-four-point bodini. A modicum of Christian justice in that, perhaps.

After the obits came "greater things"—fires, droughts, features, elections. Stories of minor consequence filled the yawning gaps between "really big stories" of human travail and triumph.

The dream of the novel faded. Not that the newsroom was a "graveyard of broken dreams," as a Canadian government commission once intoned, but the work had sufficient value and joy in itself. I loved what I was doing. It provided avenues of enrichment and growth. And it was important, wasn't it? Never mind that my landlady thumbed past my byline, moving directly to the grocery ads.

I served a stint as well on the copy and wire desks where decisions of news play are made. There I was taught by older, seasoned executives what was "truly significant." I saw also how we ladled out what our readers would learn about their world on a given day.

Often, the decisions seemed coldly indifferent to human needs and aspirations. Unlike reporters, those on the desk are a step removed from the bodies and pulse of the *hoi polloi*. The desk was a place to learn new lessons of pragmatism and compromise.

For me, the stark clash of values and expedience came to a head during the waning days of the Vietnam War. The tragedies and plundering that attended the close were part of the routine currency of our desk lives. One day a particularly heart-rending article describing the latest in an escalating series of atrocities came across my desk slotted for page one. It moved me almost to tears to process this graphic depiction of human suffering. Soon after I'd sent the edited article on its way, a stop notice came to my desk. A newer story about bus fares going up a dime would displace the Vietnam story, which was now bumped to the back.

It irked me to follow through on that decision. A story of heart-rending human pathos was being shoved inside for something I considered inconsequential. Doubts arose. What use was my job to the kingdom if I was powerless to keep a story with enormous moral dimensions from being bumped into near obscurity?

Perhaps I could better serve God applying my skills in an overtly Christian arena. Newspaper work wasn't really Christian, was it? Aside from occasionally nudging the church page editor to run a story about a Christian cause, or suggesting that the book review editor take a look at the latest religious bestseller, or perhaps pointing out the religious dimension of a general interest, how else did one "report Christianly"?

So I joined a Chicago-based religious monthly with a circulation of a quarter million. I was sure that now I could really carry out my calling in a way that would please God and advance his kingdom.

But I soon learned that the grass can be brown on both sides of the fence. I bumped up against a Christian worldview so narrow that I was now more confined than I had been at the secular papers. Moreover, I was only one of many who were available for the position. Other equally qualified people were clamoring for my job. I did not feel needed, except perhaps to push an editorial agenda that was, in my opinion, more radical, progressive and wholistically biblical than other more conservative aspirants would have.

I did feel needed later, however, within our denomination—a church that, by the mid 1970s, had produced few journalists. It appeared that I was needed at the helm of a skimpy, low-budget magazine with a circulation of less than 10,000. My family and I made the move from the fast pace of a huge metropolis to a casual midwestern town of 3,000 inhabitants.

The move seemed consistent with our understanding of what it means to integrate faith and work. My constellation of work values now seemed fuller than ever before. I was doing something that I felt to be useful at a place where I was needed. I enjoyed the work immensely. It was spiritually and intellectually enriching. My salary, though modest, was adequate in the undemanding midwestern economy.

It may have been a homecoming. My mother tells me that at the age of five I had declared my resolve to someday be a "cowboy and a preacher." The notion of a Mennonite circuit rider was an unlikely alloy, at best—always good for a chuckle at family gatherings. I was no preacher, for I was not then very devout and was plagued by a speech impediment. And I was certainly no cowboy. We had no such things in the plains of my childhood and I was far too ungainly to do well on a horse. But writing churchly articles for the denominational press somehow fulfilled that early yearning. I certainly had my pulpit—an editorial soapbox. And stirrups, too, for what journalist does not sometimes feel like Don Quixote on horseback. I pondered these things when I occasionally wore cowboy boots to the office (perfectly acceptable in central Kansas).

My work in religious publishing introduced me to a set of dynamics that had been only secondary in "secular" publishing. Many of the people I wrote about were my friends or at least friends of my friends. They were brothers and sisters in Christ. I became increasingly conscious that people can be hurt in the gathering and reporting of news. I could not blithely offend and walk away as I might have done at a secular paper. In a special way the people I was writing to and about were all members, shareholders, in the wider corporate entity that had called me. I learned a new meaning of telling the truth in love.

I gained more new insights into the use of politics in the church. I found that even Christians in the service of the Lord will sometimes lie, cheat and play power games. I learned that the secular publishing world was often more concerned about truth-telling than was the church.

I also became increasingly convinced that my idea of "Christian work" was sadly deficient. I was somehow thought to be in the "Lord's work" while my neighbors— farmers, store clerks, real estate agents—were not. They could serve the Lord after hours. I would serve the Lord from eight to five. I was called, they were hired.

At points my spiritual life may have suffered because I had become a Professional Religious Person, a PRP as we sometimes called it. I had to guard against being a Christian by rote. The things of the kingdom had become everyday tools of my work; the everyday tools of my work seemed to take on ultimate value. There is nothing wrong with seeing one's work tools as part of a higher calling to discipleship; my problem was that I saw my typewriter and blue pencil that way, but not my neighbor's screwdriver and pliers.

Sometimes I envied my friends at work in secular tasks. They were in the real world. I felt shielded like a hothouse plant from the withering elements outside, while my friends faced ethical dilemmas that, if they accomplished anything, seemed to make it possible to develop a more robust faith. How would I function in a secular profession, I wondered. Would I make profit my god, given the lucrative possibilities of the corporate world? Would I cave in to judicial compromises in the attorney's chamber? Would I use toxic substances on my farm while trying to maximize production to feed the hungry of the world? Would I use price-inflating tactics in real estate?

How did one do journalism Christianly anyway? Did a reporter for the *L.A. Times* have to be writing religion pieces? Could only religion editors like Dick Ostling (*Time*) or Ken Woodward (*Newsweek*) be real Christians in their professions?

After a ten-year absence from secular journalism, what ethical dilemmas would confront me? I had grown accustomed to defining work faithfulness as working diligently, telling the truth in love (not always easy in a Christian setting where the tendency is to tell the good and hide the bad) and challenging the church to widen its scope of ministry to include doing justice and seeking liberty for the oppressed. Were those mere peripheral adjustments or did they actually constitute a biblical integration of faith and work?

I confess to frustration on this score. I struggle with the notion that work itself is sacred. I don't dispute it, but I don't yet fully understand it. Books and sermons extolling the sacredness of work are usually written by white collar folk who already like their jobs. Those kinds of articles and books are not written by people caught in oppressive, soul-sapping tasks like Mike LeFevre, the steelworker in Studs Terkel's *Working*.

As a step toward apprehending the sacredness of work I have been striving at least to view my own profession as Christian as possible. Someone who has helped shape that vision is Wes Pippert, a seasoned United Press International reporter who is one of America's leading Christian/secular journalists. Pippert has been plying his craft in the corridors of power for years, from the state legislature in the Dakotas to the White House. I encountered his thoughts on integrating faith and work in a *Christianity Today* article titled "Faith Should Rewrite Your Job Description."

Pippert suggests that Christians who want to Christianize their jobs might begin by trying to boil their profession down to a single word definition and then examine how that word is used in Scripture. For a journalist that definition could be "truth" (though skeptics may chortle at such a lofty self-definition). When Pippert examined his work from that perspective he came away with profound insights about the integration of his Christian faith with his work. He found, for example, that the Bible saw truth as "far more than a static notion of mere accuracy" (p. 28). Truth was dynamic, energizing and inextricably connected with mercy, justice, peace and righteousness. Thus he concluded that "A reporter who is a Christian should seek and write truth that promotes justice and mercy" (p .28). A Christian reporter or editor, he goes on to say, "does not necessarily bring more intelligence or skill to the story, but he or she may have a certain sensitivity to this kind of truth that other reporters do not" (p. 29). Even a secular story thus can have deep theological implications and can help free people from all kinds of bondage (racism, injustice, war). He goes on to say:

> I came to understand that the paramount task I have as a reporter is a divine calling with tremendous spiritual implications. Thus, every time I communicate the truth, to the best of my ability—whether that story be about Poland, the president, congressional action on the budget, or merely a 'barn burner' or a 'fender bender'—I have made a theological statement (p. 29).

The "one word" tracing concept can be used in other professions, says Pippert. "For the politician, (the word) might be 'power.' Contrast, for example, the biblical view of power as servanthood with the worldly notion of power as raw force or manipulation." For the lawyer, the word might be justice, which in Scripture is more often seen as mercy and fairness than punishment. Businesspeople might relate their faith and work by trying to serve needs rather than merely to make a profit. Those workers with extremely tedious jobs might have to focus on interpersonal relationships on the job, since all are called to excellence (Phil. 1:1–10). The sales clerk at a grocery store might concentrate on seeing customers as human beings.

From Pippert I have learned a very simple but elusive insight. Being a journalist for a Christian periodical is no more a faith/work integration than being a mechanic who changes spark plugs on a missionary's Land Rover, no more an integration than a Christian doctor who prays before making a diagnosis. Being a Christian worker is more than using your skills for a church-related task (though it will include that). It is more than scrupulously maintaining professional ethics (something that secular professionals often do better than Christians). Being a Christian worker involves bringing the mind and spirit of Christ to all tasks, even to the point of challenging the philosophical foundations of a profession. It involves "pressing the kingdom" into all dimensions of the workplace.

Increasingly I doubt that we are called to any particular vocation. Scripture doesn't say much about that. But we are called to discipleship and service in the kingdom. And if we are in proper relationship to Christ's bride, the church, our brothers and sisters may often discern specific tasks, even careers, for us.

When Harold Bender, a towering pillar of the Mennonite Church, died more than twenty years ago, the pastor in charge of the funeral reportedly described Bender's vocation as one that even death could not interrupt. What a grand eulogy! Such an understanding of Christian work and vocation radically transcends a mere job or profession. It applies to all that I do, whether my hands are stained with the juice of the onion, the oregano of the pizza parlor, or even the black ink of the newsroom.

8

Is Survival Possible When Work Is Professionalized?

> The unsatisfactory mental health of working people consists in no small measure of their dwarfed desires and deadened initiative, reduction of their goals, and restriction of their efforts to a point where life is at best relatively empty and only half meaningful (Kornhauser in Pfeffer:260).

Recently a leading sociologist remarked that "the development and increasing strategic importance of the professions probably constitute the most important change that has occurred in the occupational system of modern societies" (Parsons:526).

Only a generation or two ago, the professions represented an almost negligible percentage of the work force; the professional was a rarity. From that time on, the concept of profession has expanded and the professionalization of work areas has grown unceasingly until now both process and result have become a very pervasive force in our society.

In general, universities and other educational institutions were the first to become professionalized. Then came medicine, but not only medicine: also law, engineering, chemistry, physics, accounting—to name only a few of the many occupations which slowly became self-conscious as professions. According to some experts, the most recent work area to become professionalized is business management. Many executives and middle management people now extend constant "feelers," looking for more prestigious and better paying positions; it is not unusual for a business trip at company expense to double as an opportunity for the executive to be interviewed for a better position.

Although professionalism has many implications for the societal structure in general, in this setting we want to focus on the implications for the Christian in the marketplace. However, before moving further, let us attempt a definition or two. By professionalization, we refer primarily to a change in perception, a process through which an occupation becomes self-conscious as a profession or is seen by others to have assumed the attributes of a profession.

The term professionalism, among other meanings, points to or highlights attitude. More specifically, the term refers to the tendency for those norms and values within a particular occupation or profession—either present or developing—to determine the values and behavior in the work position rather than one's own inner purpose and a given moral perspective. Still more technically, professionalism and professionalization refer to 1) increasing requirements for formal and technical training in many occupations; 2) an increasingly institutionalized mode of validating the training and competence of individuals; 3) an institutionalized means "of making sure that competence will be put to socially responsible uses" (Parsons:526).

Professionalism is, at one and the same time, a basic need of society and a serious hindrance and liability. The professions have provided a setting within which an individual's identity could flower and personal expression become a norm; professions have also brought cohesion and productivity to society. In fact, almost all social institutions have developed professions to maximize efficiency and productivity, to say nothing of purpose and motivation.

This is true even in religion. At one point, God had called out and set apart those who were to lead the Jews in their religious experience. The calling and setting apart had a clear rationale. However, from this point, it was only a short step to forms of leadership by the Jewish rabbis that settled into institutionalism.

It could be argued that the leaders of the early New Testament church, while clearly called, were still very much a part of the body. But again, the institutionalization of the Judeo-Christian faith was only a short step away. Today, the Christian clergy—in most denominational settings—have become persons set apart to specialize in religious knowledge and ritual. Without a doubt, this setting apart of a group of persons has in itself contributed to, and reflected an aura of professionalism as defined above. Of course, there have been periodic reform movements to de-professionalize the Christian clergy; even so, that work position continues to become ever more professionalized.

Our example forces us to the admission that professionalism can also become a serious hindrance and liability. When this takes place, professionalism must be subverted. But how does one know when professionalism has developed to the point where it becomes detrimental and demands subversion? The answer is simple and clear as well as profound and deserving of much more exploration: professions and professionalism are detrimental when the costs outweigh the benefits in terms of human values and relationships.

The counterproductivity of the professions and professionalism is evident in almost every sphere of our lives. I shall mention only a few to frame a context for discussion: The Jeff-Vanderlou housing project in St. Louis, Missouri, was not completed before it became clear to many that it would have to be dismantled, and indeed it was. City planners, politicians, designers, architects, builders and developers—all doing their professional best—had managed to create an unmitigated fiasco.

Or consider the artists, designers, engineers, planners, and admen who almost succeeded in bankrupting the Chrysler Motor Corporation with professionally produced dinosaurs in the face of obvious indicators that energy and pollution considerations would not allow further indulgences. (Of course, this pointing of fingers does not excuse Chrysler management; it too can be accused of only professional management rather than creative behavior.) The professionalism of warfare provides another more grisly example: in war today, the professional soldier may do battle with the kind of rationalized and professional flair that allows him to kill the enemy—not only the direct combatants but helpless children as well—without needing to see blood anymore. And of course, we could argue that if the professional soldiers would have had freedom to follow their military bent, all of our conflicts would have been solved long ago.[1]

Usually, however, professionalism affects our lives in much more subtle and refined ways. One of the most effective ways of illustrating professionalism and its problems may be a personal biographical note from one of the authors regarding his entrance into the world of professions . . .

In order to prepare for effective teaching in a church related college, it was necessary for me to obtain a Ph.D.; understandably, a specialization was required. From among various options, I chose sociology; I felt that this field would allow me the widest latitude in bringing my Christian concerns to bear on the human enterprise.[2]

In the main, I have not been disappointed, but already in graduate school I was made aware of certain professionalizing constraints. My course of study was rather focused, designed to prepare me primarily for empirical research and publication. Of course, the expectation that I would teach was also present—almost as an afterthought—but certainly it was assumed that my teaching would be at one of the major universities. Very few of my professors understood my interest in teaching at a small church college or the corresponding lack of a sense of urgency to advance professionally.

This tension grew quickly into a serious inner conflict. On the one hand was my sense of Christian calling in which human relations and human compassion through involvement in community and the addressing of social issues were paramount. On the other hand were the canons of the discipline to which I had made a commitment including the clear outline of how achievement was accomplished and measured.

The requirements to succeed as a recognized and truly professional sociologist were simple and generally accepted throughout the profession:

— to read the myriad sociological journals and books so one's discussion could be learned and the dropping of names and theories would reflect how well one was keeping abreast of new developments within the discipline.
— attendance at the most prestigious professional meetings where one's name tag informed everyone else of both the name of the renowned university with which one was affiliated and the title of one's most recent book.
— maintaining one's professional contacts aggressively and carefully in order to nurture opportunities for both advancement and publication, publication representing the *sine qua non* of professional achievement.
— being invited to the cocktail parties of the leading lights in the profession was the final professional affirmation. (For me, this created a whole new experience of ambivalence. I have never gone willingly to a cocktail party, not only because I don't drink but also because I lack the ingenuity to think of enough nonsense to fill five or six hours of frivolous socializing.)

I could add other details but, in general, these constituted the rules of the professional game.

The most stultifying aspect of professional sociology, however, came not from the status-seeking aspects of the profession, but from its intellectual paradigm. Orthodox sociology is committed to a positivist philosophy which, translated, means that human behavior and social institutions can be understood and explained on the basis of scientific axioms and procedures, much like the physical sciences. Even though, in general, sociologists are very well trained in a number of areas including philosophy, science, and mathematics, they also are typically committed to the view that human history can be understood in purely materialistic terms. For a person like myself who believed that there exist certain other dimensions of human and social reality not amenable to sociological analysis, the difficulties are obvious. As a result, of course, my alienation from the profession increased.

It is clear that I choose to live in several quite different worlds: I have chosen to benefit from and contribute to the sociological approach to life. Along with this, I have chosen also to accept the truths expressed in other dimensions of living such as the faith community and the aesthetic life. As the product of the Christian tradition I had accepted its "Weltanschauung." This, along with my commitment to basic professional objectives, caused me to walk a very narrow track as I tried to keep the two worlds together; at times, of course, this effort created a schizoid conflict within me.

From a Christian point of view this focuses on one major stress point. The problem of the professionalizing of jobs and occupations lies in the simple fact that the values, norms and practices of the professions tend to circumscribe and limit the expression of the human desire or choice to "love one's neighbor." But beyond that, professionalism tends often to compete very strongly with the first loyalty—one's Christian vocation. For the Christian, of course, it is clear that the Christian calling cannot be relegated to second place.

The professionalizing tendency affects many disciplines in fairly categorical ways. It tends to make psychiatrists Freudians, neo-Freudians, Jungians, or Rogerian variations thereof. In law, the professionalizing tendency leads an attorney to become a constructionist or an advocate in matters of legal practice and a capitalist in business matters. For the theologians, professionalism often means subscribing to a particular school of thought, like the Barthian, or Bultmannian—and separating the intellectual from the existential dimensions of the faith and placing them in compartments which do not touch. Many other professions could be described. The above are mentioned here not as objects of derision, but rather only to illustrate the problem.

Often, sensitive persons in the professions are confronted with the dilemma of acting professionally in contrast with acting like a good neighbor. Here again, a sharing of personal experience may be useful.

This recent example involved a field trip for a class studying minority religious movements. The minister of the group being visited began to expound, in a slightly evangelistic way, about how his group pictured human sin and salvation. One of the members of the class began to ask more pointed and subjective questions, indicating serious personal problems; at a certain point I was forced reluctantly to suggest to her, politely but firmly, that our class was visiting the minority group to gain sociological insight and that personal questions would have to wait.

The Problems of Professionalism

From many sources, including personal experience, we have come to develop an orientation which views the tendencies to professionalize with considerable skepticism and anxiety. Let us look at some of the issues. To help organize our discussion, four negative tendencies of professionalization will be treated.

1. *Separating personal from professional ethics.* In almost every sphere of social existence, the individual's conscience, values and purposes have tended to be subordinated to that of the organization or body with which one is affiliated. Thus Max Lerner, trying to make sense of Watergate, said, "The worst thing that has happened to professionals has been the divorce between their professional and business life and their personal life . . . The most glaring example of this dichotomy will be found in the professional mobster, who kills when he wants to dispose of competitors, but is sentimental about his family" (Lerner:12).

2. *Supporting professional values and ethics which are usually the lowest common denominator of a given collective.* Again, as Lerner describes the situation, this means that businessmen "have an ethic, but it is the wrong one. It is, to use the common business phrase, a 'bottom line' ethic, that of the bottom line of profit figure in a quarterly or annual corporate statement." Obviously, this cannot be the basis for a viable social ethic for, as Lerner says, "The bottom line is what counts, whatever the means used. It is the cancer of the professions." To separate personal from professional ethics is bad enough but to accept uncritically the ethics of the profession, especially when they are benignly immoral, is even more insidious and destructive (Lerner:11).

3. *Allowing commitment to the professional complex to alienate oneself from the neighbor.* In normal human relations—involving business, social, or personal activity—the usual encounter is direct, face-to-face, person to person. In a highly professionalized situation, persons become specialists and cases. Lerner says, "A case in point is the medical profession, which has become a cluster of highly technical specializations in which not only the patient gets lost but also the doctor." The tendency toward professionalism often creates a veil between one's self and the neighbor; what becomes especially insidious is the professional ability to pull the veil down as much as desired, while the patient is helpless to do

anything about it. No one can argue with a written diagnosis or a bill; they are indisputable objective facts.

4. *Allowing the profession to become the surrogate church.* The profession often becomes the source of beliefs, values and attitudes of the individual, and the satisfier of emotional and relational needs. In a book entitled *Trends in Education for the Professions,* Lester Anderson describes the preparation for professionals in a candid way:

> In terms of our very early statements of criteria for professionalism, socialization produces the autonomous professional who knows who he is, is committed to his profession, is motivated to serve as a professional throughout his work career. Consequently, the professional person through the socialization process achieves identity, autonomy, commitment and motivation" (Anderson:16).

This statement clearly describes the total commitment of the professional. The professions have a powerful way of becoming the ultimate church for their members, possibly because they are so economically and socially rewarding. Professionalism can thus become one of the most insidious forms of idolatry.

The Need to Subvert the Professions

It should be obvious to us that these four negative tendencies within professionalism must be resisted strenuously. Not even a secular perspective condones separating a professional from a personal ethic, nor would it condone the professional complex serving as a means of alienation from the neighbor. It is also worthy of note that a self-designated atheist, Marx, condemned the alienation that industrialism perpetrated on laborers.

But the Christian in any vocation or profession goes beyond the secular ethic; he or she is constrained by the comprehensive ethic propounded by Jesus. This ethic does not allow anything to come between a man and his neighbor. It is possible that one of the most profound interpretations of the Good Samaritan story points to the danger of allowing professionalism to become a barrier between humans (Luke 10:25–37). The Priest and the Levite both hid behind their professional identities and status, ignoring their responsibilities to the neighbor. In contrast, the Samaritan—who responded to his neighbor in an open, natural and compassionate way—was held up by Jesus as the model neighbor, practicing human relationships in a way that reflected the ethic of Jesus.

With respect to the subversion of professionalism, one could state as a principle that any expression of a social role/status which interferes in the expression of love and compassion for the neighbor is by definition unchristian and evil. Certainly, the Priest and Levite could be considered professionals; ironically, religious professionals. Without a doubt, the principle should apply to and include religious professionals. In fact, in a penetrating discussion of work and calling, Jacques Ellul makes the case as strongly as it can be put: A vocation "represents a total divorce between what society unceasingly asks of us and God's will. Service to God cannot be written into a profession" (Ellul:33).

Let us begin, therefore, with the assumption that professions and professionalism can dilute or block true service in the kingdom of God. If that is true, then the Christian must search for ways to serve in his or her profession without reducing or distorting the commitment to God's purposes. Where this prior commitment clashes with the norms and values of the profession, the Christian will engage in what might be called a responsible subversion of either the profession or the attitude of professionalism, or both.

Creative Subversion of Professionalism*

Through the years, I have enjoyed increasing satisfaction in defying a clear classification of my own professional activities. To illustrate— even though I was never ordained, I have enjoyed the privilege of preaching in many churches. This is only one example of the approach I have used to subvert the aura of professionalism with which both academics and the clergy are afflicted. If the reader allows, to help order our thinking, I would like to address the four problem areas of professionalism with specific and actual experiences. I do this at the risk of appearing boastful; rather I intend these accounts to serve as a personal testimony and confession of how I have tried to be creative in my subversion of professionalism.

1. To make sure that personal and social values and morality are not separated, an obvious tactic is to refuse to work in professions where such is demanded. Thus, many occupations and professions were excluded automatically from my consideration since I knew that they would require behavior incompatible with my fundamental commitment. Other areas were more ambiguous, for example, business. Early in my idealistic adult life, I had decided against a business career because I felt at that time that the values and ethics in the business sector could not be harmonized

*The authors approach this exploration in the context of their own personal experience. One author's first-person account of his effort at creative subversion comprises much of this section.[2] For a separate statement by the other author, see "Uncovering the Image" the excursus following this chapter. It may also be noted that this entire book is a form of subversion.

with the Christian way. In light of that conclusion, I chose education; it seemed to be a field of work in which I could retain and nurture a unified personal and social ethic.

It has been possible to maintain the integration of a personal and an institutional ethic in education, but it has not been easy. The temptation to accept the orthodox position of positivism-empiricism with its evolutionary assumptions—as indicated above, is strong in social science; by now it is clear to me that the ease of moving up in the profession is dependent in large part upon internalizing that "line."

This awareness meant that I needed to accept the fact that I would never become a bright light in professional sociology. I tried therefore to be as productive and creative as I could within the limits of my value system. So my writing and teaching have not contributed much to the so-called orthodox literature. (In general, this seems like a small loss since, in my view, much orthodox writing is trivial and irrelevant.) But hopefully my scholarly works have made a contribution to a larger circle beyond professional sociologists. Of course, I am aware that it is not always possible to choose a job or occupation where one can harmonize one's Christian and professional roles; however, that can make the challenge all the more exciting.

2. The second problem—working on the values and behaviors of the profession—is much more subtle; this deals with a commitment to the profession itself. After I began to discover that it might be possible to be in business and still retain my personal integrity, I ventured into business. I was surprised to learn that it was relatively easy for me not to buy into the bottom line ethic of business which includes such values as "all that matters is profit," or "the disparity in income between managers and laborers is a reward for risk." What made it easy was that, by then, I had developed at least two or three professional identities; I was not totally beholden to identify with any single one. This allowed me the luxury of being a "stranger" or a "free-floating intellectual," using Simmel's terms, who could dip in and out without being totally dependent upon the acceptance of any particular professional community.

Thus when I made what seemed to others like irresponsible statements regarding how businesses with which I was connected should be run, I was regarded patronizingly as "the professor who means well, and who is to be complimented for his sincere effort to understand the business world." On the other hand, when I refused to be taken in by the publish or perish syndrome of the academic community, I was usually greeted with the quietly envious retort, "You can thumb your nose at the academic rat race since you are independently wealthy." The flattery has sounded so sweet that

I've simply allowed this erroneous assumption to stand without correction.

From my own experience, therefore, I'd propose that one of the ways to be creatively subversive of professionalism is to be involved in as many streams of professionalism as possible. I am encountering increasing numbers of "professionals" who have discovered this approach to creative subversion. But where this is not possible, it is still usually possible to cultivate friendships with persons in other fields; these friends can help to provide alternative perspectives and certainly a general corrective. Incidentally, these friendships often do in fact give one entrance into other spheres.

Something all of us can do is develop a hobby; this is one of the easiest, most pleasant and rewarding ways to protect ourselves from the imperialism of professionalism. In fact, many of us are developing new counter-professions out of our hobbies. Several of my friends have developed a very creative travel business from a hobby; through these relationships I have personally developed one of my own side hobbies as a travel guide.

3. The third problem highlights a very difficult objective: keeping the profession from alienating oneself from one's neighbor. The very purposes of professionalism—effectiveness, efficiency, competency, exclusion of competitors, specializations, predictability, management of clients, along with a host of others—tend to isolate one from neighbors. I have always been grateful that medical doctors *are* in fact competent, knowledgeable and efficient. But the temptations faced in all professional pursuits are not much different than those that confront the physician: to allow the professional elements to become self-serving.

One can creatively subvert the self-service temptation by not being totally dependent financially, socially, or in terms of status, on any one profession or activity. Thus my modest financial earnings in the business world have helped me remain relatively casual about my professional academic self perception (see "Uncovering the Image" pp. 145–51). On the other hand, occupational and financial security in the university has allowed me to nurture critical attitudes with respect to business. I am helped therefore to relate to my business colleagues in ways that are less materialistic and grasping.

Involvement in community causes is another very useful way to subvert professionalism, both in terms of the role one plays and in terms of the shattering of images perceived by the community. The purpose of many community organizations is to show compassion for the neighbor; this helps to mitigate the claims and images of other professional roles. For example, I have been involved in the establishment of two credit unions. Because of these involvements, I have been asked by friends, especially bankers,

"How can you support a credit union when you are also in business? Don't you know these are in direct conflict with each other?" Questions such as these open the door for exchange and reconciliation of opposing ideologies; or they allow me to explain my own attempt to see life more holistically. I know medical doctors and lawyers who are also involved in community affairs; certainly there are many examples which show that it is possible to keep a profession from becoming the all-encompassing commitment which sees neighbors as beings* to exploit or—failing that possibility—to ignore.

4. A final problem of professionalism—the profession becoming a surrogate church. Of course, this may not be reflected in a crass, irreverent form through which one prays to almighty Henry Ford, pays tithes to the American Manufacturing Association, and sings from *Odes to Capitalism*. Rather, it comes about in more subtle ways in which one's basic world view, the nature of one's social concern and one's own contribution to the world's ills are all determined by the profession. How does one keep loyalties straight so that the question: "How am I an integral part of the local chapter of the kingdom movement?" (or the God movement, as Clarence Jordan said so beautifully) remains the central focus?

I have discovered an exciting technique which frustrates my profession from becoming a surrogate church: that is simply to bring the church and my faith into my profession. The separation of the holy and unholy is necessary, but remains very ambiguous; our attempts to maintain that separation often lead us into hopeless dualism. We are in fact citizens of two kingdoms; they are different and separate but they do intersect and interact. Within that reality, we must ask how the practice of business or other professions can be kept in a Christian context. In several of the businesses with which I am associated, we began the process towards this objective by selecting only those persons or families who had similar beliefs, ethics, and interests. Then we wrote *Charters of Purpose* in which we stated the basic objectives for our organization and how the organization would function. In some sense, therefore, the solar companies with which I am associated became the economic and business extensions of the Christian congregation and its spiritual goals. We meet at church on Sunday morning for worship, praise and fellowship; during the week some of the same people meet in board meetings working at certain corporate tasks but with a more holistic understanding of what they are about.

Another type of subversion is to involve members of the clergy in business or professional activities. This technique works

---

*really more as *things:* the I-It relationship expounded by Martin Buber, as over against the I-Thou relationship.

two ways: it educates the clerics so that their idealisms are modified and some of their unrealistic criticism is diminished; their involvement also keeps the business or professional person on his or her toes. (Obviously, this is not a sure-fire tactic, since clerics sometimes professionalize their roles in a curious Catch-22 fashion: they bend over backwards to become uncritical promoters, not only to prove acceptability but also to express long-repressed frustration at being excluded from the councils of power. Thus professional self-hatred can surface even among the *most* ordained among us.)

With reference to human experience, a common saying suggests that hindsight vision is usually 20/20. I am not sure that is always true; in fact, we may never fully understand why we do certain things. For example, I don't think I understand fully yet why I refused ordination as a young man, particularly when my professors in college and seminary tried to influence me in that direction. Was I merely calloused to the wooing of God's Spirit? I don't think so, for I did experience considerable mental anguish over that issue. My rationale for declining was simple: "that I can do more good as a lay Christian than as an ordained Christian clergyman." I still feel the same way; that is still my answer when the question comes up, as it does occasionally. With growing, although not perfect, *hindsight* I am beginning to think that I may have been acting on a creative impulse; an impulse which at the time I did not fully understand, but which—as I have argued here—is central to the creative encounter between the Christian gospel and life. (The co-author did accept ordination as a clergyman, then "subverted" that profession by serving also as a teacher, then accepting appointment as an editor—as it turned out, a preaching editor—followed subsequently by other "subversions.")

The forms of appropriate and responsible subversion are as varied as people are and as creative as determined individuals can become. A number of professional people I know have developed parallel careers—entrepreneurs who have gone into the classroom, ministers who became administrators, to name only two from among many. Other professionals have actually changed careers. When a person's identity and his norms or values come from several different positions or perspectives, there is a much greater likelihood of becoming more balanced and objective. Clearly, if the profession of sociology is only one of several of my professional commitments, I am not as prone to be subservient to that single profession; also, and very positively, my self-image and identity become multifaceted and better balanced. Naturally I am not proposing that a medical doctor become a professional boxer, but even within certain logical parameters there is still a wide range of variation applicable. Of course, one cannot ignore the opposite position in this respect: namely, that the most competent person is not necessarily the one that "eats and lives" his profession.

Nothing in the teaching of Jesus suggests that changing a career or profession endangers the ultimate state of the soul. The number of those persons who have switched careers, vocations, and professions in mid or later life is great; most of these have been blessed for it. Naturally, there are some who never find happiness and joy, regardless of the number of times they change occupations or professions, but these are the exceptions that test the rule. Job retraining programs, occupational counseling and guidance, as well as professional reorientations are becoming more prevalent and accessible; especially as the technological changes in the employment sector increase. Without a doubt, career changes or multiple career tracks are a portent of the future; more than that, however, this approach may well point the way to finding greater happiness and freedom in our work positions and opening the door to escape from an oppressive profession.

A final option for Christians to free themselves from the constraints of the professionalizing trap is to "drop out" of the so-called rat race of modern society and develop a lifestyle which is more in harmony with the gospel. This does not mean becoming parasites of the ongoing society of which Christians are members. Definitely there are obligations to be met but how they are met may well be questioned. And the consideration of alternatives is not only an option, it is a responsibility. Many people are beginning to wonder whether our present society is really that wonderful. This kind of questioning of a society can be very healthy; the Christian's answer can lead to an even greater contribution to society or to service that can be offered in a unique way. This raises the basic question of who, in the first place, should be deciding which work activities provide the best service to humanity.

Whose is the "master mind" that can determine which work is the most important to a society? Is the Adam Smithian invisible hand of competition the moral absolute that dictates what should be made and by whom? Or is it the unshackled proletariat who is competent to decide what constitutes the "good life"? Perhaps the anarchists will tell us what the ideal state of the society and the economy should be, and why one should work. Such questioning could go on, interminably and unproductively. Perhaps we might venture one opinion: that various utopians from the many centuries past have come closest to indicating what an "ideal" society should look like and how each person might contribute to it.

But so far, the utopians have fallen short of "creating" any type of ideal; it is my belief that they will never succeed. There is one fatal flaw in their argument—their assumption that the collective perfectibility of humans is possible, or at least their belief that humans can achieve greater harmony. As it relates to the world in general, this assumption is unfounded and hence spells only failure. The Christian, however, is committed to a higher authority—to an Authority who is *unconditioned* (i.e. Sovereign)—and is given norms which help to chart a course or make choices that reflect this committment. More than that, the child of God is given the will or the power to act on these choices.

It could be argued that a creative subversion of the professional structure is an irresponsible act, that such an approach contributes to social disorganization and even anarchism. Christians, however, cannot be accused of anarchism because they have a clear vision or image of the society they are hoping to achieve—the kingdom of God.

Rather than being an irresponsible act, we would argue that creative subversion of the professionalism which is corrupting our society is a Christian responsibility. With increasing satisfaction I like to confuse people when they ask, "How can you be in business when you hold down a full academic job?" Or when they miss the connection between my expressions of dreaming about service in a voluntary service program in Bolivia, my business obligations, and leading a tour group in Europe. I hope my reply, either in word or behavior, says, "It may not make a great deal of sense when considered from the treadmill point of view, but from another perspective, it is fun and rewarding." I feel confirmed in my view that subverting the professions has become an obligation, particularly when I hear many of my friends through their example reminding me of what Jesus said, "Anyone who does not take his cross and follow me is not worthy of me" (Matt. 10:38). Professions and professionalism need not be a prison; rather they can be the framework from within which one can expand and serve and help to transform the world around us.

There are no materialistic or human norms which state flatly that: "This or that specific service is the best contribution I can make to this society." The Christian, however, enjoys this particular luxury; he can know that he is making a contribution to human beings and to human society, not primarily by becoming a teacher, a doctor, a lawyer, but by being a humble servant to others in love and compassion—a servanthood expressed inside and outside a given work position.

Excursus 4
Uncovering the Image

by Urie A. Bender

I have seldom had the advantage, or disadvantage, of a precisely scheduled work day—or a vocational involvement that had "a stopping place."

On the farm, chores started as early as 5:30 A.M. and, in some of my hired-man experience, the day ended only when summer darkness fell and sheer exhaustion demanded sleep. As a milk-truck driver, my early morning beginning was always marked by an alarm clock set at the same hour but the ending could come at 3:00 P.M. or at 10:00 P.M.—whenever the job was done.

In the pastorate, days off and free evenings were only theoretical. The reality included a seven-day shepherding expectation, some part of each week spent earning a living, study and sermon preparation tucked into regular hours both early and late, thought, contemplation, prayer and caring filling most of my waking hours—particularly when many of them were spent behind the wheel of a truck.

As a teacher of English—and other subjects—in a Bible Institute, I was introduced to a new work format: only twelve hours of teaching each week. That sounded attractive until I did the arithmetic on class preparation—which, for a new teacher was considerable—as well as the reading, marking and grading of stacks of papers and essays along with classwork and follow-up, student counseling, ping-pong and faculty meetings. Three and one-half hours multiplied by twelve equaled one of my part-time jobs.

Then I was invited to become the editor of a weekly magazine for youth in a particular denomination in North America. For the first time in my life I enjoyed a schedule of neat office hours. There was a beginning hour and an ending hour, and each morning and each evening were the same. That idyllic dream-come-true lasted all the way through my orientation period—almost four months—at which point a kind of reality buzzer woke me up to the fact that I had become a public figure to a certain group of young people

145

throughout the United States and Canada and that this role entailed obligations.

Youth groups and pastors and parents and my executive editor helped me to define the extent of these obligations. Before long, I truly came to enjoy the forty hours spent each week in my office; these hours took on the flavor of leisure since there the job description was clear, weekly production schedules had their own rhythms, and coffee breaks allowed for socializing without being on display or on stage, as it were—which was the case during forty to forty-five weekends every year.

As I said, the forty-hour block in the middle of each week took on the flavor of leisure. The eight-hour core of each day was often like an elongated break from my work—early morning and most evenings—of preparing for weekends. My week in the office grew to be like a rest or respite from work, the work of representing the magazine I was editing, of speaking, of counseling, of late-evening visits in many different homes, of eating meals prepared for a guest, of trains and planes and lonely highways, of looking for ways to contain the fatigue.

Lest I be misunderstood—I was enjoying a great deal of my activity. It's just that my definition of work was tumbling into turbulent disarray. Travel became work while the activities between travel from here to there were so filled with delight and fulfillment that to call them work became a bit embarrassing. Then I surprised myself by finding that hours on a train offered their own special rewards. For a time as well, the hours between trains or planes—a necessary part of travel—were an onerous chore until I learned that all kinds of living could replace the experience of waiting. Meeting the crunch of deadlines also seemed like work until I learned that the excitements of discovery along the way to a deadline often literally obliterated the shape of a particular obligation.

Then came various opportunities for overseas travel. And I learned to live with 112 hour weeks, or more. I'm sure that some parts of these weeks must have been work but I'm still not able to decide which parts. Listening to problems, being a presence, selecting a bookstore site, starting a magazine, doing interview research for a book, traveling in the Amazon jungle on survey trips, preaching through an interpreter, teaching lay pastors, presenting lectures in public relations, planning marketing approaches in a foreign culture, proofing—line by line—a translator's work on one of my books. In all of these activities, and more, I was observed by others to be at work. My own perception is much more ambiguous; as I said, it is still not clear to me which parts of these activities could be defined as work.

Opportunities? Yes. Challenges? Without a doubt. Productive effort? In most cases, to some degree at least. Obligation? Usually, in the sense that I had made a commitment—or someone else had made a commitment—of my time and involvement.

All of it seemed—still seems—to have the flavor of living, of experience, of expression of being, of discovering potential, of realizing glimmers of insight into what it means to be made in the image of God, after His likeness. But somehow these awarenesses and my kind of life didn't fit into my childhood or early adult definitions of work. The stretchings that came with varied experiences—many of them quite difficult—also affected my understandings of work. (Perhaps my story shouldn't be a part of this learned tome on work; it may confuse the issue, as I have been confused.)

Later I had opportunities for involvement in the business world. There, in our own business, many activities focused on a single objective. Sometimes all of these activities seemed to be work; other times, none of them were.

Then there were some years spent as an advertising manager: when the excitement of a new frontier lifted long days above and beyond a simple job definition; when shaping my personal communications philosophy and an advertising ethic became my real work and all of my other activities were only necessary background detail; when creativity with words and things and people relationships was a primary obligation but so exciting that it was seldom only obligation; when living on an edge of raw life and need provided opportunity to test a whole book full of theories and conclusions about Christian witnessing and brought new horizons to most of my days; when discipleship or following Christ in an alien culture became a daily adventure.

Many years as a counselor taught me and led me into other ambiguities about work. Some of the texts, a few teachers, and certain peers created in me the impression that counseling was a vocation, a kind of work, that job descriptions could be written. But these impressions were quickly antiquated by contradictions in my own experience. Of course, there were the essential elements of a significant discipline; there were necessary learnings about human nature; there were the useful insights gained from long practice and experience. But none of this turned out to be onerous. Nor was the counseling situation itself a burden in any way. Instead of a drudgery spelled w-o-r-k, I discovered a new dimension and opportunity in relationship. Instead of obligation, I read gift. Instead of difficulty, I found new meanings for the word creative.

I discovered that selecting the right mirror to hold up before my friend became a consuming challenge; that listening led to real exhilaration and a strange, unexpected sense of personal restoration; that interaction with another human being, regardless of the circumstances of trauma or loss or anxiety, brought joy. The miracle of openness created in me a sense of awe. The gift of trust led me into thanksgiving. The simple sacrament of sharing and allowing spirits to touch each other provided strengths and a kind of personal fueling that utterly transcended the heaviness or sadness which first triggered our meeting. Instead of being burdened, I was renewed. And through some awesome alchemy which I cannot understand, in many cases, my friend in counseling was restored and made whole. Perhaps all of this constitutes a definition of work; I can't be sure.

There have also been years as a marketing consultant where every situation is immediately both problem and challenge; where rigidities need to be broken and blindness needs to be healed and creativities need to be released; where solutions are waiting for the explorer; and where success is achieved by becoming unnecessary. I suspect some of this may be work—but that's only a suspicion.

Finally, I consider my many years as a free-lance writer. In this field, disarray of all my definitions of work has now become complete. By this time, I have lost any ability I may ever have had to distinguish between work and leisure, between effort and rest, between depletion and rejuvenation, between obligation and satisfaction. I find myself at odds with most of the glib formulations. I cannot separate living from work, work from delight and fulfillment, delight from commitment or fulfillment from obligation.

In place of the usual formulations or categories. I have developed rhythms. Or perhaps, better said, I observed natural rhythms in my life and have learned to flow with them. From this perspective, I found that joy could be part of strenuous effort; that satisfactions flowered from living fully—not from either work or play; that the fundamental distinction lay not between job or leisure but rather between potential fulfilled or unfulfilled.

On the other hand, it is possible that my years as a writer have brought whatever clarities may exist. Clarity is a strong word; beginnings of insight is a better term. For it was as a free-lance writer that most of the underpinnings of a normal schedule were loosened and the parameters of expectation changed and the awesome responsibility of creative freedoms shook my soul. It was in this free-lance setting that I became more fully aware of the power of choice and the options to shape this thing or that, this word or that phrase, this idea or that vision, this concept or that result, this seed into that content and form.

It is this shaping, forming activity that others have seen me do; and they have called it work. For me, such activity is not work at all—given the definitions of my childhood or early adult years. If this kind of effort should properly be called work, then it must also be called joy, a sense of fulfillment, a delight in achievement or the realization of objective. To behold a shaped thing in the image of what one had envisioned becomes a supremely satisfying experience. None of the flavors usually associated with work are reflected in that kind of experience.

From the point of that awareness, hours were no longer divided into the categories of work and leisure, effort or pleasure, obligation or fulfillment. Every experience became a part of living. And either all of living was work—or none of it was.

Lest anyone think that what I speak of is limited to those who are writers or artists, let me say that much of what I have been engaged in during the past three or four decades has provided opportunity for the shaping of a vision into a tangible reality.

As a carpenter—I envisioned a house and brought it into being, much of it with my own hands (two of them, to be precise).

As a gardener—I imaged a garden. I saw the engaging symmetry of straight rows, spaced accurately, and contrasting colours and shapes. I delighted my mind's eye with the picture and teased my palate with anticipated tastes. Then with planted seed and my partner God, the images became reality.

As an organizer—I conceived policies, strategies and program. And then alone, or with one helper or many, I brought to pass what, in an early stage, was only a glimmer of insight into the intangible.

As an administrator—I looked ahead and saw possible results. Then I clustered the resources available to me into certain configurations and, behold, the results appeared.

Are all these adventures work? If academics do the labeling, perhaps. If the theologians insist, they may be right. If social scientists could show me a powerful rationale for such a definition, I might be convinced. Perchance, I can lay hold on some fundamental principle or focus some light on process by looking more closely and specifically at my experience as a writer. As a writer, first I create my place of work (almost anywhere) and my time of work (often scheduled but also almost any time) and the pacing of my work. Then I step into this world I have created and ready myself for other visions—a poem, an essay, a play, a story, a choric narrative, a monologue, a dialogue, a Sunday sermon, a banquet speech, a book. When the vision comes clear, then I begin the activity of creation.

But the shaping of the image into some form of reality I do not perceive as work as defined traditionally. First, I *worked* to create a setting—place and time—and pacings. Then I *worked* to create clarity of vision and purpose. Lastly, I *worked* to decipher real motivation and to plan for the disciplines that will carry me through the experience. When these elements of intense effort have been completed, then I enjoy. I allow myself the luxury of immersion in the flow of life and living, and respond expressively and creatively to all of that which becomes part of my daily, even momentary, world; including the activities and purposes to which I have made particular commitment. It is during this process, I believe, that I begin truly to reflect the image and likeness of my Creator.

Currently, one other aspect of my work claims much attention; it has the nature of a difficulty. The intrinsic difficulty is not with what I'm doing or how I'm living. It has to do rather with the fact that others insist on time frames within which my contribution to their endeavours must be placed. So what I find truly onerous is not effort or activity or work so-called. Rather I become exhausted—physically and emotionally—from the continuing and strenuous exercise of matching my *now* kind of seeking to live creatively with a clock and calendar approach imposed by someone else. And productivity is *not* the issue. I have proven to myself, over and over again, that I can be more productive—in worldly terms of quantity and quality—by discovering or creating ways to allow my method to flower and to control energy output and application, than when I suffer the imposition by others of time-driven expectations.

What is my work? My vocation? My calling?

It is not ordinary, if by that is meant attendance at a single place of work activity. It is not always productive, if by that is meant a regular or guaranteed paycheck at the end of a week or a month or a project. It is not focused, if by that is meant a single label or category—such as writer or marketing consultant. It is not sacred, if by that is meant an exclusively religious vocation. It is not secular, if by that is meant an absence of faith, meaning a dimension of spiritual kingdom awareness.

In the final analysis, philosophically or theologically, my work in this world is defined from a transcendent perspective. I am reminded of the words of Jesus, "My food is to do the will of him who sent me and to finish his work" (John 4:34). This focus on fundamental purpose gives me a cue. The *who I am* and *who I can become* relates, for me, to the sense that all of God's creatures are made in His image; and that includes me. The purpose that I perceive for my life is to discover the potential inherent in my being: to uncover and express my capabilities which are in the nature of gifts. *That is my work.* The other elements that constitute my activity are almost peripheral to any definition of work. They assume significance only as they serve—instrumentally and functionally—to fulfill purpose.

For me, understandings are enhanced but not concluded with several word couplets: in terms of the realities I deal with, there are external requirements in tension with internal commitment. In terms of the nature of my task, the words are chaos and order. In terms of a basic life principle, ingestion and expression are fundamental—including curiosity as well as risk and vulnerability. In terms of the theology I espouse, the key terms are communication and relationship.

From these I derive the core of my existence. Through these I experience life.

Work?

Yes!

9

Male-Female Relationships and Work

> A housewife is a housewife, that's all. Low on the totem pole.
> I can read the paper and find that out . . . . Somebody who
> goes out and works for a living is more important than
> somebody who doesn't . . . . Deep down, I feel what I'm
> doing is important. But you just hate to say it, because what
> are you? Just a housewife? (Terkel, *Laughs*:398).

The accumulated knowledge and literature of our culture makes practically no reference to the fact that more than one-half of all the work performed in human history has been done by women.[1] It is as though women had not existed! When work in general has been discussed, gender usually has been left out, or the implication that references to work meant male work has been allowed to stand. Even Marx and Engels, who have made such a great contribution to our understanding of the labor of humans, did not stress the differences between men's work and women's work, although they did assume that the revolution of the proletariat would erase the inequalities between the sexes.[2]

One of the most penetrating analyses of modern societies makes the following statement regarding females and work:

> It is no accident that all the critiques and studies I have
> so far mentioned refer to males or "man" and "his"
> problems of alienation and of controlling "his" technology.

Industrial societies and their pathologies are also patriarchal and have designated their most highly valued traits as masculine and accordingly repressed those they have designated feminine—cooperation, holism, intuition, humility, and peacefulness—assigning these roles to women and other low-status populations. At the same time the International Labor Organization's study for the July 1980 United National Conference on Women held in Copenhagen, estimated that women provide two-thirds of the world's work hours and produce 44 percent of the world's food supply while receiving only 10 percent of all wages and owning a mere 1 percent of all property (*The Christian Science Monitor,* July 30, 1980). Such cultural dichotomy can be stated in less sexually polarizing terms as that of the Chinese yin and yang symbols. Industrial societies have overemphasized the yang qualities and are now suffering the inevitable pathological result of such imbalance. A re-orchestrating of these yin-yang models is necessary, which will require a return of the yin (Henderson, p. 169).

Unfortunately, however, church historians, theologians and the clergy fall far behind in recognizing the uniqueness of women's participation in work. It has been argued that neither scholars nor the clergy discriminated between the sexes because they assumed that they were equal; such an interpretation cannot be defended. Even sociologists, ostensibly the transcultural and objective observers of the social scene—although they have separated male from female work concepts—have not generally recognized the unique and important sphere of women's work.

Perhaps, in this book, a distinction between male and female work should not be made. Since there is finally a movement toward opening up the world of so-called men's work to women, it may be inappropriate to call attention to differences, to separate women from men in this way. Even more to the point, should male authors be discussing female dimensions of work?

This latter question raises a moot point, for the discussion by males is now fact. However, the first question must be answered positively—with a ringing affirmative. The topic cannot be avoided. Any Christian treatment of work must include the issue of female as well as male work—no matter how controversial—or be declared inadequate.

What can be done in this chapter is to recognize the fact that "women and work" *is* a crucial issue, not only for the Christian faith, but for society at large. What must also be done is to attempt, at the least, to present an outline of one perception of the problems and possible solutions. A Christian view of work simply dare not ignore a phenomenon which has probably led to a greater sense of alienation for one-half of the human race than any other aspect of the work experience.

Some General Observations

The Opposing Worldviews of Women's Work

The work which women have done throughout most of human history has been perceived differently from that of "men's work." This statement has a double significance. First, the dominant stratum (men) has perceived that male work has been of generally greater value and significance than female work. Secondly, this perception of work—by the dominant stratum—has not been shared by the women, the so-called subordinate stratum of society.[3]

Any rejoinder that these perceptions are irrelevant because women have accepted the definition of the majority is missing the point. The sociology of minorities has shown that outward conformity does not, in itself, signify or create ideological acceptance. The fact that men have not recognized fully the value of work women have done has resulted in the development of structures which are deeply institutionalized and forms of relationship which are entrenched. Hence social change, even if welcomed by males and females alike, cannot come easily; all of us have been conditioned to think in traditional terms and to accept institutionalized advantages. In general then, men and women have conceived of work differently and the consequences of this difference are practically infinite.

The Denigration of Women's Work

In general, throughout history, "women's work" has been sharply proscribed and limited to the domestic arena.[4] Furthermore, this type of work has been downgraded and devalued. In almost all cultural contexts, housekeeping has been seen as less dramatic and less significant than the hunt or the building of a bridge. "Women's work" has almost never figured in the "gross national product" of a society. Today, even in sophisticated circles, when we ask a woman whether she is working, we mean by that does she have a job *outside* the domestic arena, is she identified with a profession, or does she at least receive remuneration for her work!

It is the men who have done the philosophizing about work and who have decided what worth work should have, and who should do it. It is women who have done much of this work but have seldom been given the opportunity to help shape a job or say how it should be done. Ironically, women have been allowed to speak (and write) about love, sex, marriage, and flower arranging.

But work as a subject for discussion by women has not seemed appropriate; thus, the mythology of women's unrelatedness to real work has continued.

The almost universal tendency to downgrade "women's work" is a very interesting and complex issue. There are many reasons, of course; following are two: (1) The work that women have done "naturally" has been downgraded by men as part of their overall attempt at subjugating females to male domination. Thus the work involved with bearing, nurturing and providing for children—having been designated as "women's work"—has been assigned a lesser significance or a lower value than other work. Through that process of definition and designation, males have been able to maintain dominance over females. One can only speculate as to how this process operates. The physical, physiological, psychological and social factors in the development of this trend are truly manifold; numerous plausible theories could be advanced.[5]

(2) Another reason for the denigration of work that women do is an approach similar to the above, namely, women have been given the menial and demeaning jobs as a simple mechanism to place and keep them in submission. This approach assumes that there exists a prior hierarchy of work evaluations, and all persons placed in the lower status work thereby lose power and esteem.

It is clear that both interpretations could be correct. Certainly the Judeo-Christian religion buttresses this view when it describes women's work as being that of childbearing and pain (Genesis 3:16). Another overwhelming example is the Muslim religion with its clearly defined and subordinate role for women. Almost every other religion also has placed the female in a subordinate position, especially in the role of work and access to sacred office. What has made the fact of male domination doubly tragic is that women, for centuries, have accepted their subordinate role as an expression of the world as it ought to be.

The Destruction of Female Creativity and Self-Respect

Although the same principles apply here which were discussed above with respect to work for humans in general, there are special nuances which should be acknowledged in a separate discussion:

1. Women have done an enormous amount of work for which they have not been recognized. As a subculture, of course, women have supported each other. Furthermore, they have privately upgraded the value of work they have done. But neither of these facts compensates for the lack of recognition from "authority figures," in this case the men. There is little point here for men to attempt to verbalize what this attitude has done to the female

psyche. Suffice it to say—those of us with mothers who lived in this type of "unregenerate" regime know the lack of self-respect which they carried around as an inexpressibly heavy burden.

2. A more ironic and bitter form of destruction of the female psyche is inherent in the fact that women have made a very strong contribution in the world of work, but men have taken the credit for it. This has been called the "redemptive role." This means that women should be satisfied with playing the supportive role since people shouldn't care about who gets the credit for important work. Further, women should take comfort in the fact that even though they are not publicly recognized for their contribution, they are in actuality "running the show." This is of course a cynical argument and reflects the thinking of oppressors. The Christian will give no time or consideration to this immoral thinking. Of course Bernard rejects the argument; she says that women must also receive recognition for the contributions they make.

3. Women have been frustrated repeatedly in their desire to move beyond the domestic arena into work allowing for a freer expression of ability and interest. There are myriad reasons for this frustration. Some are religious—women have been excluded from ecclesiastical occupations and responsibilities because of theological and polity reasons. They have also been barred from secular roles because of a generalization from religious "role typing." Thus the "helpmeet" interpretation of the creation story in Genesis has placed much religious and societal activity out of bounds for women—not fit for women or women not fit for the role.

Many have advanced the argument that women should not be allowed to enter certain occupations or jobs because that would interfere with their first responsibility, namely, the home and family. By itself, that is a logical fallacy because it is based on a dubious or false premise. That is, *if* it were clearly established by some objective standard that "women's work" is XYZ, then other work which would undercut that should be avoided, but the XYZ of women's work has never received full and unanimous agreement. Since the premise is dubious and uncertain, any argument based on it breaks down.

As indicated above, it seems impossible here to ferret out all the causes for the restriction of women to certain kinds of work; it is likewise difficult to enumerate all the ways in which female self-worth has been destroyed. What is important here is to recognize the facts and to determine that something can and must be done about it.

The Self-Wounding of Society Through Denial of the Full Range of Opportunity to Women

Whenever and wherever there is any form of subordination or oppression, it is not only the oppressed who must be set free; the oppressor must also be freed. Having learned the insight from Ghandi—possibly also from the prophet Amos—Martin Luther King proclaimed this message as a cornerstone of true freedom.

Human society has been burdened with the terrible costs of self-inflicted wounds caused in a multitude of ways. Wars are only one example. Oppression of minorities is another. But possibly the greatest self-wounding the human race has ever experienced is the way women have been barred from contributing their best to the religious, artistic, social, and economic development of society.

However, whether recognized or not, women have been making a major contribution to the various sectors of societal structures. But there is no way to measure the gap between what they have contributed and what they could have contributed if their efforts had been recognized and used more effectively. For example, at this moment in history we have the great classics in music ostensibly written primarily by men. Is it not possible to maintain, logically, that among females there could have been an equal amount of work with equal contributions to society of beauty and grace? Might we not, then, be at least twice as rich?

It is difficult to enumerate all the ways in which society has hurt itself by refusing to accept the contribution women could have made. Obviously, not much more could have been gained in the area of menial labor; women have already made the major contribution in this area. Gathering firewood, raising food, cooking meals, cleaning houses, dressing children, and similar tasks constitute the greatest amounts of hard work ever done in the world; more of the same by the same group will not contribute very much to the advancement of civilization. (Of course, a commitment to some method of equalization in this area of work is incumbent upon males.)

But it is in the areas that deal with the human spirit and reflect human aspirations where women have not been able to make the creative contributions they might have. Music and the arts were alluded to above. Beyond these finer arts, however, in our view it appears that the greatest contribution women could have made is in the public sphere: that is, the political. In spite of the "iron lady" motif, the feminine ethos might well have been of great significance in the development of nation-states and international relations. What if cooperation rather than competition would have been a dominant theme in the relationships between nations? What if mothers rather than fathers had sat in councils that determined whether armies of their children should lunge forth against each other? Would a female SS corps have sent millions of Jews to the gas chambers? How would society be different if, at certain crucial junctures in history, world leaders would have been female, instead of male?

Of course, there is no way of proving whether the course of history could have been improved if women had had opportunity to enter more fully into the making of that history. But in our conclusion to this section, one thing can be said emphatically: *Any society based upon the oppression of a significant number of its members is bound to decay and die.* Contradictory behavior of this sort is bound to destroy the structure which allows it. The moral fiber of a society is dependent upon the integration between values and behavior. If human life is a value, if freedom and equality are values, then societies that contradict themselves so dramatically cannot exist for long.

The Personal Harassment of Women

The discussion so far has focused on the way in which the *work that women* do has been understood, and consequently how women have been treated as instruments or means of accomplishing work. The other consequence for women in the work setting is the far more pervasive sexism which pertains. This dimension has many levels and nuances. Some of them pertain to prejudices against women on physical, psychological, and social grounds. Women have been and are being discriminated against because they are women, presumed to be not equal with men and therefore inferior. "Equal pay for equal work" has been one of the chief rallying cries in the effort to correct this imbalance. The fact that such a cry is necessary indicates how a basic human value has been distorted; how the rejection of this value at one point in the history of the human race has affected definitions and relationships in a most pervasive manner.

Describing or illustrating the nature and extent of female discrimination in this area performs no great service to our central arguments. Statistics on female employment in various sectors, the types of jobs they occupy, and the pay they receive are readily available, even though the insights they provide are less readily accepted. The reasons for the continuation of this inequality and exploitation are also well–known; at least in part, they relate clearly to the benefit that males experience by discriminating against females. That situation will change most dramatically as women themselves demand equal treatment; these demands are beginning to surface.

A much more insidious and difficult form of discrimination against women in work settings is, of course, the exploitation of women as sex objects. Manipulating a work situation to obtain sexual favors from women may well have persisted for as long as males and females have worked together. More recently, as women have been admitted to all levels of work, as jobs have become more closely related to each other, and as intimate associations have become more acceptable, the incidence of harrassment seems to be increasing. That could be the simple result of more frequent exposure, or greater willingness to report the problem. In any case, accounts of women experiencing harrassment at work are multiple; a number of well documented scholarly researches on this subject have appeared (Kanter).

The issue of denigration of women can be discussed on at least two levels: the moral and the cultural. The *moral* problem is rather simply addressed. Unequal or denigrating treatment of another human being is wrong; our society must exorcise beliefs and behaviors which contradict what we say we believe. Behavioral and attitudinal change is one part of the task we face. Although addressed simply, the resolution of the problem is not easy. The *structural* problem is even more difficult to solve. It may be that social institutions have not developed because the issue did not become salient enough at an earlier point. To illustrate, through certain conventions male doctors have been restrained from exploiting females by having female nurses present during examinations. This is not to deny that some normative evasion may well take place.

But in the arena of female exploitation in the workplace, institutional mechanisms have not evolved adequately enough so that male exploitation cannot take place. (Of course, this is not to assume that females do not exploit males; simply to say that the greater problem by far is male dominance over females.) If our values underscore the idea that females are equal, that they deserve to be treated as workers and not as female sex objects, it is possible that institutional structures will emerge which will protect the female from unwanted personal or sexual attention.

This issue is not excluded from religious work settings. Thus a minister-counselor is not immune from exploiting a female assistant or partner. Often religious structures are even more difficult to manage because there the norms of love and acceptance and openness may conflict with the need to retain respectful distances to avoid occasions where even unintended exploitation can emerge.

The Conflict Between Females and Males in the Marriage and Family Context

A special problem confronts those who work in the spousal relationship of marriage and as members of families. Work in this context needs to be analyzed on the basis of division of labor pertaining to the maintenance of the marriage or family internally, but also with respect to the way one's work in a marriage or family affects the larger community.

The traditional family (and marriage) has been relatively stable in its allocation of responsibilities. As the term has been used traditionally, the division of labor was so structured that the wife/mother, because of her gender-linked functions, was assigned to the home to carry out the majority of the household activities and to take care of the children—both activities considered necessary for a normal marriage-family life. "Traditionally, husbands did 'men's work,' and wives did 'women's work'" (Blood and Wolfe:47).

But the traditional family has been changing, and a new form called the "emergent" family has been developing slowly. In many ways, this change has been coincident with, and causative of, the feminist movement. Women have begun to move out of the traditional system of labor allocated to them, and increasingly are beginning to work outside the home, whether as volunteers or in remunerated settings. This phenomenon has created a massive shift in the inner dynamic and balance of the marriage and/or family. Only those which are relevant to the analysis of work can be addressed here.

The first and most obvious is that as women become more actively engaged in work outside the home, the occupational career of the male is challenged and even deflected from its usual or expected trajectory. Thus a husband who normally would follow a certain track in his advancement and promotion patterns may find his ambition limited or truncated by the added need to support his wife in her career goals. Most of us know of males who willingly or unwillingly have deferred to their wives so they could follow their careers. This is a very difficult adjustment for many males to make.

As he becomes more involved in housework, the male finds himself needing to internalize the fact that housework is necessary, hard, and often not as prestigious as his work in the marketplace. The implications of this insight for marriage and family relationships are vast and can create tensions of considerable degree. This is basically a matter of changing cultural values to accommodate the change of gender roles to include women and men in the extrahousehold work, and vice versa. How rapidly this change and adjustment to it can take place is a matter of conjecture; in some areas, rather quickly, and in other areas, very slowly and with great difficulty.

The second and even more significant issue is the experience of women in the work force outside of the home. The most obvious fact here is that a woman—married and often later with children—

enters the employed ranks in addition to maintaining her home responsibilities. If there is one thing that is being recognized by the women, it is that their new liberation and freedom to work has also become an *additional burden,* not a shifting or substitution of the domestic for the commercial. This is a difficult dilemma; it is too early to tell what its resolution will be.

A third and possibly more traumatic dimension is the community response or attitude toward an upsetting of the traditionally accepted division of labor. For women to enter the labor force, and to leave child rearing to husbands or some other arrangement has precipitated a tremendous amount of psychological and moral opposition. Grandmothers can exert the most coercive pressures of all if they subtly remind their daughters that they are neglecting their husbands and/or children. The psychological and social dynamics resulting from deviations from community practices and norms can be very inhibiting to social change.

In this setting, as in most of the others, we have been discussing women who face the logic of the "double jeopardy." That is, they are faced with an incredibly difficult dilemma: If they remain as they are, their denigration and exploitation will likely continue; if they protest and resist, they are accused of challenging religious convention or of flaunting community values and norms.

As women go to work, there is no question that readjustment in the marriage and family structure and process will be traumatic. But the necessary changes are no less important than the liberation of persons from other types of exploitation and discrimination, such as racial. Indeed, the liberation of the female is of ultimate importance! This is an issue with profound implications, an issue dealing with the fundamental question of allowing and, in fact, encouraging half of the human race to achieve its full development.

Some Propositions for the Creative Involvement of Women in Work

The Liberation of Women in Work Must Be a Joint Male/Female Venture

To suggest that men should participate in the discussion of women's liberation in work may well appear to be arrogant and chauvinistic, particularly since, it has been men who were largely responsible for the oppression of women in the first place. Certainly the organized women's liberation movement would consider this position unacceptable.

However, our position is based on the sociological recognition that the male/female relationship is so intricate, involved and intimate—especially in marriage—that no issue relating to either sex can be solved unilaterally. This may sound especially cruel when it certainly can be argued that males still unilaterally oppress females. But unilateral oppression is never fully possible, no matter how evil the oppression. Even though against her will in many settings, the female has been involved in the subordination process; it is a fact of social life that there is a reciprocity in every relationship, however uneven this may have been. Also, even though on balance such a subordinated relationship is clearly immoral, females have experienced certain compensations for their subordinate position.

In any case, in the world of work, women will not achieve their objectives through a unilateral confrontation with men. It is more likely that less progress will be made with a head-on assault than through the use of rational and reasonable approaches. This does not mean that males do not need to acknowledge their tyranny of women; such acknowledgement is essential! It is only to say that, normally, men will be brought to recognize their folly more quickly by insistent reason than by force.

At the same time, several disclaimers to this approach must be noted. First of all, to assume that men always, or that men typically, listen to reason could be a fallacious premise. Secondly, some honest men would allow or even assert that they can be rational and reasonable as well as confrontative within a specific approach to certain issues. Finally, one dare not deny that head-on confrontation can be seen as part of a process while at the same time insisting that finding answers to the current inequalities is, in fact, a joint male/female venture.

It is in this context of interaction and dialogue between the sexes that the Christian ethic comes into its full power. If the love of neighbor is to be fully functional, then the participation of both sexes in such a discussion as well as in the labor market and in the decisions of who is to work and where will be fully mutual. The New Testament, especially the Epistles, may include some limiting perspectives regarding the participation of women in religious affairs, but it contains nothing that condones subordination of women in the labor world. In fact, Jesus' treatment of women proposed the opposite, and his ethic pointed to a situation in which male and female are to be considered equal (Matt. 19:3–9).[6]

Changing the Structural Roadblocks to Women's Work Liberation

The greatest hindrance to the liberation of women in work may not be values and prejudices but structures. That is to say, we have created institutions, such as the nuclear family, which keep women in their place. With children being a usual outcome of marriage, one of the partners, (always the female for birth and usually the female in terms of childcare) is effectively, if only temporarily, barred from becoming involved in any kind of remunerated work outside of the home.

In those cases where the male takes over the domestic chores so the female can go to work, the issue is solved momentarily for the female. But the basic problem is still not solved, for what if, at the same time, the male also would like to work outside the home? It is not enough to say the male owes the wife the chance to be free. No matter how wrong males have been historically on this issue, making that right should not include creating another wrong.

In the nuclear family context, the solution to women's work liberation looks grim, for as was indicated above, either the husband or the wife will feel oppressed or restricted. It is clear that one of the reasons for the fragility of the contemporary family— where up to one-half of the marriages end in divorce—is precisely the structural trap in which females find themselves. An extended family, and a community cooperative or a commune, are promising options for many couples who are facing serious frustration because marriage and family responsibilities are limiting creative expressions in work.

There are many other structural hindrances to women's work liberation. Included are the educational biases beginning with grade school which stifle women's aspirations and tend to steer them into domestic and low-prestige jobs. Business corporations are also largely to blame because they have established criteria and guidelines for access to jobs ostensibly based on physical and mental competence criteria, but which effectively exclude women.

Of course, opening up the business and corporate arena so that women are not automatically directed toward secretarial and menial jobs but rather become eligible to compete for managerial roles is more than a structural problem alone; it also involves values and prejudices.

Changing Attitudes, Values and Norms

Changes in values and attitudes are possible! The fact that in some situations a female can refer to God as *she* and not cause all the males—including theologians present—to dive out of the nearest window is proof enough! So if it is possible for males to stretch their minds enough to entertain the idea that God can be conceived of as feminine as well as masculine, it would also seem possible for them to accept the idea that females should be admitted to the boardrooms of the business world.

Indeed it is happening, and although many such situations could be described as tokenism, there is change. Christian men in business should be the first to open up the mahogany offices to females. And if Christian businessmen are to be the leaders in this liberation process, it becomes the responsibility of the local congregations to provide moral and ethical support. If the church has any function beyond worship rituals, it is to strengthen its members to be salt and light in the world.

One reason that men and women may not have been able historically to cooperate in business and commercial relationships is the temptation of sexual involvements. It is possible that males have not allowed women into the "inner sanctums" of the business and commercial world because of fear of sexual compromise. Insofar as this is true, it becomes a matter of joint responsibility between females and males to work out the problem. There are many areas, such as medicine, where these issues have been solved structurally. Though there may be little empirical evidence as to whether the male is the initiator and aggressor in sexual intimacies in the business/commercial sector, it seems that at present the burden lies with the male and not the female.[7]

Conclusion

In our approach to the issue of women's work, we have recognized that all the principles which we have enunciated throughout this volume are applicable. But we also acknowledge that the complications of historical institutionalized violence and oppression make the subject too difficult for simple analysis. A rectification of this injustice requires the total remaking of human society—an awesome and overwhelming idea. The prospects for such a revolution are most difficult to assess. The basic values and beliefs of a social system are not easily changed or redirected. The optimism of the Social Darwinists—such as Lester Ward who maintained that human intelligence would enable social values to improve—has been practically abandoned by secular and religious thinkers alike.

An increasing amount of descriptive and statistical material regarding the world of women at work is available. But the basic issues and challenges lie elsewhere in the subconscious attitudes and feelings as well as in the cultural and religious systems of the male-dominated societies. *Women's work* is therefore still a very ambiguous and emotionally loaded concept. And it will remain so for some time to come. Any solution will demand that some agreement emerge in the following areas:

1. What actually constitutes "women's and men's work"—if indeed these distinctions may be made—and what are the bases for deciding what they shall be?

2. If there should be designated work assigned to each of the genders, how shall these areas of work be evaluated and rewarded?

That is, how will society evaluate and honor the work which is specialized with reference to gender?

3. How can society work at changing the institutional structures which have contributed to the oppression of women? What steps must be taken for resolution? This question is especially urgent for the nature of the family structure and function.

4. Most important, what special role does the Christian church have in determining the underlying values and beliefs regarding this important topic, and how can it contribute to the reformation of the institutions which have made human existence so painful for this sector of humanity? There is no question that the Christian church has contributed to the oppression of women in work. What can be done to rectify the damage will to a great extent determine the church's credibility and its ability to be relevant in the world. This may sound like a shrill voice in a civilized age. However, the contrary is true—women have endured a great deal of suffering in a shrill and uncivilized society. It is time this society acts like a gentleman! Whose job is it to wash dishes? And what is that job worth to society? How, for example, will this issue be integrated with the GNP and income tax structure?

This chapter is entitled "Male-Female Relationships and Work." It is imperative that we recognize that the actual status of women in work is the result of *relationships* between males and females which have emerged over millennia of time. Even the institution of slavery—as practiced in the American South which was then highly segregated—was developed and based on a reciprocal and interdependent relationship, often involving great intimacies; of course, the interdependent relationship was clearly very unbalanced. The female slavery in our contemporary society is based on an even more intimate though assymetrical interdependency; hence it becomes all the more difficult to eradicate. Sadly, an unequal interdependence can create a very subtle, pervasive and unhealthy dependency in which freedom may not even be desired by the subordinate. This type of dependency may well be the most dehumanizing of all. The reflections of Sophie Tolstoy, wife of Leo, say so well what must be spoken loudly, and also what must be heard:

> . . . I can't find any occupation for myself. He is lucky to be so clever and talented. But I'm neither the one nor the other. One can't live on love alone. . . .
>
> It isn't hard to find work, but before doing anything one has to create some enthusiasm for breeding hens, tinkling the piano, and reading a lot of silly books and a few very good ones, or pickling cucumbers and what not. . . .

If I am not good to him, if I am merely a doll, a *wife,* and not a *human being*—then it is all useless and I don't want to carry on this existence. Of course I am idle, but I am not idle by nature; I simply haven't yet discovered what I can do here. . . .

I love nothing and no one except Lyova. And yet one ought to have something else to love as well, just as Lyova loves his *work*. . . .

My existence is so deadly dull, while his is so full and rich, with his work and genius and immortal fame . . . .

It is sad that my emotional dependence on the man I love should have killed so much of my energy and ability; there was certainly once a great deal of energy in me (Kolbenschlag:72–73).

Marx made us aware of the opiate of religion. People became conditioned to be dependent on religion when the real issue was economic exploitation. "Women's work" may well have been the opiate for women through the centuries, whereas the real culprit may have been the exploitation of females by males, the weaker by those who are physically stronger! If force is the basis for morality, society is destined to decay.

Excursus 5
Wife, Mother and Businesswoman

by Ferne Glick

I don't remember playing with dolls. But I do remember playing store and stocking my play store shelves with empty cans scrounged from kitchen garbage—Campbell's Soup cans, beans, corn, peas, whatever Mother used in her kitchen. I'd mark the cans, arrange them attractively then try to find someone who would be my customer.

Selling is something I've enjoyed for as long as I can remember. I'm sure some part of this came to me naturally. For years, I went to market with my parents; they managed a large meat and baked goods business. I learned the various cuts of meat as well as how to satisfy people and their needs. All this while I was still a little girl. I remember how the family laughed (a few customers too) when I needed to stand on a box so I could read the weight of a cut of meat on the scales.

When our family moved to Virginia, I worked in the grocery business we owned while my sister Freda worked in the restaurant. I enjoyed my sales experience in that store. Since we had some clothing also, I sold everything from groceries to clothing.

Although working in a business was very much part of my childhood and teen years, I didn't realize then that selling would become so much a part of my life. Nor did I realize then that being in business would bring joy and conflict into my life. The times then seemed simple: they were conducive to getting married young, helping my husband, Vern, on the farm and keeping house. However, after several years on the farm, we both felt a desire to broaden our horizons; so we volunteered with our church service program and spent two years in Newfoundland. While we were there, serving in community service projects, our twin sons were born. These were happy years. When our time of service was up, we felt we were not ready to go back to the farm. So after spending a bit of time back in Pennsylvania visiting family and friends, we headed northward for service in Alberta.

While in Alberta, we became aware that our twin sons— Craig and Carson—seemed to have a behavior problem; later the problem was diagnosed as deafness. When that diagnosis was confirmed, it became clear very quickly that it would be to their advantage for us to be living closer to a metropolitan area such as Philadelphia in order to find the resources we needed for our sons; so we came back home again. This return home became a time for reevaluation: our lives, our goals, our interests and aptitudes, how best to care for our sons, how to earn a living, where?

It was clear that both of us would need to work to provide the special education our sons needed. It was also clear that if we went into business, both of us would need to contribute our energies to be sure it would get off the ground.

This was the beginning of the stereo era. So, after a lot of thought, we opened an audio shop. It seemed natural for me to fit into a combined secretarial-bookkeeping-sales role. The entire experience of being directly involved in the development of a new business was fulfilling. Of course, Vern's positive attitude toward my participation made possible some of that sense of fulfillment. Not only was I able to share in meeting our financial needs; I consistently found satisfaction in working with the public and in attending personal growth, retail management and sales seminars.

These outside contacts became increasingly important to me as our children were growing up; they helped me keep a balance within. Of course, I had inner conflict. Our two sons were away from home for long periods of time and, consequently, needed extra attention. Now also, we had a daughter, Tina—two and one-half years younger than the boys. She needed special attention as much as the boys for she had to learn how to relate to a family—parents and brothers—where the only siblings she had were living with a handicap. And where the only parents she had were spending a lot of their energy earning money to pay for the special education they felt their sons deserved.

A second crucial time in my life emerged when the children grew older and demanded less and less of my time. Now, where did I fit in? Although working together with Vern in the audio business had been very satisfying in many ways, my inclination was to pull away from what had always seemed to be Vern's realm, and to discover what I could manage on my own. So in 1978, with Vern's support, I decided to open a dress shop with a double challenge—one floor with new clothing and one with consigned clothing. Applying the ideas in selling I had learned in the stereo field was exciting, but also a difficult challenge. Some of the things I had learned applied; others didn't. The training I had received in personnel and management seminars was very helpful. Although neither hiring nor firing ever came easy for me, I had learned something about proper procedures. But learning to deal with a different clientele was a truly stretching experience; I needed to make some mistakes of my own. Although much in my background was helpful, I must admit that it didn't truly prepare me for the next several years.

The decline in our U.S. economy and the mistakes I made during the early period of testing my own wings forced me to realize that I must take a hard look at the direction the business was going. Subsequently, I decided that although the part of the shop with the new clothing was a delight to many, it was not something that I could continue financially. I decided to change the entire shop and to run it as a consigned clothing shop. Even though I had put in fifteen-hour days and worked very hard to make the new clothing store a success, I became convinced that closing that store was the direction I needed to go if my business was to survive.

The struggle for survival turned into an education. By turns, the struggle was exhilarating, challenging and frightening. I learned what it feels like to awaken in the middle of the night and in the moment of awakening to agonize: "Am I going to make it? Which of my decisions have led me to the brink of failure? What changes can I make so I can become more successful?"

However, making the necessary changes was also a struggle. Deciding to change course was one thing; educating the public—my customers—and my own employees was quite another. Giving up a new clothing boutique and concentrating on consigned used clothing, even though of a high quality, seemed to my employees and certain customers like a step down instead of a movement toward success. but I persisted and had the pleasure of seeing this change in focus develop into a very acceptable and successful way of merchandising. So acceptable and so successful that we have opened a second store on the same premises—this one offering fine furniture.

My feelings are mixed as I look back over my business life and the metamorphosis of my self during those years. My mind is filled with questions, with an awareness of some of the problems I've faced, with a rather sharp sense of what I would say to a young woman who might come to me for advice or guidance before entering a wife-mother-business woman career. My ideas may not be new and they will certainly not fit everyone else; but they are my ideas, drawn from my own pilgrimage and, in some cases, hammered out in the heat of anxiety, or uncertainty, or pressures in marriage, family or financial need.

First, a few questions: Is business a legitimate form of expression for the Christian woman? Should one rather not be present all the time for family? If financial necessity requires a second income, would a vocation such as teaching or nursing be more "right" and perhaps easier to manage? Should husband and wife be in business together?

It doesn't seem necessary to detail a response to each question. I think my story suggests the answers I have found. But I will say that some parts of the male dominated business world would be better for a woman's viewpoint. Also, I believe that the church is richer in dimension and understanding because there are women in a congregation who are having firsthand experience in business. Finally, I'm convinced that women have gifts which should be called forth through involvement in many different kinds of activity, including business.

But there are problems: A businesswoman married to a businessman. The demands of each business. The possibility of the male feeling "his" business is more important than "hers." Differences in management style. The "stretch" between a husband-wife business relationship and their marital relationship—the need to be fully objective, professional and decisive at work and then at home to allow emotion, subjectivity and vulnerability.

There are personnel problems: the unwillingness of younger persons or males to "hear" a woman boss; the superior attitudes of those with greater technical expertise; the ability to be objective in hiring and firing procedures.

And problems in the financial realm: Bankers who want to talk to the "man of the house." The need to bite one's tongue and be silent sometimes when men talk to men, knowing full well that the wrong word from a woman or the wrong timing for a legitimate comment could sabotage an absolutely essential line of credit.

I mentioned technical problems. Sometimes I wish I had learned more about audio components so I could have held my own better in that field. Instead, I chose to start my own businesses.

I've hinted at the attitudes of others, particularly a certain type of employee as well as those who hold seats of financial power. But an even larger problem was my own attitude. It took me a long time to feel secure in the business: to believe that my word really meant as much as my husband-partner's word. I was afraid to be labeled as an aggressive woman so I ended up not being as straightforward as I might have been. I deliberately squelched my emotions at times because I knew that if I showed the least bit more emotion than my husband, male heads would nod at the solemn statement that "women are too emotional to be in business." That was not only a problem; it was a loss—to myself and others.

There was the big problem of family versus business. Which comes first? Guilt often follows either answer people give to that question. There was the wonderful and satisfying picture of a husband committed to doing the best he could to offer his children—handicapped and not—everything possible so that their growing years and educational experiences would fit them for life; there was also the wistful plaint, "Daddy's always working." There was the mother's finding fulfillment in joint business ventures with her husband and in businesses established on her own initiative—needing this challenge and fulfillment, in fact, to avoid being overwhelmed with her sons' handicaps—at the same time, torn when a sick employee kept her from fulfilling a Saturday promise at Hershey Park. Of course, there were always also the balancing factors: children who knew how to give— children who learned early how to respond when a great deal was expected of them.

Have I learned anything from all of this? Although I think I know the answer to that question, the reader may also judge from the quality and meaning of whatever insights appear here. I do know this: if any woman ever approaches me about what to watch for as she pursues a wife-mother-business-woman career path, I'd plant a few suggestions that might possibly serve as signposts.

1. You must be willing to accept responsibility for your decisions. Know what you want; admit the likelihood of mistakes; accept responsibility for making them and correcting them.

2. Be ready to be misunderstood. Since few others, if any others, have walked intimately with you as this part of your pilgrimage evolves, they won't know how you have agonized over your decision-making. Perhaps the label "aggressive woman" will be the hardest to hear and bear with grace.

3. Have the courage to risk. There are financial risks, risks in the area of relationships, even a risk that the objective

demands of the real world of business will tempt you to submerge or block the flowering of your femininity. That need not be so, but it is a risk.

4. Be sure of your motivations. Why do I want to be in business? The answers here will affect your staying power when the going gets rough. You'll need both a solid motivation and stick-to-it-iveness as well as stamina and a high commitment of energy to get you through fifteen-hour days and multiple demands.

5. You must enjoy your work!

6. If you're in business with your husband, establish clear areas of responsibility and clear lines of authority. Who is responsible for what to whom? Be sure you have similar understandings about goals, basic policies and procedures. Keep the lines of communication open.

7. Be smart. Set aside times for play, fun and personal rejuvenation. Scheduling this kind of time is as important as meeting your banker to apply for a line of credit.

8. Don't forget your husband! Nurture your relationship. Don't slip into the rut of "business all the time." Watch for the trap of business patterns of relationship overwhelming your private marital relationship. Plan special events for the two of you. Discover each other; rediscover.

9. Your family is important. Each child needs you. The whole family needs to "feel" like a family. That takes work. Your ability to see employee needs and organize elements that respond to those needs must be applied at home as well. You can and must remain sensitive to the needs of your children.

10. Be prepared to give up certain desires: lengthy vacations, leisurely travel, lazy afternoons, extra time with friends. Sometimes a business can be like a "child" needing constant attention from the "parent."

That's quite a list, I know. I'm sure I was involved in business before I thought very much about what it meant. Or before I realized the cost. It was just something I liked doing and, without a lot of thinking, I was there.

If I were starting over, these are some of the signposts I'd take a look at. But knowing me, I'd probably do it again. I can think of no other work I might have done that would have offered the challenge, the potential for personal fulfillment or the rewards of many kinds that being a businesswoman has brought into my life.

Being wife-mother-businesswoman is work! No question about it! I love it!

10

The Changing Nature of Work: A Contemporary Challenge

> Times are changing, and I think it's a mistake for a kid to start out in computer training as a freshman in college and that's all he'll ever know. As a matter of fact, what I am doing now is getting a master's degree. As a general rule I think you should always have a hip pocket career along with your main one because you don't know what's going to happen. Our society is changing so drastically, in my lifetime (a 40-year-old entrepreneur) we've gone from an industrial society to an informational one (Interview by Authors, 1985).

We have been defining jobs as the work that people do to earn a living. Using this definition, it is clear that jobs have not always been available to all who need them. Unemployment and underemployment along with a general lack of adequate economic opportunity have plagued most human societies. It is within this context and for this reason that the United Nations' "Universal Declaration of Human Rights" addresses the topic of work, maintaining that access to work is a fundamental right.[1]

Point one of article 23 states, "Everyone has the right to work, to free choice of employment, to just and favorable conditions of work and to protection against unemployment." Beyond this fundamental statement, the declaration places heavy emphasis on the right for equal pay without discrimination (article 23, section

175

3), the right to fair remuneration (section 2) and the right of rest from labor (article 24). It is not difficult to project oneself into the mood of the framers of this "Universal Declaration" in 1948. Obviously, they were aware of the "yearning" that mankind has felt for the liberation of human beings from various kinds of social bondage and their growth as a group into a more just society.

This is not a volume on the history of work, so we are simply reminding ourselves that the writers of the United Nations Declaration reflected a strong consciousness of how humans have been deprived of work; also that often they have been dehumanized in the experience of work. There is one motif, however, which can link our analysis of work with the struggle to find meaningful work: that is the premise that *the nature of work is changing*. Even though much work done today is similar to that done for centuries and even millennia—as for example, sweeping floors and cultivating gardens—much remunerated work has changed dramatically. Most of these changes are the result of a rapidly expanding evolution in technology.

Specifically, the changes may be categorized as follows: (1) the types of work available, (2) the amount of work available, (3) the remuneration for the various types of work, (4) the impact of the various types of work on humans and (5) the implications of changing work for human society. In this discussion we will deal with the work on the job, or employment work.[2]

The Transformation of Work

The changes in the nature of work parallel very closely the development of technology. An excellent example of this truism would be carpentry. For centuries the work of building a home from wood required hammer and saw; these tools may have been refined or changed to accommodate certain new materials or processes, but in essence and foundational principle they remained the same. The technology of cutting and fastening changed very slowly—until certain types of power became available.

Since that point, changes have been dramatic. Much cutting has been taken over by a variety of high-speed band saws and circular saws. The hand-held hammer is almost obsolete in some settings; instead a pneumatic tool nails roof shingles or framing pieces or sheathing at great speed. Using power saws and pneumatic hammers, mass-production techniques in various building applications literally change the face of a construction site. Crews build trusses in standardized forms; other crews complete stud wall sections, including sheathing; still another crew with a crane sets the sections quickly in place and caps them with finished roof trusses ready for roof sheathing and shingles. Of course, many other types of work reflect changes just as dramatic as those found in carpentry.

As a matter of fact, Louis Levine, in an article entitled "Effects of Technological Change on the Nature of Jobs," concludes the article by saying, "The upheaval in the job market is so tremendous that the nation has yet to take the measure of its social, economic and political impact" (Herman, Sadofsky, and Rosenberg:106). One of the most pervasive ways in which technology has changed work is mechanization—a change which has displaced and replaced thousands of people. In the twenty-five years before 1968, "A full two-thirds of the nation's farm famlies yielded to machines, chemicals, and capital of agro-business" (Luecke:48). These families obviously took other work, which for them meant drastic shifts in work habits and activities.

But technology didn't stop by replacing people with machines. It continued on to automation. In this setting, people began to serve machines. Since machines still needed some attention, automation began to demand that people be matched with the dictations of the machine. Until recently, cutting steel bars required a person to tend the machine, to feed it, to oil it. Now a modern bar-cutting machine is controlled by a computer tape and the "operator" is there mainly to report if anything unusual happens.

However, automation has brought an even greater change in work: it has changed drastically the social relationships that used to exist in the workplace. Historically, much, if not most, productive work has been done in work groups—situations where persons worked together and performed the work through a cooperative effort. A threshing bee "down on the farm" would be such an example. This was usually a community or an extended family affair. Today wheat harvest implies a combine operator sitting in an air-conditioned cab, listening to hard rock or country western, with another person hauling the wheat from field to storage in a big truck. This setting barely allows for a social structure to exist or socializing to function.

In the factory, individuals tend huge computer-controlled machines and talk to fellow workers only at coffee break time. Even the building trades—traditionally a collective or group activity—have become more specialized; specialists put in the basements, or walls, or roofs. Each person does a specialized job and relates only briefly, if at all, to his or her fellow workers.

Within a few short years, mechanization, automation and computerization have changed the nature of work so completely that the machine has now become the worker. Now also—incredible irony—the machine dictates the work arrangements of the human accomplice. Instead of the human controlling the machine, as has been the case during the early years of technological development, the human is forced to adapt to and serve the rhythms of the machine.

Another significant change has to do with the interactions of persons working in the same department. At one time, there was considerable opportunity for social involvement with other human beings. Now the individual is paired with a machine instead of with other persons. Now humans, for example, are "married" to the computer and often isolated almost completely from the social context of work.

Developing technology has also affected the organizational structures of management. The older bureaucratic structure has been replaced by a specialization which—according to Read— "represents a staggering change in thinking, action and decision-making in organizations . . . . " He continues by saying that these changes present "new arrangements of people and tasks, . . . which sharply break with the bureaucratic tradition" (Toffler, 1970:140–41). Technology is moving us toward a "working society of technical co-equals" where technical knowledge is determinative of what one does and how one relates to other people (Toffler, 1970:142).

Technology has brought other changes. It has increased the ratio of white collar to blue collar jobs, with the routine work of other years having been taken over by machines. It has increased the need for higher education, especially of the technical variety; in turn, this feeds the technology already in hand. It has increased the demand for information processing and communication.

Of course, not all work has been transformed; there is still much work that is similar to what has been done for hundreds of years. A mailman delivering mail from door to door does relatively the same work he did when the post office first came into being. The work of preparing and cooking potatoes for the family supper will probably never change much. But the changes in work that have taken place in the last number of decades, in themselves, become the prognosis of significant changes to come—in the family, community and societal structure.

What we have pointed out above is not intended to depreciate the way in which mechanization and automation have taken the drudgery out of many work positions. There is no merit in backbreaking work for its own sake, nor in work which is difficult, debilitating and enervating. On the contrary, wherever possible, this aspect of technology and automation is to be welcomed and applied.

The Deletion of Work

The advent of technology is bringing with it a rather significant shift in the *type* and *amount* of work that will be available. As indicated earlier, automation is deleting productive work in many sectors. At the same time we are witnessing a dramatic increase in the development of service and related industries. Transportation, communication, and human services represent only a few of the categories of work that are burgeoning. At the same time, many heavy production jobs are disappearing as automation usurps that role.

More and more work will shift to the electronic sector, which pertains to communication and information sharing. Indeed, as Alvin Toffler proposes in *Third Wave,* many jobs—some already existing and others now emerging—will be done at home in "electronic cottages." This new category will include sales work, professional work such as consulting and counseling, architecture and a host of activities which allow for decentralization.

Many of the new jobs will be highly technical and professionalized. Computer technology will demand specialized training in learning the language of the new society; the knowledge industry—which includes schools and universities—will need to become conversant with these new technologies. However, with all of this change, a basic fact still remains: that a major layer of production, service and distribution work will continue, still relatively traditional in form. The futurists may picture a rather dramatic shift in the future world of work, but the overall picture will retain numerous similarities with the past.[3]

The debate as to whether the modern transformation of work has affected the total amount of work available is still going on. One position acknowledges that technology destroys some jobs but insists that other new ones are created. Another position holds that the net result is clearly a decrease in the total number of jobs available. Still others argue that the total amount of work is actually increased. The debate cannot be resolved easily because of the complex factors that help determine the amount of work actually available. One thing is clear, however: technology has created and continues to create tremendous dislocations in the total work force and unemployment of individuals as they get caught in the many changes being made in the forms of production.[4]

Since there is not yet convincing data regarding the question of whether technology is actually deleting jobs and creating a net loss, the debate cannot be resolved. Even so, the fact still remains that the loss of work has been a fact for many people in North America and around the world for many years.[5] Lack of work is a massive problem in many countries and has never been fully solved by any except the more primitive societies. Of central importance to us is the human anguish and sadness that unemployment causes, and what we can do about it.

Being unemployed brings to the surface the tremendous significance of work for the human being. Most of us have had some contact with persons who have been deprived of gainful and secure employment. We have observed that the cost to self-worth and interpersonal relationships is profound. In the next chapter the personal account of being unemployed for a short while portrays some of this feeling.

We have pointed out also that employment is an international and national political/economic problem. However, that fact should not diminish our concern; there are things that the Christian should and can do. On the most general level, of course, no one should be deprived of the necessities of life and the capability of shaping a decent self-respecting way of life. In occasional emergency situations we may be called on to help a person or family in need; and we should help. But we also have an obligation to deal with the larger and more pervasive conditions that cause unemployment. That is a much more difficult problem, although there are approaches that can be developed. Work sharing or increasing service work to solve human suffering are two such approaches still largely undeveloped. Of course, innovations which will create work of a useful nature is the greatest challenge, a challenge to which Christians especially should feel called.

The Quality of Work

Work is changing not only on the basis of the technological innovations which are affecting many aspects of our lives. Rather, some of the changes are taking place because of a "rationalizing" tendency which, according to Max Weber, is characteristic of our approach in modernizing history. Briefly stated, rationalizing work means that it is being structured increasingly on the basis of rational criteria concerned with increased awareness of our own human activities and performance.

Even universities are affected. The dean of the university where I teach sends a packet each term with an enclosed note saying, "I am distributing the course evaluation forms for the Arts Course Questionnaire. Please return them to my office as soon as possible." These standardized surveys are computerized and coded by machine, and reflect a rational approach to the evaluation of teaching effectiveness. With the advent of empirical social science, statistical analyses, computer technology and administrative theory, a host of scientific analyses of work and its effectiveness has invaded even the university.

Frederick W. Taylor's concept of "human engineering"—a pioneer effort which produced a whole new approach to work—has been expanded in almost limitless ways and applications. Even management processes have become subjected to scientific analyses. Consequently, numerous theories of effective management have emerged, such as management by objectives (MBO).

Work in almost every sector has been described, defined and become subject to "grading." Job descriptions are developed almost endlessly by personnel departments for every job in the plant. Job promotions and wage or salary increases are measured against these technical criteria. Although Ellul spoke of the effects of the "rationalizing" process in society in general, it nevertheless applies to work also:

> A progressively more complete technical knowledge of man is being developed. Will it liberate him? Man's traditional, spontaneous activities are now subjected to analysis in all their aspects—objects, modes, durations, quantities, results. The totality of these actions and feelings is then systematized, schematized, and tabulated (Ellul:395).

The experience of work as a spontaneous expression of human response to the things that need doing is thus subordinated to the rational definition of the work, and to the evaluation of its achievement.

Because the norm is productivity and efficiency, the individualistic or esthetic elements of the work situation tend to be downgraded. The concept of the craftsman producing a quality product which expresses the philosophy and emotions of the creator is not very feasible in the context described above. The technique itself becomes the judge of the work done, for the goal of technique is efficiency. And ultimately, within this frame of reference, there is only one best technique for any one job—the technique through which is achieved optimum efficiency.

Numerous philosophers and scholars have promoted the idea that, in large measure, human beings are the product of their experience. More specifically, men like Karl Marx and Adam Smith have suggested that the "mode of production" determines the kind of person that will emerge as a result of that context. This does not make humans the helpless victims of the socio-cultural environment, but it does say that if we create certain situations, they will, most likely, in turn, affect us in significant ways. Karl Jaspers expresses this concern well when he says:

> Wherever people are reduced to the position of those who merely have to perform an allotted task, the problem of the cleavage between a human creature and being a worker

plays a decisive part in the individual's fate. One's own life acquires a new preponderant, and joy in work grows relative . . . the vital question is how far this process of rationalization can go and how far it is self-limited in order to leave scope for the individual to act on his own initiative instead of blindly obeying instructions (Jaspers:64–65).

As we have emphasized elsewhere, the worker and his work are part of a creative process. In the first instance, creating something out of an unformed or unordered situation was an expression of the love of God; this mode of creation continues to be reflected in man's being. Rationalization of work—by which the challenge is removed from the worker and his work and transferred to a mathematical and mechanical system—takes from the human being the opportunity of "creating" as he works. Numerical control (NC) machines—in which every part of the process of drilling a machine part, for example, is done automatically—leave no challenge for the person attending the machines. The glib retort that this fact allows the attendant to relax or read a book, or think of the good wage he is making completely misses the point to be made about meaningful work.

Technology and Depersonalization

The "goodness" or "badness" of technology has been argued for a long time. In discussions we have witnessed, the issue was usually dismissed with the cliche: "Technology is neither good nor bad: it is neutral. It all depends upon man and how he uses it." We have never been totally satisfied with that kind of glib argument. First of all, it tends to justify the production of anything. For if what is produced is neither bad nor good, then what criterion shall we use to decide whether it should be produced, or whether a new technique should be employed? (Using the argument of neutrality, nuclear submarines are neither good nor bad and there is nothing wrong with producing them.)

More problematically, however, this threadbare cliche begs the real question. To say that it is the people who use the technology that create the moral problem transfers the issue into a subjective land where technology is irrelevant. The problem is then reduced to an issue of individual ethics. What is considered bad ethics for one person may be acceptable for another. Furthermore, if there is no objective criterion for deciding whether a technique is good or bad, and personal ethics become normative, then the issue becomes as broad as the reform or renewal of all individuals in society. This may in fact be true but represents a totally unmanageable condition.

Finally, the most pernicious consequence of the neutrality stance toward technology is that it throws up a smokescreen around the fact that technique and technology *do* influence us, and that technology *does* have a life of its own. Violence on TV *does* influence our own behavior. The ready availability of handguns *does* influence the *kind* of violence that is perpetrated, if not the *amount.* It is clear to us that the reason social science has not come up with clearer proof of the impact of technology on our lives is that there exists a powerful ideological, institutional and existential bias in favor of technique and technology.[6] Put another way, the reason why technology is seen as either innocuous, or more probably, as good, is that most people gain so much from the benefits of technology itself; benefits in our work and in our professions; benefits reflected in our achievements, in our power structures and in our personal advancements; benefits known by their other name of increased profits. All of these create a harvest of blessing from new techniques. These pervasive benefits tend to dull our senses to the adverse consequences of the growth of technology without essential controls.

This tendency to rationalize (that is, to shape our perceptions with a bias in favor of our own interests) is not generally admitted, but most serious thinkers are aware of its pernicious and subtle pervasiveness. Indeed recently there has been a growing thread of awareness of this problem in the social science literature.

A survey of much of the social science research done over the last number of decades by Berelson and Steiner concludes with the summary observation that man has been tempted to deceive himself to suit his own ends. "Thus, he adjusts his social perception to fit not only the objective reality but also what suits his wishes and his needs" (Berelson and Steiner:664). Based on the evidence of much sociological research, the authors concluded that "man's need for psychological protection is so great that he has become an expert in defense mechanisms" (Berelson and Steiner:664).

A new technique, procedure, device, machine or process is truly fascinating and *can* be healthy to humans, but it may also be very dangerous. To know the difference is crucial, and to be certain that one knows *which it is* is probably impossible at least until much after the fact.

Numerous factors in technology are able to create depersonalization. The most obvious, and probably the most significant already covered is that modern technology removes individuals from social work groupings. A numerical control machine operator, a computer programmer, a forklift operator, a line production worker, a line draftsman, and thousands of other jobs can be described as depersonalizing precisely because the person works less with other humans than with machines. The history of human work has been labor in human groups, whether it was hunting bands stalking a elephant in Africa, Inuit on a seal hunt in the Artic, peasant farmers tilling their plots in Medieval Europe, or a family farming in Iowa. Much if not most of the work done for a living across the human landscape is still being done in work groups, but technology has been bringing about inexorable changes in this pattern.

Televising introductory classes at universities is a sad commentary on the way in which technology has depersonalized education. This is all the more galling when, at the same time, many professors are being laid off for lack of finances. It is an example of how a supposedly useful and helpful technique is depersonalizing basic human activities, and how "convincing" technology has become.

But there are more covert ways in which techniques and technology depersonalize, interjecting a subtle but powerful element into human relationships. Everyone has experienced the imperialism that the telephone exercises when one is waiting in line at a service desk or counter. Or, during an appointment—regardless of how intense the discussion—when the telephone rings the person invariably picks up the phone and gives the telephone caller priority, even though the other party may be calling about a relatively trivial matter. Although people try to be polite to the person being sidetracked, it is clear that we have not developed any cultural norm to downgrade the power of technological intervention. Another powerful but not so subtle example is how the telephone can intervene with and in fact eliminate face-to-face interaction altogether.

Memoranda and computer printouts, along with the entire system of communications which has evolved in the name of efficiency, have tended to place a material intervention between persons within an organization, persons between whom there could be a relationship. In these modern communication settings, one relates less and less to people and more and more to papers, charts, orders, notices, specifications and other impersonal elements. The computerization of many elements in human institutions tends to place the machine and various processes at the core of the determining action, and makes persons less prone to be at the center of things."

Finally, however, the most pervasive consequence of technique and technology is the reduction of human problems and thinking to a binary perceptual system. Everything ultimately can be broken down into yes or no, plus or minus, 0 or 1. It is of more than passing interest that "computer thinking" possesses this relentless logic and that recent attempts to reduce human thinking to computer models is also moving in this direction. A mathematical orientation thus begins to permeate social structures, especialiy within the producing structures.

Thus, the goals of an organization are quantified, and the achievement of these goals is reduced to verifiable measures, which in turn can be subjected to and reduced to binary thinking. Goals and means have become numbers, manipulable by computers. The spirit of an organization, the latticework of human relationships, and all the human expectations and feelings are subordinated to technical means. In the words of Jacques Ellul,

> Technology cannot put up with intuitions and "litera-ture." It must necessarily don mathematical vestments. Everything in human life that does not lend itself to mathematical treatment must be excluded—because it is not a possible end for technique—and left to the sphere of dreams (p. 431).

Technology and techniques are the end result of the relentless search for a rational (or *efficient*) way of living and thinking. Feelings, emotions, attitudes, perceptions—and all the other elements of the human spirit, especially as they impinge on interpersonal relations—have been sacrificed on the altar of ration-ality. The least effort, the quickest and least costly method, the most "elegant" approach, the most logical procedures have become predominant.

This orientation does have functional value and has led to certain positive results. One could point to the almost infinite variety of work. There is also a movement away from homoge-neous segments of work such as assembly line work, or mining jobs. A number of changes—particularly the increasing variety of jobs—are due to mechanization, technicalization and automation. Insofar as this trend represents a movement away from great masses of people working at dehumanizing tasks, it is to be welcomed.

At the same time, it must be said that within this *rational* orientation lies one of the ultimate ironies of human culture: the most rational and most efficient technology seems to be turning out to be the most costly and destructive! Huge gas-guzzling tractors are one of the most inefficient ways of raising food; the automobile is one of the most inefficient ways of transporting people; the mass production line is one of the most inefficient ways of producing goods—when all the social, human, environmental and resource costs are included. Finally, when all the resource, environmental, social, economic, psychological and political costs are honestly tabulated, nuclear power (a questionable technological advance) may well be the most disastrous human venture ever devised.[7]

To say the least, these dysfunctional offspring of the mechanization, automation and technicalization of work are not attractive. Aldous Huxley's *Brave New World* uses a fictional form to describe the world he saw becoming a reality. It may well be that Huxley's novel was not very palatable because it was so negative about the consequences of the modernizing world of technology. In response to requests that he reflect on the impact of the first novel, Huxley wrote *Brave New World Revisited* in 1965. It is sobering to hear what he has to say about the message of his first book:

> Twenty-seven years later, in this third quarter of the twentieth century, A.D., and long before the end of the first century A.F. (after Ford), I feel a good deal less optimistic than I did when I was writing *Brave New World* (1965:11).

> During the past century the successive advances in technology have been accompanied by corresponding advances in organization . . . In order to fit into these organizations, individuals have had to de-individualize themselves, have had to deny their native diversity and conform to a standard pattern, have had to do their best to become automata (1965:38–39).

A Christian Humanization of Work

Up to this point we have discussed some of the ways in which remunerated work has changed. (Of course, changes will continue in the future.) We have also identified a few positive results. And we have pointed out a number of the bleaker aspects on the work scene and in our contemporary culture.

However—and this viewpoint has been reiterated at numerous points throughout the book so far—the Christian cannot be limited by the state of affairs that appears to exist in the world of work. First, he must change the nature and meaning of work for himself; then he must work toward changing it for others in the community and in the society at large. In the final pages of this chapter a few practical steps will be outlined which may be helpful as we respond to the challenge of making work meaningful.

One could take a number of perspectives in tackling the problem of how to "humanize" the dehumanizing aspects of some types of remunerated work, but as has been stated a number of times, we are approaching the issue of work from a Christian point of view. What difference does this make in how we approach work that is dehumanizing? If we assume the perspective that Christians as a group are not different psychologically from those who claim no Christian commitment, then there is no great difference. But, emphatically, Christians *are* different in their life goals, motivations and values.

When faced with the kinds of situations outlined above, it is natural for many people to "blame the system" and to spend their energies and emotions trying to undermine it. Others have a more positive orientation; they will attempt to change the system, and resist continuing depersonalization. In spite of that, however, the "walking wounded" are legion, as a look at Terkel's *Working* makes plain. These victims of the system are a reminder that the results of the dehumanization are vast and run deep, regardless of what people have tried to do about it in the past.

Christians, however, have resources available which should make their reaction somewhat different:

1. They recognize how personal faith resists cynicism and fatalism about the work situation. Christian eschatological consciousness will remind them constantly that an eight-hour shift on a machine is not a meaningless period, but a segment of life which can help to achieve God's purpose in the work world. Most legitimate work includes some aspects of meaning and fulfillment.

2. Even though much work—in terms of self-image and self-acceptance—tends to be disparaging and therefore dehumanizes, Christians have a source of affirmation available. The supporting fellowship of believers provides the worker with both acceptance and affirmation; it also offers him a perspective on the importance of serving Christ even in the menial things. Furthermore, difficult work can be made bearable when an individual's reference group extends acceptance not on the basis of the prestige or status of the work position but on the basis of that person's importance to the kingdom of God. The significance of the reference group as an anchor for self-acceptance has long been recognized; this principle works effectively in the world of work. The church, of course, can be and should be the ultimately important reference group.[8]

3. But the subjective difficulties of dehumanizing work are not the only problem which the Christian community can help solve. The Christian also has resources to make objective adjustments and changes in dehumanizing work positions. If he is an employer or an entrepreneur, he will be helped by his support group to become conscious of the dehumanizing aspects of the work he provides and will do whatever is within his own power to make the various work positions amenable to the human spirit. It is easy to ignore or downplay the power that employers and/or entrepreneurs have available to change the nature of the work positions in which their employees function. The "quality of work" literature is very extensive and documents how much is being done to bring humane and personal elements back into the work position. Christians should be on the forefront of this thrust.

Admittedly, it is easier for an entrepreneur (defined as the innovative small businessperson) to provide for more participation of employees in the work experience than it is for the boss in a huge corporate structure, but it is possible in both types of work setting. Furthermore, since we know that in the larger organizations there is a greater tendency for dehumanization, the Christian employer or entrepreneur should seriously consider smaller scale businesses or organizations that are more prone to allow humanizing tendencies to express themselves.

This suggestion is based on insight into the future of large corporations. The almost universal values and norms that emphasize growth, expansion, consolidation, merger, vertical and horizontal integration, acquisition, pyramiding (and all the other euphemisims for greed) are moving slowly but steadily toward a crunching halt. Our finite globe and its limited resources will not allow for continued cannibalism. The environmental prophets are calling mankind to discover that "small is beautiful," and that we can live better with less.[9] Others are saying that only by decentralizing and developing small local industries and organizations will we be able to maintain our level of expectations.[10]

To argue then that the Christian employer/entrepreneur should try to humanize work by recognizing the beauty of the small scale is not only conforming to biblical ethics; it is also anticipating what natural forces will force humankind to do. Hence, there is nothing really heroic about the Christian entrepreneur "going smaller." One can merely acknowledge the fact that the Christian won't be the last convert to the new ethic—even though too often changes are made for business reasons rather than because the entrepreneur has brought Christian understandings to his or her decision-making in business.

Those who are not employers or entrepreneurs also have resources to make their work more human. They can change jobs! That is not a very novel insight and certainly not limited to Christians. However, many people do not take the step of changing work because they lack the courage and resources to tide them over until they find a better job. Christians may be able to make this objective and bold step more easily because they have access to a psychological and spiritual support system. Ideally, the Christian fellowship should also provide both the psychological encouragement and the financial resources for an individual to make the shift.

4. If changing jobs is difficult or impractical, the Christian has another resource. Because he is not as totally dependent on his job for self-definition and acceptance as others, he may be more straightforward to discuss with his superiors the problems existing in his job and what can be done to solve them. One of the clear conclusions of research on the workplace is that many employees do not exert themselves in improving their work positions simply

because they cannot afford to jeopardize their jobs (*Work in America*).

A member of a Christian fellowship—whether that refers to a congregation, Sunday school, small support group, house church, to list only several of the many possibilities—will have a different attitude toward the autocratic institutions of the work world than if he or she were standing alone. In the past, unions have provided certain support for the individual in the fight for better working conditions. But the union is proving to be increasingly ineffective in facing the complexities of the post-industrial age. The specific nature of any problem in most work positions makes a more individual or local approach to dehumanization much more effective.

5. The Christian who is facing dehumanizing work has another important option: that is to stop being an employee and become his or her own boss. Of course, theoretically, this option is open to everyone, but has been the ideal of many Americans for years. In a provocative chapter entitled, "To Thine Own Self be Boss," author Paul Dickson states:

> If one is so inclined, an alternative to waiting for a new world of work to be brought to you by the same folks who created the job you now have is to split. That is, chuck it, strike out on your own, buck the tide (Dickson:315).

Dickson states that the perennial American dream of being one's own boss has not fared so well during the last three decades, but he suggests that, increasingly, it will become an option for the reasons cited above—the simple but powerful ecological limits with which our world is faced.

Here again, the Christian has particular resources which should be recognized and used in his or her congregation. This support group can serve many functions as the option of self-employment is contemplated: (1) the group can act as a sounding board and critic of the "dream"; (2) it can help to provide the member with the emotional and informational data needed to take the big step; (3) the group, or individual members of the group, can often serve as copartners or investors in such ventures. Many Christian denominations have some type of organization already in place, established precisely to achieve such ends. However, even if no formal organization exists to provide a range of essential services—from technical advice to economic loans—there are many resources in a local Sunday school class or small fellowship group. The power and helpful support available in the congregation is a major resource.

One final resource that an individual makes available to himself by "splitting"—the term Dickson uses—is the strength inherent in cooperation. Traditionally, the American dream has focused on individual achievement. But many people have experienced the limitations of this model and are now discovering the power of cooperation. Two or three people, pooling their ideas, enthusiasm, expertise, experience and resources can become self-employed much more easily than one individual. Unfortunately, and strangely, it appears that Christians are often less prone to work cooperatively.[11] If that is true, we must discover why Christians are less willing to accept this approach than others.

Sociological research tells us that the Christian church is a rather close reflection of the societal values and structure. If that is correct, then it is doubly important that an effort be made to break that mold. The church should lead the way in freeing individual employees from the constricting straightjackets of dehumanizing employment and in helping them become free to choose work which will express the Christian faith.

Excursus 6
Then Suddenly I Was Out of Work

by John D. Yoder

For six weeks I had been working at a small advertising company. One afternoon the manager called the staff together to announce that our office would be phased out over the next two months. He told each of us when our last day would be. Then two weeks later we met again. The president of the company had changed his plans: our office would close the next day. With frightening swiftness fourteen people were out of work.

I was one of them. And I soon discovered that being unemployed, when you want to work, is a bittersweet pill. I would not wish it on anyone.

True, I was now free to work on writing projects I had put off for years. But I despaired of earning enough from them to buy a gallon of milk. I also enjoyed the extra time I had to spend with my wife and daughter. Yet all the while I had to repress a sense of panic. How would we survive? Would I be able to find another job in a depressed economy? What would other people think? Where was my faith?

Today, months later, although I still have periods of high anxiety about the future, I am more hopeful. I see opportunities in the midst of uncertainty. Being unemployed has given me a chance to analyze my skills and explore career options in more depth than ever before. More important, it has changed my attitude toward the world of work.

But before I saw any good in being unemployed, I had to reorient myself to what Robert O. Paxton (in another context) has called an "altered universe of expectations." My formerly stable life seemed suddenly out of control. Cherished plans came crashing down. What I thought was a ride on the career escalator started to resemble a trip through a macabre funhouse. An unmarked trapdoor had suddenly opened, and I found myself in a large room surrounded by desperate people.

That brought some comfort. Even though I was frightened, at least I was not alone. Not since the great Depression have so many Americans been out of work.

My immediate concerns were financial. Overnight I started to think like a materialist. Providing our family with food and clothes became a consuming passion, even though we had resources many people do not have. Except for the mortgage on the house, we had no debts. Since my wife worked part-time, we also had some income. I was eligible for unemployment compensation for twenty-six weeks. I soon picked up some part-time jobs too, an income one is obligated to deduct from any unemployment compensation.

We were also fortunate to have family and friends who offered to help if our money ran low. The church offered to help pay our medical insurance premiums if that should become necessary. And money in our savings account would buy groceries for several months. So between family and friends, we had the safety net the U.S. government is fond of talking about for the truly needy.

Yet while we did not crash financially, we were stunned by a 65 percent drop in our income. Since we were not living overstuffed lives before, this economic belt-tightening was painful. We agonized about decisions we scarcely thought about before. Could we afford a plumber to fix the furnace that refused to heat the bedroom? Would our daughter's earache go away, or should we take her to the doctor? Could we take a chance on the tires lasting another 5000 miles?

Since my finely tuned sense of responsibiliy detects irresponsible behavior as easily as a weather satellite sees an ocean, these questions had a tremendous impact. To think them at all seemed a crime. Naturally, if your tires are worn, you replace them, and a child's earache gets attention as promptly as a fire in the kitchen. You do not, I have always known, take unnecessary risks with your life and your health. Now we *were* taking risks, and I began to live on a steady diet of guilt.

Being preoccupied with questions of money changed who I was in other ways too. I had always thought of myself as a good steward in the Lord's vineyard, planting carefully and harvesting wisely so that we would have enough to give to the church and others in need. From the number of calls we normally get asking for money, I suspect our family is on every solicitor's list in the county as a certified easy touch. I don't recall ever turning away anyone who came to the door selling roses, candles, or light bulbs to promote their worthy community project. As a family we were also fixtures at fund-raising fish fries, pancake breakfasts, chicken barbecues, and spaghetti dinners.

After I was laid off, I started to act like Scrooge. With increasing frequency my family heard me say, "No, we can't eat out; no, we can't go to Indianapolis; no, we can't buy that toy." And when letters asking for money descended from church agencies and schools like a December blizzard, I shoveled them into the wastebasket, while the ghost of Christmas past—myself as a giver—haunted my mind.

While financial problems were difficult enough to face during those first weeks, a greater one was my loss of self-esteem. Being laid off was a blow to my pride. It cut to the core of who I was as a responsible husband and father, opening a mental and spiritual wound. By comparison, economic problems became superficial bruises.

Every decision we made that was related to money became a subtle reminder that I was not the provider I had been before. Even though I was not responsible for being laid off, I still felt I was a failure. Other men and women my age, with my education and skills, were working. What was the matter with me?

I also missed the affirmation I had received at work. Like most people, I derived my sense of worth, at least to some degree, from my job. When performing a useful service, I felt needed and valued. On occasion, jobs had even transported me to the upper room of personal fulfillment.

But take away my job, or give me a meaningless one, and I am much less certain that I have value as a person. I begin to doubt my worth. (Women who work at home know what it means for people to consider them unimportant because they have no "real" job.)

Very quickly I discovered that the central issue I needed to resolve for my mental health was the relationship between my work and my sense of self-worth. Was my worth a reflection of my work? Was my work (or lack of it) a measure of my worth? On the one hand was my conviction that I derive my primary value as a person from being a child of God. On the other was my experience of knowing that meaningful work gave me personal satisfaction.

Compounding the problem is the attitude of our society toward work. Most people identify a person's work and his or her worth quite closely. Jobs are a reward for those with good skills. The conviction is as powerful as the belief in nursery school that Santa brings toys to good girls and boys.

Unless you live in a cave, it is impossible to escape the force of this idea. We use it every day. When we meet new people, we automatically begin our small talk by asking them what they do. There is nothing sinister about this question. Knowing someone's job tells us something about his or her interests; it helps us find common ground. Without a job people don't know how to classify you. At first you don't know how to classify yourself.

I remember going to the hospital for a blood test about a week after I was laid off. The nurse filling out the insurance form, obviously new at the job, asked me where I worked. My mind went blank. After several long seconds, I managed to say, "I work for myself." Since that wasn't exactly the information the form asked for, she turned to her supervisor and said in a voice that echoed through the waiting room and down the hall, "He says he works for himself. What do I put down?"

From the number of heads in the room that turned to hear the answer, you would have thought that E. F. Hutton himself was about to give an inside tip. I leaned forward too, because more than anyone else I was anxious to hear who I was and what I was worth.

But the more I thought about the relationship between what I do and who I am, the more I became convinced that society and I were both wrong in equating job skills or employment with personal worth. During this time I was meeting once a week with a group of unemployed Christian friends. We talked about our problems and encouraged each other to explore jobs in areas that really interested us. Specific suggestions helped one person pursue her interest in theater, another his interest in broadcasting, and another her interest in sales. The group encouraged me to try some writing projects.

Looking around the room at a group of highly motivated, competent people who were, nevertheless, struggling to find work made me realize how absurd it was to think their value or mine depended on what job we did or did not have at the moment. They were all valuable to me, and I to them. We were helping each other identify our skills and think about places to apply them.

At heart, equating a person's worth with work, is an adaptation of social Darwinism. In this scheme society is a jungle. The fittest species find the best jobs and rise to the top of the corporate tree. Those in lower-level jobs are less able (and worthy), while those without jobs are just too inept (and worthless) to find them.

The problem with the jungle analogy is that it distorts the way hiring and firing actually works. For example in the

Midwest, many skilled and diligent laborers are idle not because they are poor workers, but because persons who direct General Motors and Ford made some poor management decisions. Though their decisions of the past ten years have not reflected superior competence, they still have jobs.

After I saw my value reflected back to me from this small group, I was ready to put together a plan to find work based on my skills. What society might think about my unemployed status became irrelevant.

I reread the classic books on job search by John Crystal and Richard Bolles. They are emphatic in saying that the responsibility to find or create a job is up to you. Those who rely on a nonexistent "employment system" to match them with a job are dreamers.

My experience at the state employment office confirms their thesis. I had a twelve-minute interview designed to put me into two job categories, which the employment office could then match with job openings that came to their office. But the counselor I saw was so burned out from talking with desperate people I could see the ashes in his eyes. For the first eight minutes of the interview he told me how bad unemployment was in the county and how difficult it was for him to hear the stories of so many depressed people.

"They sit at my desk with three dollars in their pocket and say they're contemplating suicide," he said. "What am I supposed to do?" I had no answer, but I did my best to sympathize with his plight.

With difficulty I steered the conversation back to my situation. He looked through a huge book of job categories and found two that seemed to describe my interests. He said they would call if they heard of any openings in those areas. So far no one has called. Obviously I would have to find a job on my own.

Well, if the choice of jobs were mine, what did I want to do? Here was my opportunity. I looked at my skills and interests again, the things I enjoyed doing. On my desk was a file of ideas I had always wanted to write about. I got them in order and started writing. I contacted local businesses to see if they needed any writing done for them. Slowly I got assignments—and a few checks.

Although I haven't begun to make a living by writing yet (and I never may), the experience of concentrating the job search in areas that I enjoy has changed my concept of work. I've learned that doing something I love isn't "work" in the usual sense of that term. It's more like play—something I would do even if no one paid me to do it. Though the pay is low, my job satisfaction is at an all-time high.

As I continue to explore employment as a writer, my goal is to find or create a job that uses my skills rather than accept whatever happens to be available. Because of the need to earn more, that may not be possible, but it is my goal.

In the final analysis a good job does not determine our success or failure as a person. Our status as children in God's family guarantees our worth. But we inevitably enhance our well-being when we are able to exercise our gifts in response to God's call to build his kingdom. Some of us have the ability to drive nails, others to plow and seed the fields. Still others can compose a symphony as easily as others among us paint a wall or comfort a child.

Looking around at our ragged world, it is inconceivable to me that there is not an important job for all God's children. It is up to us to help each other find our unique task.

11

Re-entry: The Critical Search Repeated

> . . . a number of young 'C' and 'D' stream school-leavers
> were followed into their first jobs in factories and shops. One
> of their most bitter complaints was that while at school, they
> had been encouraged to appreciate and to write poetry and
> that the world of imaginative possibility that had been opened
> to them was obscured when they began doing the jobs that
> they knew they would have to do for the next forty years
> (Anthony:155).

A toddler on the beach heaps wet sand high. With his little pail
and shovel and his hands, he shapes a castle—in the eyes of his
childish storybook fantasy—a magnificent castle. In great delight,
he calls for his mother to see the structure he has built. Just then a
renegade wave, signaling the rising tide, washes through his
creation, crumbling turrets and walls, and retreats, leaving only a
watery rounded mound as a reminder of what was.

On the sand, he marks the reach of that wave and starts to
build again, this time a little higher on the beach. But not high
enough; another wave first laps the base like a warning then,
suddenly, a great crest sweeps across the place where he stands and
tumbles him and castle into a puddle of sand and water, leaving no
trace of his proud moment.

In sad disgust, he picks himself up and walks away, pail and shovel in hand—his quivering lip hinting perhaps that a young mind is trying to grasp the fact that life has waves and that castles are not for always.

There may be nothing more shattering than to discover that one's childhood experience on a long-ago beach can be repeated in real life decades later. Yet that is the brutal fact.

Mounting statistics of unemployment, of occupations and career tracks that have suddenly become obsolete, of corporate bankruptcies and organizational collapses that change the face of a community overnight—all this, and more, in these turbulent decades weaves a sad tapestry of heartache, frustration and uncertainty. The brilliant hues of promising careers turn to a sickly gray; the careful design of a grand career plan is lost in a moment, swallowed whole in the chaos of new, unpredictable and ever-changing patterns; the symbols of worth and value which were part of the careful shuttling on each loom are now lost in the grotesque, misshapen globs of foreign material caught in the warp and woof of life.

Now instead of a wall hung with beauty and meaning and profound fulfillment, there are only the dangling ends of high expectations, broken dreams and well-laid plans frayed beyond recognition. The harsh reality is that many of us will find ourselves forced to make choice of career and job not only once, but twice or three times, or even more. What was unthinkable a half-generation ago has now become reality.

Caught in a web of specialized training or narrow experience or geography or absence of new opportunity or lack of courage—or a thousand other bindings of genes and circumstance or happenstance—we struggle weakly, if at all; or we thrash about in anger at the fates that have stolen our achievements and our dreams and, for good measure, our hope as well.

There is likely nothing more devastating in one's adult and seasoned years than to have carefully laid plans and a seemingly secure career path suddenly fall apart. Even though making the initial critical choice of career or occupation appears to be difficult, and often is, for many persons to repeat the search and make a critical choice all over again seems at first impossible. In the flush of young adult excitement and with the high levels of energy available then, there is at least a kind of momentum that moves one across the thresholds of uncertainty and fear. But when enforced change strikes the worker in mid-life, he or she may well feel sucked into a swamp of despairing questions and self-doubt where initiative and momentum literally cease to exist.

This fact forms the second basic purpose of our book—to speak hope to those who find themselves mired in the trauma of change in the workplace during mid-life. Lest the reader expect more than we are able to offer, let us say quickly that we do not bring any magic panacea, not even any profound insights about the particular problems such a mid-life stress can create. However, we do believe that our attempt at dialogue, so work and the workplace can be redeemed, will contribute useful insights to the person forced again and again to carry out the search and make the critical choice.

A careful reading of all the personal testimonies included in the book will reveal that change is threaded through each person's story. Some of the stories may not reflect as much trauma as others, but most of them hint at the stress that accompanies change. At least two deal forthrightly with the upheaval and dislocation caused by unexpected turbulence in their work experience. The story that follows this chapter is undoubtedly the most graphic and may therefore be the most helpful.

The authors believe that such a personal approach to this difficult subject will serve our purposes best. (Certainly, it is not within our area of skill to suggest approaches to the psychological turbulence which may issue from the need to change jobs during the middle years.) However, before releasing the reader to walk with Menno Friesen through his mid-life crisis—"How He Works and What Happens When He Doesn't'—we would like to take note of a few facts that outline the current reality.

The first obvious reality is that the choice of work—which hopefully leads to a useful occupation and a life's vocation—is becoming increasingly temporary and unpredictable. We are in a period of "future shock" driven by technical, cultural and social changes. This needs little documentation. One expert on the future of work states: "The unskilled, semi-skilled and skilled manual jobs, clerical administrative and managerial posts and the whole information industry workforce are all at risk" (Jenkins and Sherman:105). Obviously, little is left totally untouched. Job classifications are changing so rapidly that even government agencies cannot keep up with the shifting system. What is more, the jobs themselves are being deleted and replaced by new jobs so rapidly that organizations have come into existence by the thousands—public and private—structured to help people retrain and retool for the future. Unfortunately, even this "retooling" may be obsolete within a short period of time.

Job change, job redundancy, automation, obsolescence, and new technology along with a host of other factors have brought about the changes that are now affecting the stability of the world of work. An organizational revolution has come as well. Changes in organizational procedures; mergers; vertical, horizontal and conglomerate integration and many other managerial changes are affecting the nature of work for those who move in the white-collar world. Except for the few top managers who can write their own personalized "golden parachute" into their contracts, almost all of management and staff people are susceptible to the vagaries of the shifting sands of employment and job creation.

The traditional axioms and criteria of work seem no longer to hold steady. Old loyalties to workers—and from workers—customary within family-owned businesses in earlier times have almost disappeared. In this day of competition and self-interest, some companies will raid pension reserves if they can get by with it; or even borrow heavily from pension funds, then declare bankruptcy, leaving the workers' retirement depleted. Employees are often deleted like unnecessary digits, if the bottom line dictates such drastic action, regardless of how long or how faithfully they have worked for the company. "I worked for the Wilson Tile and Brick Company for thirty-six years, and I never got a penny of retirement set aside for me. I am not a union man, but I kinda wish we would have had a union; it would have forced the old man to lay a bit aside for us, for he made very well" (Interview, December 8, 1986).

Future shock is now as taken for granted as was the earlier stability in the job market; indeed, so taken for granted that we are no longer shocked by it. When a relative loses his farm and begins selling real estate, we say it is the way things are. When a professor friend loses his job at a college because his department was closed down to save money, we thank God it wasn't us. When a company goes bankrupt because it can no longer compete with foreign goods, we feel free trade may not be good but it helps keep prices down. Of course, the truth underlying all of this change is simply that technology is taking work from millions of people who need to find new ways of making a living. Many people resist the idea that technology is replacing workers. However, the evidence seems overwhelming, even in face of the admitted evidence that new work opportunities emerge in other sectors as a result of or as a response to this technology.

But technology is not the only culprit; the greatest revolution may be in the way we move, both physically and socially. In time past, work and residence were closely related and relatively stable. Occasional mobility may have been present but was by no means so pronounced. Today, however, most of us will move at least once if not many more times. With these moves our lives will change, since most moves also bring changes in employment.

It is clear, of course, that social mobility—or upward mobility as the sociologist says—is a great motivator for all of us; that is, we attempt to move up the social ladder to more prestigious levels. This drive is very strong; in fact, many theorists believe that the urge to move up is the most important motive force in Western society. Clearly, the most significant single indicator of an upward move is the changing of jobs from a less prestigious level to positions that are more highly respected.

The impermanence of work is no longer an abstract idea; it is becoming real to many families and to many individuals. As long ago as 1970, Alvin Toffler talked about the life expectancy of a job which then was claimed to be 4.2 years by the U.S. Department of Labor (Toffler, 1970:108). The report continued, "the average twenty-year old man in the work force could be expected to change jobs about six or seven times. Thus instead of thinking in terms of a 'career' the citizen of super industrial society will think in terms of 'serial careers'" (Toffler, 1970:109–110). During the intervening years, the statistics have not changed much; if at all, they have moved toward a reflection of even more instability.

We must assume that many or most of the readers of this book will change jobs at least three times in their lifetime. How will this make a difference in the way the problem of work is approached? The reader can decide. Another factor which is further complicating the change in work roles is the entrance of a vast contingent of females into the work force, especially married females. This is a relatively new phenomenon which is creating much greater occupational adjustments and shifts in the family than it has previously and deserves much greater and more thoughtful attention (See chapter 9, "Male-Female Relationships and Work").

Marriage relationships are also becoming increasingly dependent upon the happy resolution of occupational and career aspirations of both partners. When changes at work occur, family members are directly involved; relocation often results in many losses, including the disruption of friendships and changes in school activities. There are also many new and anxiety-creating prospects. All of these elements can make a job change a most traumatic family experience.

The crisis being caused by the impermanence of work is as serious and as important as the crisis related to the meaning of work itself. This is true because of the cruel dilemma which confronts us—the natural desire for a secure and predictable future in our employment track, and the way that desire can paralyze us when the setback comes. But that is not the worst part of the dilemma. During a time when there is so little security in the world of work, that very desire for security can cause us to shrink back and to settle for much less than we are capable of accomplishing. Jesus made a profound comment about "playing it safe" in the parable of the talents; the person who simply preserved what he had been given was criticized because he had not risked what he had been given in order to grow to the greatest possible stature.

This second crisis in job search—and the third or fourth—

confronts us with a number of challenges. But perhaps none are more real, or more urgent in terms of dealing with them properly, than the presence of impatience and anger when our plans and career track are devastated by one kind of job market turbulence or another. Of course, the challenge relates in part to our need to feel secure again, and the fact that the kind of security we felt before may not be possible.

Even though they must be acknowledged and processed, neither impatience nor anger are helpful responses, particularly when the anger turns into hostility—either towards others or, even more devastatingly, towards ourselves. Either of these understandable responses, allowed to run unchecked, may not only hinder the search for new employment; they may also destroy us.

For that reason, we need to be assured that to reopen a decision which was made long ago is not necessarily moving backwards. To start over again with some basic life decisions often means a more successful and more fulfilled life. The life story of Yorgy in the prologue is a model for us as we pursue this challenge. Yorgy made the decision to follow a certain career and vocation, but found that decision constantly buffeted and challenged as time went on. He changed his direction a number of times, and truly found a happy life, but almost as an afterthought.

We believe that this confidence can be ours as we investigate together the promise of work to bring personal fulfillment and thus to make us happy. The excursuses by Menno Friesen (pp. 203–13) and John D. Yoder (pp. 191–96) are typical of the rewards of starting again and quite possibly, finding an even better and more rewarding occupation and career. Finally, what we hope to accomplish above all is the enhancement of our vocations which—if they are virtuous, as Aristotle said, or responsible to God's will, as Jesus promised—will make us full of happiness.

This may be an appropriate place to emphasize that this is not so much a "how to" book; instead it is a "why" book! A book that informs, provokes thought and leads to certain understandings which then help us to make decisions that issue in both personal and collective happiness.

As Christians, we believe that the right decisions will bring about growth toward the image of God in us and help us build the new community—according to what God originally intended for us.

Excursus 7
How He Works and What Happens If He Doesn't: A Look at Mid-life Crisis

by Menno M. Friesen

I have worked very hard ever since leaving Meade, Kansas. I was determined to replace the austere life at Meade with an education that would lead to new beginnings. It worked. After earning a Ph.D. in English and after four years of lecturing in Drake University classrooms, I—at age 37, along with my wife, Shirley Penner, and our children, Paul, Laura, and Julia—sailed for London on the S.S. *United States* to begin a four-year period in an apparent promised land. London seemed very far from Meade—much more than half a world away. We had come a long way.

In this account, I observe how my early years led to a teaching career, how uncomfortable that career became even while it provided much-needed prestige, how I escaped from that career track, how London provided space for giving up a career even while I was trying to keep it, how the mid-life crisis intensified, how my mental health was restored after the crisis and, finally, how I started a new career.

The first eighteen years at Meade were formative ones. Some were devastating, some were mediocre, and some were good: the old swimming hole in Sand Creek, the primitive tennis and basketball courts we set up surreptitiously on our farm, homemade ice cream at birthdays of those close to us, the influence of fine grade school teachers, and good times with family, friends and particularly cousins.

In my working world at Meade, harvest work reflected the greatest intensity—both urgency and some satisfaction. During harvesttime, aggressive truck driving was not only acceptable but encouraged. The sense of power and speed and the rattling, vibrating snorts from a no-muffler exhaust on an eager Model A truck became their own reward. Fine farm meals were brought to the field; men sat almost as kings at lunch during the harvest to be served well and amply. The threshing days seemed the best of work times because they achieved a momentum that lifted hard work above drudgery. The shared efforts of neighbors made it a festival; the muscled young men—Rempels, Reimers, Bartels, Classens, and Friesens—their camaraderie, their jokes, their pranks and their orchestrated pitching of wheat bundles led to roast beef and cherry pie. No wonder dinner time had the marks of celebration.

Work between harvest seasons seemed more aimless and boring. Although we still had to grind barley or maize for the hogs, mend a few fences, brand some cattle or haul them to the Dodge City livestock auction, these miscellaneous farm tasks could never trigger the exciting harvesttime sense of urgency. That was gone. If there were rewards for these ordinary chores, they seemed remote indeed.

In our restricted community, where options were scarce and the atmosphere was stern and oppressive, I failed to find enough materials for a dream. Instead, my days were often soured by boredom. The most boring of all my tasks was driving the tractor alone in a large field, a ten-foot swath across a 320-acre field at four miles per hour. It seemed hopeless. Plowing was done in circular fashion, from circumference to center, with only limited signs of progress. I missed the companionship of other people. That's why I liked harvest. I could relate to people several times per load of wheat hauled. But all day alone on a tractor was devastating.

During these years, work, and success in work, could be measured: bushels per acre, straight rows, good equipment and adequate tools. Ours was a proud farm, but ways to measure individual success were scarce in our system. The family benefited, of course, but I felt too much like a cog in a wheel. There was not enough room for my personal dreams.

I had no hope of changing that until I was fifteen years old. I had finished grade school and was helping on the farm with no thoughts of going on to high school. In September of my second year at home, I found myself on the tractor sowing wheat—in pleasant weather, relatively happy.

One day at noon another world broke in. Coming in from the field for lunch, I found that school was the topic of conversation. My sister, Margaret, had just enrolled at Meade Bible Academy. She was happy with all that prospect promised. Then it happened. Dad turned in my direction and dropped a stray remark: "Menno, maybe you would like to go also." That was the extent of the discussion—no dialogue or even encouragement, just a casual comment—support for education was not strong in our family. But that casual comment shook my world apart, made windows in my day. I returned to work that afternoon wearing matching shirt and trousers in tan cotton twill, happy with my neat non-farmlike appearance, enjoying the autumn weather, hardly noticing that I was sowing wheat. I sat a bit straighter on the tractor during those afternoon hours; the field was shorter; the tractor ran faster. It didn't matter that my whistling wasn't audible; I could hear it in my brain.

The next day I left for school while Dad was doing chores. To this hour I have not learned what time of day he discovered my absence. I can remember nothing about enrolling for classes that day. I do remember that Dad was upset with me for having obligated him to pay tuition on the basis of that stray remark. My quiet disappearance that morning didn't help. But I had made up my mind quickly— Dad's remarks sounded so good to me that I wasn't going to risk any discussion that might somehow shatter an opportunity. I really wanted another kind of life.

Of course, I had had other fantasies of escape before this apparently impulsive decision. Often, while plowing, I had dreamt about having a car and going away, but I had no idea where "away" was or what it looked like.

This lunch-time event began a long and torturous course of education, a course more arduous than any farm operation I had ever known. In a sense, education seemed to provide an escape, but I had no idea where it would lead. I simply wanted to build my own dream and I needed some fresh material for my dreaming.

Without knowing it at the time, I did have a model for my long struggle. Dad's fierce determination, required for success on the farm, gave me a model for securing an education, even though since, I have considered the model detrimental. Nevertheless, these work attitudes nurtured by my father's example turned into beneficial survival techniques during my years on university campuses.

From Meade Bible Academy, I went on to study for four years at Tabor College and one year at Goshen Biblical Seminary. These study years were followed by two years of teaching at Holyrood High School and two years at Pratt Junior College.

Then, at twenty-eight, I took another major step in my dogged pursuit of an education. I was accepted as a doctoral candidate for a Ph.D. in English at the University of Denver. This educational process was monumental, both in difficulty and in scope, considering particularly where and how it all began. Dad's one remark unleashed a powerful force, far beyond what either he or I realized at that time. In sharp contrast to my liberation from the farm and the much-needed ventilation in high school, I was now, in 1960, firmly locked into an esoteric program in American literature that—as I was able to confirm only relatively recently—went counter to my soul and spirit. I didn't really know it then, but my dream was no longer liberating; it was calcified. My stubborn desire to succeed had served me well as a vehicle of escape, but was definitely not an adequate vehicle to carry me toward authentic self-realization.

After three years in the program toward my Ph.D., I was scheduled for the final interrogation by five professors. Although the prospect was awesome, I felt brave; a Baptist friend of mine had traveled the same route with flying colors a few months earlier. Now it was my turn. The hours passed. And suddenly my day turned dark when my interrogators announced, after a huddle, that I had not regurgitated my heavy diet of literature properly. My spirit was crushed. In the gloom of the evening, I returned to our bleak house where Shirley had invited guests to help with our celebration. Instead of celebrating, I needed to anesthesize myself. I went with Shirley to a movie. The movie didn't work—layers of gloom and depression insulated me from the pulse of life in film—I needed something considerably stronger.

Three months later, however, I had bounced back; I had taken two written examinations to make up for two weak spots in my previous oral interrogation. My self-respect was soon restored; after the lenient professor told me I passed his test, the difficult professor jokingly/seriously told me he would pass me also, at the same time confiding that he hadn't yet read my exam. Such approval in advance bolstered my confidence. But there was still another hurdle. I needed to write a two-hundred-page book and be questioned about why I wrote it.

The pressures of academic life weighed heavily upon me. Within three days of having passed the make-up tests, I developed a detached retina. The stress of doctoral pursuits may have helped bring about this condition. This legitimate medical delay gave my soul space to breathe, but the atmosphere in that space was not the best.

After two unsuccessful repair attempts in Denver, I flew to Boston for a successful retina repair. A year later I completed the dissertation. With considerable and deserved fanfare, we celebrated my graduation. In August of 1964, I was granted the ultimate degree, DOCTOR OF PHILOSOPHY, "with all the rights and privileges pertaining thereto." That was a tremendously gratifying experience.

Dad's noticeable approval of my celebrated achievement meant a lot to me. I was pleased that he could recognize my academic struggles, even though in a subdued manner. But sometimes I think I paid an unconscionable price for his approval. Was the doctorate really enough of a reward for all the hell I went through? There must have been an alternative which I overlooked.

In any case, a new era lay ahead. Armed with a fresh doctorate, I had greater confidence now than when I escaped the farm. Then came my first big test of work after the Ph.D.; of course, at first, it didn't seem like a test. Seeking a new professorial position, I visited seven universities responding to invitations for an interview. The plane flights were exciting; so was all the attention I received at the universities. It made me think I was good. How little I knew! After several campus visits, I found myself at one university where the atmosphere was more sophisticated and the professionalism more impressive. Naturally, I wanted to go first class; nothing less would do.

So, in my mind, Drake University at Des Moines was the university for me. It was the most prestigious university I could muster. I anticipated the glory of carving out a career, and most of my successes so far seemed to support my plans. I suppressed the memory of my failures; they seemed parallel to the complaints of my friends about their own vocational dissatisfactions.

The first year or so at Drake University was difficult, though now, at least, we had an income. We had had one before, of course, but now we were also released from the pursuit of other degrees.

The difficult part was to prepare well enough for lectures to gain the approval and respect of my students. At Denver University, I had had a high regard for my professors; I didn't know why my students at Drake didn't have an immediate and equal admiration for me. However long I prepared for lectures, there was always more preparation to complete. There was never any clear way to determine when I was fully prepared. In my view, there was never enough time to do it really well. My highly developed perfectionism became part of my downfall.

Before the lectures at Drake started, I sought a hobby that would provide some relief from the academic. So I enrolled in an evening woodworking class. Here, even before I had a chance to use my beloved Ph.D., I started on a new learning process. This course was exacting, demanding and measurable. Woodworking also reached back to the physical work at Meade; it provided an effective contrast to my less satisfying experiences in teaching.

The Friday afternoon after classes started, I was walking across the campus with a heavy briefcase in hand when I met a professor who invited me for a drink at four. I was pleased. I arrived home at two and worked on my lathe as a break from my busy week. At four I dusted my coveralls and started on my way to the professor's home. It turned out to be a full-scale cocktail party. But my coveralls survived and I was fine. The juxtaposition of farm and school may have gone beyond the eccentric. It may have been symbolic of unresolved clashes between my gifts and the career I had so forcefully adopted.

A few months into my first year I began my first struggle with ulcer symptoms. I knew the tensions in my work were severe but I didn't understand the physical signals of those tensions. My teaching improved somewhat as I moved into my third year. Then came another signal. The dean informed me that I was not being granted tenure; not enough community involvement, he charged. That was a major jolt. My pride was sorely damaged, but the pain soon lessened; perhaps I was getting a necessary message. Tenure would have locked me into a lifetime of suffering. I didn't need tenure; I needed escape.

I decided not to submit to bondage for seven years; I needed a sabbatical now, and a way out. It had been a long, grinding climb. In thirteen successive summers (1956-1968), I had had no relief from academic pursuits; I was either going to graduate school or teaching. With my mind casting about for a "sabbatical" escape, I learned about a position involving international students in London, England. We took it.

In retrospect, London was a glorious interlude; however, it was also a time for reassessment and a time for the extremely painful awareness that further adjustments would have to be made. London allowed me to de-escalate; actually, it became a kind of moratorium.

When our boat-train arrived at Waterloo Station, we took a taxi to 14 Shepherd's Hill in North London. There our family established a new home. We had a large flat in a Victorian three-story "mansion," the London Mennonite Centre.

The primary responsibilities Shirley and I had been given—under the auspices of the Mennonite Board of Missions at Elkhart, Indiana—were to nourish a Christian community among, and relate creatively to university students from Turkey, Iran, India, Mexico, Brazil, Peru, Malaysia, Ghana, and Hong Kong.

Our small group of international students, fourteen to sixteen, had many informal encounters with each other; with us as staff, with visiting Goshen College faculty who stopped in before or after a sabbatical, and with Mennonite tourists as well. Casual as this may sound, these were the methods and means of an international ministry. There were planned meetings and, of course, Sunday dinners were special. Students were more relaxed on Sundays and enjoyed a good home-cooked meal, but on Sundays the dialogue was usually even better than usual since frequently both they and we had invited other guests. Shirley and I were hosts and eager participants in their stories and lives.

Our work went well for several years. The highlight of that period was the planning that led to a peace conference in Dublin and Belfast; that led, subsequently, to the establishment of the Mennonite church in Dublin.

At the time of this planning trip to Ireland, I was still hanging on to my teaching career. I gave a guest lecture at the University of Belfast on the contemporary English novel on the same day that our group engaged in peace discussions at the Baptist seminary. And I was still dreaming of a lofty tenure track at a prestigious university.

My dream emphasized the fact that when the London sojourn came to an end—if indeed it must—I would be unusually well credentialed with my doctorate and my London experience to claim a highly desirable professorship that would put the old haunts and shadows forever behind me and lead to the steady fulfillment of all my hopes and dreams. I would come to be acclaimed and respected; I would have time to devote to scholarly pursuits and leisurely conversation. In the end I would be handsomely repaid for my blood, sweat, and tears and, certainly then, all my striving would subside.

So I fantasized and rationalized and, in the rationalizing, denied the tiny cracks, the uneasy reservations, and the shadows of doubt that insisted on creeping into my consciousness. Books and essays remained unwritten. Worse, there were no stacks of invitations to vaunted and desired professorships. A flight back to the United States to generate applications and to strengthen old friendships—all the old connections in colleges in Wichita, Fresno, Los Angeles, Missouri, Denver and Goshen—turned up nothing but some friendly support to offset the embarrassments of finding no leads. I was ready for the world, but the world wasn't ready for me! Teaching positions in colleges were not to be had.

After our four-year term stretched to five, we decided finally to relocate our family in the U.S.A. We had never planned to stay beyond this period. So the time came to pack our suitcases. This task requires a certain sense of order, something which was scarce at this time. In Kansas we could fit the truck to the size of our worldly goods and move to Indiana. But moving from London to Goshen, we needed to adjust our belongings to the size of our suitcases. I turned out to be totally useless for the task. Somehow it all seemed symbolic of the future.

Questions abounded. Had I spent all my life trying to establish my worth by improving my work? Without work, what am I worth? It seemed that my work and my self-esteem were inseparably married; now that my work had died, my self-esteem was no more.

Returning to U.S. on the famous ocean liner, THE FRANCE, should have been a great experience, especially with both lobster and filet mignon being served in the same meal. But aside from momentary pleasures, the voyage was very painful—it was a passage in a dark tunnel, leading nowhere. The time with my family during this return voyage should have been relaxed; instead, I felt anxious and helpless because I did not know how I could support my family or find worth again.

The trail to an intermediate summit—London—had been clearly marked, if steep and arduous. The western slope before me now seemed utterly unmarked, inhospitable and impassable. Returning from London, I should have been on a friendly trail home, moving with confidence and joy. Instead I felt myself an intruder with nowhere to go, a stranger with a needy and deserving family whom I could not support, a home-seeker with heavy boxes and suitcases, but no sense of where to look for home.

When a grown man's life falls apart, how does he put the pieces together again?

During these weeks and months, my being suffered a shock that measured six on the Richter scale. The quake shook me to my foundations; I became aware that it takes a heavy quake—almost as heavy as death—to slough off a profession to which I had given my life and blood.

A first step was to return to old friends and friendly environs in Goshen, Indiana. During our early months there, our friends provided a context for things to happen, but they did not make them happen. Their support could not solve the problems. One feels so helpless in such a transition; my friends felt just as helpless; useless as well. To be consoled by friends lessens the pain only slightly, if at all. But as depression diminished, the value from friendships seemed to become more effective.

Yet, even while making some feeble attempts to put the pieces together again, I remained depressed; I found it difficult to take steps which might have led to a new career. Overall there lay another heavy awareness: my hesitation, my lack of initiative and my depression were so diametrically opposed to my earlier aggressive assault on the educational program I had pursued, leading to a Ph.D. in English and American Literature.

A few months after our return from London, I checked in, reluctantly, at the Oaklawn Mental Health Clinic; there I started out with a few weeks in their daytime treatment center. Having had my first degree in psychology, I had some appreciation for the help that might be available. But it wasn't easy. I asked Shirley not to tell Paul, Laura, and Julia where I was going; they weren't supposed to know that Dad needed help. Gradually, however, our entire family became conversant with depression and possible solutions. We speak freely about it now.

The counseling, the exchanges of problems within the Oaklawn groups, the programed interchanges between patients, the work and recreational activities which were structured to put us in touch with all aspects of life, slowly renewed my hope. I could easily have remained a stubborn adult and thus denied my need for help. The humiliation of becoming a child in making the request for help is enough to keep most of us from seeking it. At least, it was so for me. My strongest inclination was to solve my problem with sheer effort. But the unreliable perception I had of my own problem required that I let go, and allow trained therapists to help. Until I relinquished my own solutions, I was stymied. When I let go, I was no longer forcing my own interpretations of my relational problems on my family and others.

As an adult, I could have walked out of the treatment center at any time. But, I soon began to sense that it was a miniature, monitored social order; at the same time, I felt the need to submit to this helpful order in hope of success. Before I could leave, I needed to argue my case for leaving. Specifically, my argument was that I would begin slowly to make small commercial commitments in the community. In other words, my plan to enter the antique business would provide work obligations that would renew my suspended role in the community. I expected this step-by-step process gradually would put me in direct contact with the community in a way that the general support of friends could not do.

The negotiated release became effective. These agreements to work—whether a large job or small, provided an organizing factor in my life. In the past, I have worked because I was told to. Sometimes, I have worked for the pleasure of it. But I achieved a new respect for work when I began to work hard toward stronger human relationships in a desperate attempt at survival. I had known of course, theoretically, that work was beneficial and necessary for human beings, but I had never known from experience how a series of work commitments could be so essential in the renewal of my strength after the crisis.

After a number of years in the antique business and selling buildings for a construction firm, I began my own construction business in 1980. I chose a corporate name bigger than I; and I placed my family name strategically: FRIESEN BUILDING CORPORATION.

When the second career became a necessity, I improvised. I looked at the existing resources again. Having had highly sophisticated training the first time around, I could hardly put up with happenstance and feeble training for my second career.

My approach was to get help, advice, and expertise whenever and wherever I could find it. This required some humility because a contractor is expected to give answers rather than ask questions. At first I consulted local businessmen—frequently those in our local church—or my favorite banker about general business practices. When it came to construction procedures or plumbing options, I would ask subcontractors, such as the plumber, what they would recommend. Some contractors start their careers at state universities, but I started with monetary rewards or losses at my heels. No more Ph.D.s for me. I like on-the-job training, especially when it works out.

The second career came hard. It was like a painful rebirth, where I had to learn to walk again, starting out hesitantly, a few people holding my hand; but it was I who had to walk and to take my own steps at my own pace.

I chose teaching as my first career because that was the only one that came to mind. It seemed prominent at Tabor College and I could think of nothing else. I took the necessary education courses thinking they involved relatively few hours and they might be worth some money.

As I look back now, I can see that my business career,

apparently, was more rooted in my past than my teaching career had been. I deliberated longer and consulted more carefully in choosing my business career. My teaching career decision was made as a sophomore is likely to make that decision, with some thought but very little research. My business career was formed with much more awareness of my abilities and my inclinations in early years; I was then able to take my history and my personality into account.

At this stage of my life, I enjoy modest success. I have a peace of mind and minimal stress considering all the risks in a contractor's business. But I hear time's winged chariot hurrying near, and I know that I dare not make an idol out of my present business. Neither do I want to work slavishly and mechanically to avoid a possible future failure in business, or a future emotional crisis. I do not wish to be driven only by my past; now I know that the future must remain open to nourish other dreams.

> The Wounded Deer—leaps highest—
> I've heard the hunter tell—
> (Emily Dickinson, "The Wounded Deer")

BOOK THREE

WORK IN THE KINGDOM OF GOD

12

When Is Work Christian?— A Sociological Analysis

He who labors as he prays lifts his heart to God with his hands (St. Bernard of Clairvaux).

God never calls a lazy, disgruntled man to a job which requires the finer qualities of real manhood. Every worker may make the commonest job an immortal task (Charles Stelzle).

A careful look at the subject of work will include a number of frames of reference. Of course, each of these frames of reference will be perceived—understood or misunderstood—against the background of an individual's work experience. Indeed, one's experience in the workplace tends to become the primary frame of reference, shaping and flavoring most of the considerations a study entails.

There is advantage, of course, in discovering how work actually functions in one's life. Personal experience and observation offer insights that academic discussions sometimes bypass. Grit and boredom and anxiety on the job test the positive, unbruised definitions that social scientists sometimes formulate. Grassroots realities provide windows of understanding for the theorist—the historian, the sociologist, the theologian. Grime and tedium and power politics in the work setting confront propositions, help to

217

establish or confirm principles, illustrate problems and often rescue glib theory from irrelevance.

At the same time, anyone searching seriously for answers to the work dilemmas of our time must find some method of distancing himself or herself from the limited purview of personal experience. There must be a way to identify fundamental elements present in work settings for centuries; a way to extrapolate principle from the great range of worker experience; a way to respond systematically and rationally to the dynamics and the problems millions of workers live with every day.

In our view, sociologists have done all of this; they have taken a long step toward providing anchor points of principle lifted above the narrow confines of one person's experience or one occupation. They have laid broad and solid foundations useful to both an individual and a national overview. They have shaped logical structures that tend toward the universal—at least within industrialized societies. Conscientiously and competently, they have studied many of the issues relating to work and have recorded a great many valuable and significant insights.

However, also in our view, the value systems assumed in these worthwhile studies are often not adequate for the Christian. Christian scholars neither deny nor ignore many of the basic insights developed in the field of sociology; rather they bring their Christian commitment and understandings to bear on both the body of sociological principle and the work experience. From this perspective, they seek to shape a Christian response which utilizes and incorporates recognized principles of sociology while at the same time fulfilling the unique understandings put forth by the gospel: that the Christian's primary calling is to build the kingdom of God and that work choices reflect that calling.

That is the approach we attempt in this chapter and in all of Book 3. Indeed, in a nutshell, these few paragraphs represent the thesis of the entire book: that there is—*that there must be*—*a Christian perspective of work.*

The questions engendered by this thesis are real and urgent. Many of them have been addressed already in previous chapters, directly and indirectly. Others remain.

On the following pages, we will attempt a precise definition of work, outline one approach to the analysis and evaluation of work and look at some of the factors we need to consider if we are to fulfill our Christian calling as defined above.

Four Types of Work

Although we seldom think of its varied dimensions, most work involves at least four different elements: physical, mental, psychic and social. When we are at work, these four aspects of our human experience usually come into play, although in different proportions.[1] The most pervasive aspect of work is the physical dimension. Almost always, work involves the exertion of some form of physical energy in order to achieve a desired end.

Physical work is defined as the *result* of force exerted and is measured by the movement of any object through distance ($W = Fd$); in this formula, $W = $ work, $F = $ Force and $d = $ the distance that an object is moved. Energy is distinguished from work in that energy represents the ability of the "work-er" to do work. The implication above, of course, is that a work-er can exert force only through the use of energy; energy, which is measured in ergs, is the means by which the work-er does work.

On this level, humans accomplish a result called work in the same way that mules and internal combustion engines accomplish a result called work—that is, through the use of energy. All types of workers utilize energy to exert force on an object through distance, whether it is to lift a shovel, turn a pump or pull a cultivator. However, physical work has implications for the human worker that are not present for mules or the engine, particularly in the psychological, social and spiritual realms. For example, physical work has often been meaningless for humans. This could not be true for an engine; nor can it be true for animals in the same way it is true for humans, even though a mule may have some "feeling" for or about work.

In addition to the physical, human beings are capable of other types of work; this capability separates them further from animals and machines. One of these types is mental work, often referred to as cogitation. This is the work called "theoria" by the Greeks. In this thinking sphere, humans expend energy also (literally physical energy) to do work which does not necessarily move physical objects. Mental work involves the manipulation of symbols and ideas in the brain to achieve a certain result; this activity can eventuate in physical work such as moving a pencil, pecking at the keys of a typewriter, or building a bridge. Throughout history, some people have maintained that mental work has been more powerful than brute force. This type of work has been limited largely to human beings, even though recent research indicates that certain primates are able also to conceptualize and manipulate symbols.

A third type of work in which human beings engage is psychic work. This type of work, which has not been widely discussed, refers to the energy humans expend in subjective processes and feelings such as worry, frustration, hostility, anxiety, bereavement, empathy, or sympathy.[2] Not least among the many other elements of psychic work in which humans engage is that of interpreting and reacting to signals, messages and communications from others. Each of us can vouch for the reality of this kind of psychic work in many areas of our lives. Who of us has not spent energy trying to interpret what Joe or Mary meant by a certain statement? Or who has not experienced the enervation or even fatigue of trying to relate to a friend who is mired in deep frustration or despair? Who cannot recall how tired one may become dealing with the loss of a friend or relative? Sometimes psychic work is derailed into physical work—often as a natural response to psychic "overload," other times when prescribed by a psychiatrist.

The fourth type of work is social work: the activity we engage in to discharge our obligations as members of the social community.[3] Human beings do a lot of work to maintain and strengthen relationships with others and to discharge social responsibilities to each other. The repetition of the phrase "Good morning" when we would rather not even recognize another's presence, or the task of writing a note of appreciation to the gracious hostess who cared for us during our last visit to a distant community are trivial examples of social work. Social work runs the gamut from the work we do to keep human institutions running smoothly so society can survive—for example, work in, and through, political and educational institutions—to visiting one's neighbors, whether out of duty or for sheer pleasure.

A great amount of social work is also done (i.e., energy expended) to keep up with, or get ahead of, relatives, friends, neighbors, and members of society at large. The same is true on the international scene. Nations trying to move ahead of other nations in the military arms race may well be motivated partly on ideological grounds—a form of competitive intellectual work—but such a race is also greatly influenced by the social struggle of nations. The recent campaign slogan of a presidential hopeful, "Let's make America great again," seems to make that clear.

To this point, work has been described from four different perspectives. This approach could suggest that work may be identified as belonging to one of these types; indeed, classifying work activity under the types noted above does contribute to understanding.

However, work must also be described from a singular perspective; this would mean that work cannot be classified simplistically under one of four headings but, for human beings, almost always involves all four types of activity. This latter definition of work refers, therefore, to the combined physical, mental, psychic and social activity required to achieve a desired result—all flowing from a beginning expenditure of *physical energy*.

A job familiar to most of us will serve to illustrate the multiple levels of activity present in a singular approach to work experience.

A person driving a bus is engaged in physical work—he manipulates the bus controls; in mental work—he calculates which lane of traffic will move the bus along its route most rapidly; in psychic work—he represses his irritation at several ruffians creating a disturbance in the back of the bus; in social work—he maintains good relationships with passengers on the bus so reports of his performance and good relationships with his riders will filter back to his manager.

As members of the human community, we engage continuously in all four types of work in varying mixtures and proportions. Our jobs—occupations, careers, professions—even our Christian calling, involve all four types. Of course, some of us find ourselves doing more of one type of work than another. And all of us recognize that societies have developed elaborate systems of values regarding the status, significance and contributions of the various types of work. In the West, sociological research has shown repeatedly that intellectual work is ranked higher than physical work, illustrated by the professor and the garbage collector.[4] Hence, to speak of "work" as merely making a living or as a necessity for human existence—even though that is true—obscures the complexity and richness of the reality and meaning of work.

Another area which calls for careful definition as we search for a Christian understanding of work has to do with a cluster of four familiar terms—job, occupation, profession and vocation or calling—terms which are often mistakenly thought of as synonyms. What is often referred to as *job* is the first term that requires precise definition. For many people the job is the sum and substance of work. Those of us who grew up in the Jimmy Durante age remember his capstone one-liner when he tried to find a niche in a conversation, "Albuquerque? Why yes, I used to *woik* in dat town!" Willy Loman* wrestled with the concept of work, occupation and career in the limited terms of reference provided by one person's view of one kind of job, that of a salesman. It is true that work and the job can sometimes be equated, but they must also be distinguished from each other in order to open up the many related issues.

The *job* is defined as a specified amount or piece of work designed to achieve a specific objective for which a specific remuneration or reward is stipulated.[5] A job includes the piece or pieces of work a person does, whether employed in a firm or self-employed. These pieces of work are structured to achieve a particular purpose. A job can be a formally structured activity or it can be a one-time type of activity, like digging a hole for a privy. A job can be a very standardized piece of work, such as driving a

---

*in *Death of a Salesman.*

truck; or it can vary from an activity like sweeping floors (with only the simplest requirements) to the tending or operation of boilers which requires specialized training, formal examination and a license.

The term *occupation* derives directly from a certain understanding about job; it refers more precisely to the track an individual follows in the pursuit and fulfillment of certain types of work. An occupation is thus a standardized set of expectations regarding a specific task which renders services to the society and for which the practitioners of that occupation receive social prestige and esteem and monetary reward. An occupation is the specialized system of work elements which cohere to provide the guidelines for the person performing the work—guidelines that must be learned.[6]

A *profession* derives from the occupational system, but has the added characteristic that the members or practitioners of a given occupation develop criteria for the acceptance of persons into that occupation. In brief, they determine what kind of training and other requisites are necessary, and they establish what are considered to be minimum, adequate or professional standards of work. A particular professional community may also often attempt to control access to the knowledge and techniques relative to that occupation in order to protect the monetary rewards and social status of the members of that profession.[7]

A *vocation,* our final concept, derives its name from the Latin, *vocatio* or calling, and is the most general concept in our analysis. It pertains to the overarching purpose or goal for an individual's action and life, expressed not only in the job, occupation or profession, but in all the other activities in which a person engages. Hence the vocation for a Christian might be spoken of as "being a disciple of Christ." This would mean that in all actions—on the job, in his recreation, in his family life, and in a variety of general activities—the Christian would act so as to "love his neighbor as himself."

Martin Luther's concept of *calling* alludes to vocation, but he tended to equate it with job, occupation or profession. In fact, one's vocation is the encompassing circle of life's activities, into which the smaller circle of job or occupation *can* (but does not automatically) fit. The apostle Paul referred to the *vocation* or calling of the Christian as the entire life-action system, and not merely the job or occupation. He expressed it majestically in Romans 12:1–2: "Therefore, I urge you, brothers, in view of God's mercy, to offer your bodies as living sacrifices, holy and pleasing to God. . . . "

Guidelines for Evaluating Work

All humans, by virtue of their material and human existence, must work to exist and survive. But this principle goes far beyond the mere individualistic actions of gathering roots for bodily sustenance. Humans have also needed to work at creating a social order which has made the physical, psychological, and cultural aspects of human existence not only possible but also more effective. Every human institution which serves mankind requires enormous effort on the part of workers to keep it functioning and adapted to changing circumstances.

However, as Christians, we are not satisfied with the facts about work, we must ask the question of "why" certain work can and should be done; further we must ask how that work fits into our understanding of the Christian's calling. We propose, therefore, that the four categories of work be subdivided into eight subcategories by asking two questions of each type of work: 1) What are the purposes for this particular type of work? and 2) What are the real or true consequences of this particular work activity? The Christian must always ask the ends *and* means questions, not just one or the other. For the Christian, the means are judged by the ends, and the ends are judged by the means; they are fully and irrevocably interdependent. (See Table 4)

Table 4. An Ethical Evaluation of Work

Perspective	Reasons for Working	Consequences of Work
1. From the Worker's Point of View	← – – – – – → Agreement?	
2. From the Community's Point of View	← – – – – – → Agreement?	
3. From the Perspective of the Kingdom of God	← – – – – – → Agreement?	

Agreement? ↑ ↓

To illustrate our paradigm, physical work (as one of four types) must be evaluated from two perspectives: 1) Why does one engage in the particular work? and 2) what are the larger or unintended consequences of that work? Thus, for example, the suburbanite who plows a garden (physical work) should be asking two questions: Why I am preparing the garden? and What will be the consequences of my activities? The answer to the first question could include reasons such as: To augment the family budget, or to provide more nourishing food for the family, or to get wholesome exercise (which is often the only goal). Answers to the second question *might* include: Although it may not pay financially, working in the garden provides a good discipline for my children who need to learn to work.

At first glance, this distinction may not seem to be very significant. But it is. In sociological analysis, this is called the difference between the intended and the unintended or unanticipated consequences of an act. Many, if not most, human activities are comprised of both. Most of our actions have specific purposes or intentions. But they also have unanticipated results. Let's assume that I work at GM. To provide a paycheck for my family's needs answers the *why* or for what purpose question. The *consequence* question may be answered in a variety of ways: I will develop emphysema from fumes in the paint shop; or I experience total loss of dignity and sense of self-worth, because all I do is I put nut x on bolt y and give it 3 turns 713 times a day, and over at Plant No. 9 they have a robot doing the same job. When we look at actual cases, the *why* question and the *consequence* question are seen with greater clarity.

Similar questions need to be asked and answered for the other three types of work in which we all engage. If the latter of these two questions—the consequence question—is not asked, the work experience may become contradictory, or destructive, or meaningless. Worst of all, it can actually interfere with or disrupt the worker's realization of his or her Christian calling.

It should be noted also that the answer to either of these two questions can be approached from at least three perspectives: the point of view of the individual contemplating the work, the view of the community which provides the work and is also the beneficiary of the worker's efforts, and third, the moral (Christian) point of view. Table 4 describes these added dimensions to the analysis of work which we are proposing here.

The justification for these three levels of analysis derives from the fact that our lives and actions have at least three systems of meaning.

1. Our own personal self-conscious perspective regarding the meaning of our lives and the role of work for us.
2. The community perspective. No man lives unto himself, not even in our extremely individualistic society. The

human community has a tremendous claim on our lives, since it nurtured us and has provided us with the total apparatus with which we understand reality and live in it. So the community perspective must include all the other persons who have in a direct or indirect way influenced us and provided us with the means for, and the purposes of, life.

3. A belief system. Even the social community is not ultimately normative for the Christian; of course the same is also true for the nonreligious person. Each person and human community operates on the basis of what the anthropologist would call a *charter* or a belief system, which includes some conclusion about the ultimate reality, authority or absolute. For the Christian, this ultimate reality, authority and absolute is the Judeo-Christian God, Yahweh. He is accepted as the creator and sustainer of life and, in the spiritual realm, the finisher of our faith. Every thought is known to him and every human activity takes place with his knowledge; in turn, we are responsible to him and are judged by him. So any human activity, including work, needs to be considered in the light of what God's will is, along with the individual and community perspectives outlined above.

As we look at Table 4 it will become clear that all four types of work can and must be analyzed in terms of both their purposes and results from the perspective of the individual, the community and one's faith or belief system. To illustrate, let us assume we are looking at mental work, such as is required in the writing of a novel. We could say that the writing of novels is approved uniformly from both the individual and community perspectives; approved also in terms of both purpose and results. At the same time, from the moral perspective, the results of writing novels could be disapproved, if, for example, the contents of the novels would foster violence and cynicism.

As a general norm, an ideal job, occupation or profession would involve work which is acceptable to the individual, to the community and to moral beliefs. But rarely do jobs or occupations qualify in a total sense. In real life, jobs or occupations often involve trade-offs; this means that the Christian often has to make compromises. For example, a person might have both the individual inclination and the community support to become an influential politician; however, from a religious perspective he or she might decide that the moral dilemmas would be too great. Or, to use another approach—a given individual may respond to the challenge inherent in his or her belief system and make a commitment to the ministry or some other type of Christian service. However, if he or she does not have the essential aptitudes and interests required by that role and, furthermore, does not have community support for this noble activity, that person will not likely be a successful pastor.

Now that we have demonstrated the functions of the working schema, we are ready to see at closer range how work in the marketplace can be evaluated, and how work must be understood when a Christian perspective is used.

The first principle, from a biblical perspective, is that there is no hierarchy of status among the four types of work. The Christian gospel honors alike physical, mental, psychic, and social work. In the parables of Jesus, the laborers are neither upgraded nor downgraded, nor is the manager/employer held up as being of more merit. The point at issue is always *whether the individual or neighbor is benefited* and whether the *moral dimension is satisfied.* The apostle Paul, the leading spokesman of the fledgling Christian movement, worked with his hands as an example to fellow believers. It is likely that all the apostles also worked from necessity. The point made by this principle is simple and central: *Christians do not choose jobs, occupations, or professions on the basis of status of work, for all work activity is honorable if its purposes are to serve fellow human beings and ultimately God.*

The second principle is that a job must always be evaluated not only from the perspective of its ideal purposes and goals but also on the basis of actual results. There are many examples where the two dimensions of work do not coincide. From the individual perspective, a simple example would be the man who honorably earns a living in a chemical factory only to discover that, as a result of exposure to toxic elements, he has contracted an incurable disease. A more contemporary example of an occupation which seems to be acceptable from an individual point of view but may be totally unacceptable from a societal point of view, is the international development worker. This person teaches the principles of modernization to a third world community, only to discover that—with reference to the people in that country—he has created greater dependence on foreign multinationals or dominant nations.

The Christian gospel is replete with parables which teach the importance of consistency between the purposes of work and the results. One such parable describes the man who wanted to build a tower but first needed to sit down to decide whether he could finish it (Luke 14:28–30). A more graphic example is found in the story of the rich man whose goal evidently had been to amass considerable wealth and who was congratulating himself on having achieved this goal. But Jesus implied that the very wealth he amassed had "ensnared" the man and destroyed his spiritual being (Luke 12:16–21). All four types of work may in themselves be honorable (principle number 1), but the consequences of the work must also be consistent with the goals. Assuming that the objectives of particular work are moral—it is possible to be engaged in work that is unquestionably honorable but nonetheless is wrong because evil consequences destroy the good intentions of the work.

Using the perspective of consequence, it is much easier to conclude whether a particular job, occupation, profession is acceptable or unacceptable. Clearly some are wrong for the Christian: for example, could any person committed to walking in the way of Christ be a hangman, a professional soldier, a drug dealer, a thief, a prostitute, a pimp? But aside from work in categories such as these—other obvious examples could be added to this list—many types of jobs can be acceptable from several of the perspectives in our paradigm, yet fail the complete and comprehensive test. This means that each job, vocation and occupation must be evaluated from a number of perspectives using the Christian gospel as the norm.

A third principle is that work position* which is acceptable in terms of both purposes and consequences in one aspect of work may be undesirable and incompatible in another. Thus it is possible that the mental work involved in a certain job may be acceptable in its objectives and results or consequences, but physically may be totally unacceptable. An illustration would be working in a position where the results are so significant that a mistake could be disastrous; thus emotional and psychological strains are created that lead to a nervous breakdown. On a more subtle level, this principle could be illustrated in certain work positions where the emotional demands are so high that they lead to psychic "burnout"; recent studies have shown that this has been taking place in professions such as teaching and nursing.

In this context, the mental and physical work of the job has become destructive of the psychic dimensions of man, thus, man has become "dehumanized" and alienated, not only from his own work but from himself. Where this takes place, "work" has become something externalized and not an expression of his inner reality and creativity. To be integrated, work cannot satisfy one aspect of a person's life while destroying or undermining the rest. Hence, if the physical and mental aspects of a job are destructive of the person's psyche, that job obviously undercuts the important social aspects of work which pertain to the self-identity and self-acceptance of the individual.

This principle suggests that work positions are highly variable

---

*"Work position" hereafter will be used to refer to the work that is performed either in a specific setting, in context of a job or in a profession.

in the way they combine the four levels of work and in the way these four levels are harmonious or disharmonious in their effects.

A fourth and final principle states that the moral perspective supercedes both the individual and social perspectives in evaluating the appropriateness of any type of job, occupation, or profession. That is to say, the type of physical, mental, psychic or social work which a person does—as expressed in the specific job, occupation, or profession—must be judged above all by the moral (Christian) criteria of purposes and consequences. Work, as expressed in the job, may be personally fulfilling and rewarding, may be socially acceptable and provide the individual with a great amount of psychic identity and self-acceptance, but it may still be wrong, or at least relatively unimportant. Hence, neither the *honorableness* of physical work, nor the *importance* of mental work, nor the *healthful aspects* in the psychic dimensions of the work, nor the *relevance* of the work for the social community may, *in and of themselves,* create a sufficient base for working in that particular job.

Not any job, *ipso facto,* is work for the honor and glory of God. If the criteria we have described above are valid, the concept that the job is the natural "calling" in which we serve God clearly has to be revised! Jobs, occupations, and professions cannot be seen as simple monolithic systems of activities which submissively allow themselves to be used to express a person's wishes to serve God. The alienation of the work in a job is not only questionable from an individual and societal health point of view: from a Christian point of view it is immoral. Beyond the four typical frames of reference, one could also speak of a fifth type—spiritual work which affects the relationships of men to God and to their fellow men. Thus, physical work could be considered as having spiritual dimensions as well as having mental, psychic and social dimensions.

From this vantage point, therefore, social work in any job— social work being defined as the creation, maintenance and enlargement of social relationships in the social fabric—must be of such a nature that social relations are enhanced rather than weakened. To be explicit, if a job—such as an administrative job in a large firm—is so competitive and fraught with so many physical, mental and psychic demands that the human relations are neglected or weakened, that job is suspect from a moral (Christian) perspective.

The moral dimensions of the specific work position are therefore crucial when the relations of the individual *vis-a-vis* his comrades—whether equals, subordinates or superordinates—are being considered. If the work position demands that the individual as boss underpay his employees, or brutally compete with colleagues, or deceive a superior to "get the job done," then that work position is immoral. Work positions which are so structured that they cause the incumbent to exploit, hinder, deceive, downgrade, frustrate or hurt the neighbor cannot be contemplated. The social and moral problems which stem from the social structure dimensions of various work positions are facts which many of us, including evangelical Christians, do not want to face.

However, we must be very careful not just to blame "the system" for the evils that exist. As individuals in the system, we may well be part of the problem; partly because we have helped to shape it and partly because we continue to condone it for personal reasons. We dare not judge the work position as the only culprit when, in fact, the individual's insecurity or motivations of greed, lust for power and desire for prestige contribute to, enlarge and maintain the evil. Often the structures and work positions are used to enhance personal advantage. On the other hand, in our experience, structure often helps to keep us moral.

Let's look at an example: As a carpenter, I could succumb easily to the temptation to take shortcuts in building a house, thus increasing the profit but lowering the quality of my work. But certain external and structural restraints such as building codes and inspectors and project foremen keep this from taking place. So societal structures are not necessarily and in themselves evil; nor do they necessarily and of themselves bring unmitigated good. Often, the individual has the ability to choose what he will do ultimately in his work position.

Of course, the question of which job, occupation, or profession passes all the criteria for the Christian must be more fully answered. Many Christians consider many if not all of the principles we have outlined above in eliminating many possible work positions from consideration. This still leaves many work positions from which one can choose. Unfortunately, however, work positions are often then selected on the basis of secular criteria: that is, which of the acceptable work opportunities offer the greatest financial returns, or the highest prestige or the most long-term security. For example, by most norms, teaching would seem to be a commendable and legitimate profession. Is it not true that teaching performs an important and honorable function in the larger social system? Yet it is probably not incorrect to say that prestige, pay and perks are often the dominant factors as the individual teacher decides which position he or she will take.

If in fact a society represented the exact blueprint God had in mind for humankind, then one could argue that most of the jobs, occupations and professions would be pleasing to God.* But this assumption cannot be made unequivocally, especially in light of all

*Interestingly, however, even the functionalist sociologists admit that not all institutions and work positions are necessarily helpful to the larger system.

the institutionalized violence, deceit, oppression and competition that exists in work positions in most societies. Assuming that the basis for deciding what is moral is "what is good for the society in question," this approach still begs the question. The real issue is that a society by itself cannot decide. Even the most organicist sociologists deny this thesis simply because it assumes a type of moral "collective mind."

Christians especially cannot agree that morality evolves out of the collective human experience, since God's own people, the Jews, were not able to develop their own system of morals, and had to be given a set of codes at Mount Sinai. Contrary to a persistent belief, morals do not evolve by themselves. The Old Testament prophets were so powerful and timeless in their pronouncements because, though they spoke in a cultural context, they proclaimed a message which came from outside the system.[8]

Nevertheless, even Jesus taught a new understanding of this moral code. While the code remains the same, each generation seems to require prophets to show how to "Act justly and to love mercy and to walk humbly with your God" (Mic. 6:8).

It is clear, therefore, that jobs, occupations, and professions must ultimately be evaluated from a range of perspectives—not only in terms of the personal and social perspective, but of the moral as well. It must be admitted without reservation, that both individual and societal perspectives can be and often turn out to be self-serving rationalizations. Certainly, the individual's abilities, interests, and biases often enter into work position decisions. And, without a doubt, the community's values, objectives, and interests will obtain when the community perspective is taken into consideration. But of the two, the community is probably more objective than the individual.

Thus, from both perspectives, an individual might be justified in considering a work position of truck driver as the best, given all the considerations. But the moral perspective might dictate otherwise. The moral perspective might dictate that the Christian's calling could be better expressed in other work positions. For example, there could be a shortage of firefighters in the community. But, even more importantly, when the Christian begins to ask the kind of questions we are proposing here, he or she may well begin to see that there are problems in the community which are not being responded to at all—problems such as child abuse, broken families, unemployment, recreational needs, or care for the elderly.

This suggests that the Christian's purpose, as outlined above, is to "present his body a sacrifice" to serve the purposes of God's kingdom. It suggests also that original plans for a particular job, occupation or even profession may need to be discarded to engage in this higher service. Furthermore, this could also mean that one's calling may exclude a specific job, at least at certain times in an individual's life. Dorothy Day, the noted Catholic humanitarian, whose funeral was celebrated with tears of hope as well as sorrow, would be an illustration of this point.[9]

A second point is involved here, namely, that earning a living—an objective or purpose almost always associated with employment in a work position—is so powerful that the idea of "vocation" as suggested above and the need to make a living are often incompatible. In this regard, it may be instructive to recall a fact of history: that those individuals who truly believed in a cause usually discovered ways to stay alive. Artists in the Middle Ages found "patrons"; revolutionaries have almost always found persons who would support their "thinker." Of course, John the Baptist and Jesus also illustrate this type of orientation, while the mendicant orders, as well as the Gautama Buddha show that, around the world, people are ready to support others who are following a conviction.

Conclusion

We have argued in this chapter that work has four dimensions, each of which is relevant when one is analyzing work. Further, we have suggested a number of questions which must be asked when a person is deciding what type of job, occupation, or vocation he or she will follow. Finally, we have proposed that work can contribute to the destruction of personal, social and moral good. It is obvious, of course, that we have not discussed how a given individual can "humanize" his work if he is not able to choose a work position which allows Christian convictions to be practiced or fulfilled. That would require a study of cases and settings.

However, in spite of that, it is our conviction that a Christian must somehow become the master of his work; otherwise he capitulates as an individual. When a worker relegates the largest block of his waking hours to elements outside of himself, he literally abdicates his autonomy. Of course, it is clear that not everyone can choose work which is precisely and totally consistent with the Christian faith; in fact, very few persons enjoy that privilege. For those who cannot choose, there is still the possibility of making changes in the nature of the work position and its demands. There is also the great challenge for individuals to find ways to alter the influence of their work positions to bring them in line with Christian beliefs and thus embody commitment to the view that work choices should reflect the Christian's primary calling to help build the kingdom of God.

13

A Christian View of Work— Historical and Theological Perspectives

> God saw all that he had made, and it was very good. And there was evening, and there was morning—the sixth day . . . And God blessed the seventh day and made it holy, because on it he rested from all the work of creating that he had done (Gen. 1:31; 2:3).
>
> For God will bring every deed into judgment, including every hidden thing, whether it is good or evil (Eccl. 12:14).

Many young people are plagued by the indecision and uneasiness that often accompany the choice of occupation, profession or vocation. As well, numerous adults in midcareer have second thoughts about their vocation or the specific job in which they're engaged and begin to wonder if they should continue. Still others develop concern about the ethical problems associated with their positions. Many more are afflicted with a form of job-related depression; they live constantly on the edge of a corrosive despair because their work seems so meaningless.

After counseling with young people and older folk on such questions for many years, we have developed a number of ideas and convictions regarding the nature of work for the Christian. Using as background the various views of work presented earlier, we would like to present a perspective on the nature of work for the

Christian—a perspective which recognizes the historical sources and sociological understandings about work but which, we believe, remains true to the claims of the Christian gospel.

From the Christian perspective, work is not only a physical and social fact; it has transcendent aspects as well. Since the human being is created in the image of God, work should and can reflect the same creative and pleasurable facets which God enjoyed when He worked.

In that frame of reference, proper work, by definition, is creative and not, therefore, destructive of creation—including both the natural environment and God's human creatures. Also, from the creative perspective, a Christian view would include consideration of all the activities in which human beings are engaged.

In the following pages, a Christian view of work will be presented in the form of propositions. These have been gleaned from various sources, but they do express our own convictions about what work can and should mean for the Christian.

Proposition 1. Work was Instituted by God.

Work is defined as the expenditure of energy to achieve a desired end.* Perhaps nowhere else is this definition of work displayed more simply and dramatically than in the biblical story of creation. Even though some of us have read the creation story many times, we often miss a surprising fact: our first information is a simple statement that God worked. He created; he expressed energy to achieve a desired end. He acted; indeed he could not create without acting.

After God achieved His intended end, he stopped working. Genesis 2:1 reports, "Now at last the heavens and earth were successfully completed, with all that they contained. So on the seventh day, having finished his task, God ceased from this work he had been doing" (LB).

God's own pattern of work was reflected in everything else he created. In His dialogue with Adam after the Fall, he said, "By the sweat of your brow you will eat your food . . . . " (Gen. 3:19). Food for the sustenance of life was a desirable end. Later in Exodus, where the rules of the covenant are delivered, God told the children of Israel: "Six days you shall labor and do all your work . . . . (Ex. 20:9). Almost as an afterthought, it seems, God told the people that He also had worked for six days and deserved the seventh day for rest. It is clear that work, being ordained of God, also had limits set by God's example as well as by precept.

So, in order for the entire drama of history to begin, God had

*Work is defined operationally in chapter 4.

to work. The expenditure of energy to achieve a desired end became a fundamental principle of creation, easily observed in its application. That principle continues to function, for to this day all living things must expend energy merely to live. Beyond that basic need, human beings are programmed as it were: they must work to achieve any desired end.[1]

However, the drama of history did not only begin with work. God not only instituted work by making it a requirement for the emergence and maintenance of creation; He exemplified the creative expenditure of energy by His own actions which at the same time set certain guidelines for all work.

Proposition 2. Work Can Be Good and Honorable.

God blessed the work that He did in creation. Since that time, He has blessed much of the work that humankind has done. In the building of the Tent of God, God told Moses, "Also I have given skill to all the craftsmen to make everything I have commanded you" (Ex. 31:6). Jesus said, "My father is always at his work to this very day, and I, too, am working" (John 5:17). The apostle Paul wrote, in response to some who were avoiding work, "He who has been stealing must steal no longer, but must work, doing something useful with his own hands, that he may have something to share with those in need" (Eph. 4:28). And to those who felt that work was second-rate to the laborless euphoria of the kingdom of heaven, Paul said, "Make it your ambition to lead a quiet life, to mind your own business and to work with your hands; just as we told you" (1 Thess. 4:11).

Work, therefore, is not sinful, but rather an ethically desirable fact of life. All work which is not harmful to the self or neighbor is good and honorable. There is no intimation in the Old or New Testaments that some work is more noble or honorable than other work. The act of working is foundational to human existence and therefore must be good. The Talmud states: "Greater even than the pious man is he who eats that which is the fruit of his own toil: for Scripture declares him twice-blessed."

Proposition 3. Work Can Be a Loving Act.

The first proposition addressed the issue of work being instituted by God. This proposition must begin with God rather than with work. Who is God? is the prior question. Of course, we cannot here enter a lengthy philosophical or theological discussion. But we can appeal to a simple identifying statement from the epistle of John: "God is love" (1 John 4:16). The New Testament

Scriptures offer many other affirmations of this fundamental viewpoint. Along with Old Testament Scriptures, they provide us with a body of material from which we derive our understanding of God as love.

Sometimes, the Old Testament is seen only as a body of threats of punishment for wrongdoing since these are so pervasive in the prophetic literature. But there are also strong statements of God's love. Deuteronomy 7:9 says, "Know therefore that the Lord your God is God; he is the faithful God, keeping his covenant of love to a thousand generations of those who love him and keep his commands." This meshes perfectly with the later words of the apostle John who could say with great assurance "How great is the love the Father has lavished on us, that we should be called children of God!" (1 John 3:1). However, even without direct references to God's love in the creation story, that perception is essential to the form of His biblical identity if we wish to understand creation and work.

Accepting this identity of God as premise—God is love—we see creation of the world as a loving act of God. Since God cannot deny His nature, His work was and is a loving act. And in an ideal sense, if it is truly creative, all work is a loving act. "There is no excellency without hard labor" was the message on a motto an accomplished musician friend had hanging in his studio. His life and work affirmed both elements of the motto: excellency and hard labor. His creativity was almost entirely the result of his love for the work he was doing.

To work after God's pattern is to create. And to create is to work out of love. It is difficult to think of God's creating as an unloving act; that is true simply because God is love. However, since man is not fully love or totally loving, he may work toward ends that are neither creative nor loving. This dark possibility must be kept in mind during any attempt at a definition of work.

Proposition 4. Work Helps to Define Man's Creatureliness.

To speculate endlessly about what our world would have been like if man had not sinned may not be very helpful. At the same time, the condition of humankind before the Fall in the world God had created does provide some insight about work itself—as does the fact that God himself worked. In that prefallen state, *the human beings God created needed to work,* although not "by the sweat of their brow." In fact, the requirement that men and women should work is related directly to the fact that they are created beings, to their creatureliness. Our creatureliness is clearly indicated by our need to live by the exertion we bring forth.[2]

God's definition of human existence included making work a condition of survival; all living things needed to exert energy in order to live. In some sense, therefore, our very existence is fueled or made possible by work. This is true, not only in terms of individual physical survival and for the perpetuation of the race, but also in terms of psychological and sociological well-being and meaning for life. A world in which no one needed to work would be meaningless. Work both defines the boundaries of human creatureliness and provides it with meaning. Of course, meaning can refer to that work which will allow one to eat tomorrow, or the work that helps us to achieve some form of perfection, say on the violin. Creaturehood and work are twins.

However, this principle must not be misapplied or taken to one of its possible conclusions, namely, that all work or only work defines creatureliness and that other things do not. Certainly, leisure and "re-creation" can also give meaning to life and are part of the creaturely condition. At the same time, work cannot be exempted from any analysis of the limitations of humankind. It was Leonardo da Vinci who said, "God sells us all things at the price of labor."

Proposition 5. Work is a Means for Human Fulfillment.

"Occupation was one of the pleasures of Paradise, and we cannot be happy without it," was the way Anna Brownell Jameson describes the role of work in human happiness and fulfillment. Many images come to mind that express this fundamental observation. The painting of a man praying over a loaf of bread and a cup of wine—hanging in many dining rooms—conveys to us a feeling of thankfulness for the fruits of daily work. The simple joy of returning to the farm kitchen after a hard day's work is portrayed impressively by O. E. Rollveeg in *Giants in the Land*.

But we cannot depend merely upon such observations of our own or the reactions of others to wholesome work and its satisfactions. Arguments about the nature of human beings and of God's intentions for them should also be considered. God was pleased with what He had made; there seems no higher principle than that. He was fulfilled by what He had done, especially by the creation of man who was a reflection of himself. Men and women, each a reflection of God, should thereby also find joy and pleasure and thus fulfillment in the results of their labor. To be able, then, to create makes possible one of the highest joys of which human beings are capable.

The fulfillment of work is composed of several strands. One is the joy of work itself—exerting energy to achieve an end. "Good for the body is the work of the body, good for the soul the work of the soul, and good for either the work of the other" (Henry David Thoreau). The joy of working is a God-given pleasure. But the other strand is just as rewarding—enjoying what one has created. A child will cry out with delight and summon all to "come and see" when he succeeds in building a little block house. A man will enjoy for a lifetime a black walnut deacon's bench he has made. As God himself was fulfilled by work, so can we be also. But a caution must also be inserted here. As well as having the potential for human fulfillment, work can also be degrading and dehumanizing; more than that, the product or results of work can be ugly and alienating. This means that we must look at the work we are doing with a very careful eye lest we be too easily seduced.

Proposition 6. Work is for the Benefit of the Community.

Work is a social fact, for almost all work done by everyone affects other people. Whether I work with a selfish motive–for example, to increase my bank account—or a noble motive, the work I do normally affects other people, often in many different ways. There is always the possibility that my work will have negative or destructive consequences for others, but even negative consequences prove that most work is social in its impact.

John R. W. Stott believes that "work is intended for the benefit of community. By cultivating the Garden of Eden, Adam will have fed and perhaps clothed his family" (*Christianity Today,* May 4, 1979). An interesting example of work serving the community is the building of the ark of the covenant in Exodus. Here are described the craftsmen and the jobs they were to do; in this setting the foreman was God! "The Lord said . . . Make a chest of acacia wood—two and a half cubits long, a cubit and a half wide. . . ." (Ex. 25:10). The Lord concludes by saying, "I have filled him . . . with skill, ability and knowledge in all kinds of crafts . . . ." (Ex. 31:3). The ark of the covenant was clearly intended for the spiritual benefit of the community of Israel.

Many other references in Scripture point to the fact that work is for the benefit of the community. Without exception, Jesus worked to help the members of the community. When He called the twelve disciples (Luke 9) and the seventy (Luke 10), Jesus gave the same instructions: to preach the kingdom of God and to heal the sick and to be satisfied with what was set before them at mealtime. The modern idea that work is the exchange of personal labor for another good *which then becomes a personal right* is not emphasized in the New Testament.

The social benefit of work is nowhere better exemplified than by the apostle Paul himself, who in his self-definition as the servant of the church says:

> We proclaim him . . . To this end I labor, struggling with all his energy, which so powerfully works in me. I want you to know how much I am struggling for you and for those at Laodicea, and for all who have not met me personally (Col. 1:28–2:1).

As we know, the Socialist credo has maintained for decades that work must always be for the benefit of the community. The same has been true, of course, for the Christian faith; in this case, the principle has been modeled for centuries. The crucial difference is that the Christian work ethic is motivated by the love of humans reflecting the love of God to others while socialists claim that they do not need God's love to work for others.

Proposition 7. Work can be for the Glory of God.

There is an enduring tradition which has maintained that work is one of the ways of glorifying God. St. Bernard of Clairvaux said, "He who labors as he prays lifts his heart to God with his hands." Some have questioned the glorifying value of work by asking: How is a menial act, such as scrubbing a floor, an act that brings glory to God? Or what difference does it make in the economy of God? Or, to use another kind of example—when we sing an anthem of praise to God, what is a shout of praise beyond expenditure of energy to produce sound waves?

There is a nonpractical dimension of life which we call the symbolic; symbols are signs that stand for another reality and are often as important as the practical. Just as singing can convey a reality or a meaning beyond the song itself, so work can convey some ideas, feelings or meanings which the work itself does not contain. Brother Lawrence, amidst the "noise and clutter of his kitchen" which he disliked, worked not only to submit himself to God's will, but to state thereby that he was willingly offering himself to God.

Through our work we symbolize a number of realities. We are saying to God that we accept collaboration with Him in His creative endeavours as being significant. We say to Him and our neighbor that we acknowledge work as part of the created order. We signify that work and its result were part of what God affirmed when He said, "This is good." We also proclaim our willingness to be identified as members of the species for whom work is an essential part of survival. All this and more we symbolize through work.

Man derives pleasure from acts of pleasing God. God derives

pleasure from the worship and praise of His creatures. Work is one such instrument of praise. To work is to please God.

Proposition 8. Work Gives Structure to Interpersonal Relationships.

No one has argued with Aristotle's early dictum that "Man is a social being" (he used the word political but meant social). The best proof of this profound dictum is perhaps the fact that one of the greatest punishments known to humans is solitary confinement. Of course, certain eremitic soul types seek aloneness, but even that practice has been shown to have definite social implications. One could say: Man is truly man because he is social—nurtured in the bosom of loving tender relationships. Or that humankind is helped to be more fully human by being part of or enjoying relational experience.

As indicated above, most work involves relating to others simply because very little work can be done in total isolation. The "hunt"—a vital activity in many traditional civilizations—was a social or group affair. Nomadic and agricultural societies were formed by tribes and clans working together to extract an existence from the earth. Modern societies structure a great deal of their work in group situations whether it is coal mining two miles below the surface of the earth, or launching a space shuttle.

Since sleep is not a very social act, work remains the major sector of existence where we relate to other beings. Though our leisure time may be spent in informal relationships, in work we are usually related to others in more or less specifically defined role-relations. These structured and formal relationships may involve many differences in status, authority, power, and influence.

Regardless of these differences, however, these formal settings do include social relationship. They also provide a most challenging arena in which humans can come to terms with the myriad dynamics related to satisfying our own subjective needs for creativity and productivity and our relational needs. That work is social is indicated by the almost universal appearance of informal or primary type relationships in the work setting. It is normal for us to become attracted to, and to develop affinity with, others with whom we relate. In fact, a major sociological theory about the emergence of the social group is premised on this understanding.[3]

It is interesting to note that both work and social relationships are essential elements in life and well-being. Further, that they are interrelated: work is a setting in which social relationships become possible and are nurtured and the social setting is a place where work can be done joyfully and with fulfillment. It seems that structures are needed where people can relate to others for mutual stimulation, inspiration and encouragement. In societies such as ancient Greece where work was not highly developed or valued, other structures existed to meet this need—such as planned games or other public events.

Human beings develop their human characteristics through the stimulation and promptings of other humans. A baby becomes social as it experiences social reality around it. A human adult becomes fully human as he or she experiences the vast gamut of social stimuli in the fully rounded orb of life; this includes leisure and play but above all work. To work is to relate to others. Work is the structured context for many interpersonal relationships, and therefore provides the setting in which part of man's need for interaction with others is satisfied.

Counterpoint

To this point, our proposals have sought to shape a Christian view of work. However, this book would not be complete without specifically recognizing and focusing on a counterpoint to the essence of what we have presented so far. Simply stated, this counterpoint proposes that some work is evil and has evil consequences; that some work is a denial of creativity and destroys the worker and others; that some work is totally antithetical to and does not reflect the image of God.

None of this should be interpreted to mean that work is intrinsically evil, or that somehow work is second best for man. On the contrary, God hallowed work by His own activity in creation and ordained that His creatures should work for the fundamental reasons already noted. But throughout the fabric of God's creation run the ugly strands of fallenness. Work is not exempt from the distortions of sin, nor from the willful acts of those who choose to turn from God's will and purpose. Both the created world and God's creatures suffer from such disobedience. Sometimes God's creatures bring disaster upon themselves by their own thoughtless choices. In many settings the choices of a few ungodly persons visit misery and destruction upon whole populations.

Work can become the channel for this misery; that is to say, work often provides the context for great unhappiness, alienation, exploitation, repression, dehumanization. Although God intended work to have a holy character, like other parts of His creation, it has been sullied by sin. In spite of God's purpose to enhance man's dignity through creative work, it has often become the means through which that dignity has been destroyed. Instead of work resulting in creativity, pleasure and rewards, this area in which man can reflect the image of his Creator has become the setting for man's oppression by man in forms that have brought incredible suffering.

Many who read this book will be able to cite their own examples where work has seemed evil. But few of us will know much about being part of exploited masses living and working under primitive conditions or political circumstances where humanity is brutalized by a definition of work that bears all the marks of sin—sin against humanity and sin against God.

Be that as it may, all of us can remember times when work was not a blessing, when it did not bring unmitigated good. Instead we experienced work as a chore, or we saw it as punishment; or we found ourselves obligated to serve under conditions where work became almost unbearable. I remember one such time early in my own life.

As a lad of fourteen, I was hired out by my father to work on a hay baling crew. I sat on the baler half-covered by chaff in a terribly hot and noisy situation, day in and day out trying desperately to keep up with the tying of wires as the bales moved by. It seemed the bales moved faster than they could humanly be tied. I worked for $1.50 per day; since our family was very poor, these wages went to my father. The only joy I remember from that work experience was the half-hour lunch break when we could eat all we wanted, including some store-bought bread, which was a delicacy to me at the time. I remember another thing: telling myself that I would go to college so I wouldn't have to work so hard and in such miserable conditions ever again.

In prehistoric times, work settings have been used by masters and lords to enslave people and extract their last ounce of human energy. Merchants and traders have hired men, women, and even children in the pursuit of gain for themselves. Industrialists and financiers have sent people into mines and roads to build empires, leaving corpses buried in the earth where they toiled. Ballads such as *Big John* send shivers down the spine for they depict the horribly brutish working conditions and the sheer cruelty of human taskmasters. Negro spirituals such as "Soon I'll Be Done" epitomize the tragedy of slave labor.

When we acknowledge elements like this in society, we are forced to conclude that work can be "hell." In the words of Arthur Kornhauser, a long-time student of work, "The unsatisfactory mental health of working people consists in no small measure of their dwarfed desires and deadened initiative, reduction of their goals, and restriction of their efforts to a point where life is at best relatively empty and only half meaningful" (Pfeffer:260).

It is this final principle—cast in counterpoint—which causes us to concern ourselves with the nature and condition of work; for those of us who claim a Christian commitment it is doubly important, for we hold to an ethic that calls us to a redeemed life which affects not only ourselves but also our neighbors.

God not only loved to do work, but he loved what he had created. In similar fashion, Christians should see work as a loving act, doing good deeds for the created order and for mankind and loving what they create. Jesus interpreted His Father's will as feeding the hungry, clothing the naked, healing the sick, and preaching the gospel of peace. As Jesus' followers, we will interpret work in the same way. We should not work at things which contribute to the misfortune of others; rather, we will engage in activities that show our love for them.

God's work was good, beautiful and creative. Man's rebellion, however, has sullied God's work. The pollution of this earth which is the Lord's is a strong reminder of that fact. Thus man's present work, although it reflects God's work, must be seen basically as "repair work" ordained by God to help restore the creation which mankind has tainted.

This idea sets the stage for a whole new dimension of work. Originally, God worked in creation and called us also to work creatively for love of Him and for love of others. When sin became a reality through willful disobedience, the image of God in the human race suffered grievous distortions. All creation suffered and continues to suffer. In this setting of failures and brokenness and pain, God has instituted a new dimension of work we have come to know as redemption—that is, the restoration of His creation so the divine intention can still be fulfilled.

Man is now called by God to work with Him in this new activity of redemption. Although He has initiated the redemptive activity and although, through Christ, He has opened wide a door to the redemption of all creation, God still places much of this work on man's shoulders. The restoration of the created order has become our task: to make whole again the damaged relationship between man and God, to reconcile man with man and thus heal estrangements, to change the exploitative relationship that man has come to have with his physical environment and to discover again the original and natural partnership between all created elements and entities. (The idea of domination and exploitation of the earth—and with it the domination of man—is a pernicious theology which must be destroyed.)

God's will for humanity and the created order is clear. It was shown fully in the original creation. It has been mirrored in every part of God's redemptive activity since human fallenness became a reality. It is reflected finally in the promise of heaven—an ultimate Shalom where through His work in redemption God's intention in His creative work is fully realized. To be workers together with

God in bringing about the fulfillment of His purposes represents the highest kind of calling.

Thus, in point and counterpoint, we confront reality. On the one hand, we see the reality of God's intention in creation and His activity in redemption so the divine intention can be realized. On the other hand, we admit the realities of the world in which we live, the problems in the societies of which we are a part, the sins which we continue to perpetrate in our thoughtless, selfish lives.

The Christian must choose: choose to turn blind eyes on the pervasive destructiveness of certain ways in which work is being used, or choose to be partner with God in His continuing work of creation and redemption.

In 1972 in Peru, I stood at one of the Inca fortresses in Cuzco and marveled at the massive boulders which had been chipped and rubbed to perfection and placed in a wall in a way which no modern twentieth-century technology could duplicate. I tried to imagine the human labor involved in placing one such boulder; I was told it took the lifetimes of numerous individuals to prepare a single rock for its place in the wall. I tried to visualize the nameless, faceless slaves who worked and died in the creation of this Inca empire. And I had to ask myself: Was that labor creative? Was that work done for the glory of God? Did those monumental efforts lead to the creation of Shalom? And I saw—perhaps more clearly than in any other setting—the contrast between work that is holy, creative, joyful and a fulfillment of human dignity and of God's purpose and work that is debasing, dehumanizing and evil because in the process it destroys a part of God's creation.

In conclusion, we venture to suggest that as an expenditure of energy work is not intrinsically holy or intrinsically evil; *God's purpose for work was and is holy* and His purpose hallowed His work; and the only way for humankind to experience work as creative and holy is to align our will with God's purpose.

For Christians and non-Christians alike, the crucial question about work is for what purpose does one exert energy? Through work, humans have built cathedrals; other humans have destroyed them with bombs. Through work, people have exercised incredible ingenuity and invented awesome devices and powerful machines; others have used these devices and machines to stalk soldiers on a battlefield, leaving only the litter of their broken bodies. Clearly every Christian ultimately must choose whether his work is to be creative and redemptive, or whether it is to be thoughtless, oppressive or destructive.

14

Work and the
Kingdom of God

> As long as it is day, we must do the work of him who sent
> me. Night is coming, when no one can work (John 9:4).

During the three short years of His ministry, Jesus went about
Galilee announcing that the "kingdom of God is at hand" (Matt.
4:17). Probably, the full meaning of that statement can never be
understood. But certainly those few words—the kingdom of God
is at hand—must have contained the essential core of His message
expressed through His preaching and actions. His emphases on love
of neighbor, sharing with the needy and compassion for the sick
were, without a doubt, a reflection of this kingdom of God.

Even though Jesus made no explicit pronouncements about
work, it is clear that He saw work as a common thread throughout
His references to the coming kingdom. His parables depicting
faithful stewards, obedient servants, the shrewd businessman—and
a host of other economic teachings—can only be understood as
recognizing the centrality and importance of work in the kingdom.

Implicit also in His activities was the emphasis on work! For
how were the sick to be healed? How were the naked to be clothed?
How was the gospel to be preached? Was it not through work? In
three short years, Jesus provided a classic model for His followers
who were committed to the realization of the kingdom of God. No
matter with what transcendence His listeners heard Him speak of

245

the kingdom, His example reflected a very human expenditure of
energy to begin making that kingdom real!

Toward a Theology of Work

Although we have presented a Christian perspective of work
in chapter 13, it is necessary to conclude our discussion of the role
of work for the Christian by relating it to the grand purpose of
creation itself. This may seem like a presumptuous intention.
However, there is a justification for such an attempt: the obvious
conclusion that *not* trying to fit work into the larger picture is an
even worse presumption, for that would ignore the very center of
human existence.[1]

One of the most comprehensive theological and philosophical
perspectives on work and, at the same the most intuitive, is
provided by the biblical material about the kingdom of God. The
understanding of the kingdom is itself immensely rich and
controversial; witness two of the major paradoxical emphases
which are included in the Scriptures—that the kingdom of God is
already here and that the kingdom of God is still to come. Both
emphases need to be retained (Brauer:198ff.)

It is possible that our best understanding of work emerges
from this paradox! Through the atoning work of Christ, one can
view the kingdom of God as *already come*. At the same time, there is
a perspective that emphasizes both God's continuing work and
human work as instrumental in fulfilling kingdom intention and
potential; thus one can justifiably view the kingdom of God as *still
to come*. There is no question that, in one sense, God has done all the
work necessary to make peace with man! However, with the same
degree of certainty, one can state that the process of implementing
this peace continues and must continue until all things are "united
in him" (Col. 1:14–19).

So human work is not ultimate: only God's work and purpose
have that distinction. But human work is nonetheless indispens-
able—the kingdom that is to come cannot be realized without
work on the part of kingdom citizens. The psychological, social
and spiritual dimensions of work described earlier thus become
more meaningful if we place them into the larger purpose of God's
kingdom. In this way, man's work is contingent and conditioned—
it is derived from God's basic purpose for His creation. But it is
also fundamentally important, for God cannot achieve the kingdom
He envisions without the cooperation and compliance of His
kingdom citizens.

Another central fact about the kingdom of God is how it
symbolizes the relevance of *all* life. The very term "implies a close
relationship to analogous structures of life and history. Of necessity

such a concept must deal concretely with the day-to-day affairs of living men and women. Furthermore, this symbol, by its very nature, must include the personal and social aspects of life; to be less inclusive would do violence to the symbol of 'Kingdom' or of 'rule' " (Brauer:199).[2]

For our purposes, the kingdom of God implies that there is a first mover, that there is a purpose, and that there is an order. "Insofar as it is the kingdom of God, it stresses the freedom and sovereignty of God the creator, the sustainer, and the redeemer" (Brauer:199). But this is more than simply a statement of authority and power; it involves the kingdom subjects as well. "It transcends the totality of this life, both personal and social, and demands that the Christian take a stand against this life. It appears as a completion of this life, as a fulfillment, as the final meaning of history; yet it is God's Kingdom, God's work and not man's . . . . " (Brauer:199).

The nature of this kingdom which God is creating is open to diverse interpretations. It is not possible here to comment on or to make evaluations of these interpretations. It might make better sense to suggest that all the various ethical systems which religious groups have espoused together point to a fuller-orbed view of the coming kingdom. Certainly, the common emphases on compassion, peace, love, freedom, sharing, faith, trust and hope need to be included in any interpretation of the content of the kingdom of God. But there are many other elements in this kingdom that deserve consideration. One of these is work and how it may be applied to the varying emphases of the kingdom of God. This we will do in the following sections.

Work as Worship

All earthly kingdoms, all human orders and all organizations are structured on a certain division of authority and labor. Human life is impossible without the presence and function of authority to bring about and maintain order. Regardless of the intrinsic worthiness of the person holding an office or an authoritative position, the fundamental requirements for order are the facts of office holding and authority figures.

Within the Christian tradition, the Judeo-Christian God has always been accepted as the ultimate authority and the creator and sustainer of all life. All of the Christian creeds begin from this point. The Apostolic Creed begins "I believe in God the Father Almighty, maker of heaven and earth. . . . " Wherever there is order and structure, respect and honor are paid to the holder of that authority. In sociology, authority is explained as the "internalization of norms"; this means that authority truly exists when people accept the legitimacy of the authority someone else is exercising over them and act accordingly.

In any kingdom, it is assumed that citizens will respect and revere the king. One can grant that the history of God's rule over His kingdom has included a lot of rebellion; in spite of that, however, there has been general recognition of God's rule. Many forms of this recognition have developed, the most natural of the entire institutional practice being so-called worship rituals. Of course, from God's point of view, the most comprehensive recognition of His authority is when men obey Him totally. Indeed, at times God has been angered by the hypocrisy of His people—when they carried out rituals of worship that symbolized homage and obedience but at the same time were being rebellious and disobedient—times when, in fact, men's hearts were far from Him (See Isa. 58:6).

If God is honored and respected most when people obey Him, then insofar as work is a way of obeying God, work becomes a *central form of worship*. In the coming of the kingdom of God, as we have shown, work is a central element. Thus, when men and women obey God by doing the work that He has called us all to do, that work becomes worship of the most intense and holy nature. In the natural order of things, submission to authority always implies obedience; that means a literal submission of the inferior to the will of the superior. In a setting where the respect for authority is motivated by love—as it is in the God-man relationship—then submission is voluntary, willful and joyful.

Throughout Christian history, the worship of God through work has been a central response of God's children. *Ora est labora* is a form of worship. Work is the creature's expression of love, reverence and joy to the Creator; work is the Christian's response to the King of Kings. One of the simple but profound motivations for such expressions of love, reverence and joy is God's great gift to us.

In the setting of the kingdom, that gift has special meaning. Through faith, we step into a new realm of experience. We are given a part to play in God's kingdom. We are placed in a state of belonging; we are given the status of "belonging-ness'. We enjoy the security of being members of the household of God. This wonderful sense of position—of being a part of something greater than oneself—is the underlying and true basis for thankfulness and joy. Being called by God to work represents status in the kingdom of God, a place of importance, a high position. When we understand that, we will respond accordingly.

That response can be spoken of as work, or as worship. As an act of obedience to God, work constitutes worship. As an act of thankfulness to God, work confirms our position as citizens of the kingdom; work acknowledges that indeed we are sons and daughters of God, that indeed we have status and a place of belonging. In a complementary sense, work stands with ritualistic forms of worship as one of the ways through which people give thanks to God because He has made them a part of His holy economy. In a fundamental sense, work is worship—one of the highest forms of honor a Christian can give to God.

Work as Service

However, to engage in work as a freely offered gift of love and as an act of worship to God does not represent the whole truth. As significant as that perspective may be, it does not fully define the role of work in the kingdom of God.

Members of any kingdom are constituent parts of that society; in a truly fundamental sense, they make it possible for the society to exist. Even the establishment of all the institutions of human order is possible only because of the subjects who live in a given realm or kingdom. Since a kingdom needs subjects to exist, one could say that persons perform a service to that kingdom simply by being part of it. They help to make that kingdom tangible.

But the subjects of a kingdom or members of a society cannot just be present. They must become supportive of the human order in which they exist. For the human order to function, work must be done. Work is central, in fact; it enables the continuing existence of human community in the broadest sense of the term. Even more than that basic function of work, however, the work of subjects is important to the fulfillment of that kingdom's purposes or its objectives.

The same is true in the kingdom of God. Without loyal subjects, God's kingdom cannot be built. Only through the subjects of that kingdom can God's objective be realized. They must become supportive of the order in which they exist, just as a human society is supportive of the order in which it exists.

God's idea of the kingdom is directed toward a state of being where Shalom, or perfect peace will reign—where the will of God will reign supreme.

> It is clear in the New Testament that the concept signifies the kingly rule, the sovereignty, or the rule of God. Its basic intention is to affirm the fact that God reigns in all aspects of personal and social life (Brauer:197).

God's total will can be conceived of only as a condition where love informs all thought and action.

Service in the kingdom of God, therefore, simply means doing the work required of citizens to help the "nation" achieve its purposes. From this perspective, every Christian has a service to give to help the holy nation achieve those purposes. As was indicated above, Shalom or peace is certainly one way of describing the *end state* of the kingdom of God. But Shalom, as the Jews understood it, meant more than a spiritual condition; it included the full satisfaction of human needs.

> Shalom is not only a spiritual condition, but the condition of well-being intended by God for all creatures. For humans this includes food, health, security from danger, means of livelihood, shelter, clothing, family, community and relationship to God (Birch and Rasmussen:150).

Service in the kingdom of God thus implies that Christians see their work as creating Shalom across the full range of its meaning. The *work position,* therefore, becomes the channel or means by which you and I fulfill our role in the purpose of the holy nation to which we belong. Again, from this perspective, the work position of truck driver takes on a totally different character. Even though the work position serves a function of providing transport for goods from one place to another, the driver—as a Christian—is transporting goods so that Shalom can be realized.

Thus, the Christian's service must be seen to function in two spheres at the same time: the material sphere where work is done to maintain earthly existence and the heavenly sphere where work is done so that Shalom may come.

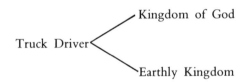

As is made more clear in the diagram, some work positions and services are out of bounds for the Christian, for they do not contribute to Shalom. Service in organizations, institutions or structures which tend to destroy or create disharmony should not be engaged in by the Christian. Ultimately, all activities that are not uplifting or in some way contributory to Shalom must be held in question. Such questionable activities can never be part of that sphere known as the kingdom of God.

It should be clear then that, in itself, holding a work position is not a guarantee that our work is service in the kingdom of God. The truck driver delivering goods in a society whose national objectives include the exploitation of weak or underdeveloped third world nations must seriously question an activity that is not building the kingdom of God. In other words, work positions as such cannot be conceived of as "divine callings" as Luther believed. The consequences of our work must be evaluated as well.

Therefore work as service in the kingdom of God must be work which is not used for destructive ends.

This argument forces upon us the sharp and painful conclusion that Christians have an awesome responsibility in their choice of work, for that choice determines and reflects whether or not they are working in the kingdom of God. It means that as we fill work positions we must understand the consequences of our work— not only directly, but also its more total and far-reaching effects. And if we believe the ecologists' creed that "we cannot touch a flower without troubling a star" we are indeed profoundly responsible.

Is this not too great a burden to place on the rank and file of human beings? The answer is an emphatic no! For work is the basic shaper of our own personal existence and that of human society. To say that certain human beings are not "up to" participating in the ultimate meaning of human existence is an insult to God and far from complimentary to any person who believes that. Furthermore, to suggest that the average person is not able to participate in the ultimate issues of existence reflects an elitism which has no foundation in the teachings of Christ.

If we are citizens in the kingdom of God—a most hallowed privilege and status—then each of us is obligated to fill our place in a way that is worthy of that citizenship. Jesus taught the importance of every human being in God's kingdom. But he went far beyond that. In fact, he emphasized the importance of every human being in God's kingdom by reminding us that God *knows* and *cares* about every bird of the air and every flower of the field. And if, as Jesus also said, the very hairs of our heads are numbered, whether few or many, it is certainly consistent to suggest that the work position— and all the work we do in it—possesses profound and eternal significance.

The human social structure is such that it is almost impossible for individual persons to survive without the help of others. Only in the most limited and primitive circumstances can an individual survive by his own efforts alone. Rather, in general, through cooperation and mutual service, mankind has been able to achieve a relatively good life, even though the distribution of that good life has been both unequal and very unfair.

Work in the kingdom of God benefits the worker, but also benefits others who can share in the results of that work. Producing food, or furniture—beyond what one needs for oneself so it can be shared—is productive work and one of the bases of civilization. Producing chairs, for example, so that others can also sit, is kingdom work. Producing destructive implements of war is not kingdom work, and does not fit into God's economy. God told the children of Israel that they should "beat their swords into plowshares" (Isa. 2:4). Producing dependency-creating luxury items also is not productive work in the kingdom of God. And certainly, in the same vein, creating dependency on these items through mass marketing techniques is also not kingdom work. In fact, creating any need for self-serving items which make people "soft" and cause them to focus on self-indulgence and self-gratification is far from kingdom work.

The Personal Nature of Work

We have suggested above how work contributes to the psychological and social aspects of man. In the kingdom of God, work needs to be useful if it is to contribute to the objectives of the kingdom. But what is useful work? Some of us think we know and have prided ourselves in avoiding useless work. Is an artist who paints originals more or less useful than the farmer who plows the same fields year after year? Is the classroom teacher who attempts to make learning an exciting event more productive or creative than the person who works in a coal mine? What are the criteria for determining utility of work in the kingdom of God?

First of all, productive work must be helpful for the individual doing the work, for if it is not, it defeats its own ends. How can a Christian be working for the kingdom of God if he is destroyed in the process? Hence, since humans are composed of body, spirit, mind, and soul, work must protect and enhance these dimensions if it is to be consistent with kingdom ethics. Although we have already spoken extensively to this issue, it may be useful to review what this means theologically.

God created humans as physical beings and spiritual beings; all are called to reverence themselves as a creation of God. It is as sinful to destroy oneself as it is to destroy another. God's loving-kindness in preserving the weak and broken informs our love for others— temples of God's presence. Work must not debilitate and incapacitate the human body. Contracting black lung disease at work is contrary to kingdom ethics. Conditions like this must be corrected; work must be purified so it is not destructive to man's body.

The psychological dimension of man must also be fulfilled in work; each of us as humans should have access to the means for becoming fully human. Work was not a result of the Fall or sin; the Fall only made work more central in man's search for salvation. Work must provide a person with a feeling of accomplishment, of productivity, of creativity. As this transpires for all those working in the kingdom of God, the kingdom itself is being achieved for them. Beyond this, the good and positive sense of self-acceptance and a feeling of worth will radiate out to others who are being brought into this kingdom.

Finally the soul must be nurtured in work. The soul (the spirit which God has given us) will be fed as each person experiences being a part of the "economy of God" and understands that he or she is contributing, in a grand master plan, to a city "whose designer and builder is God." In his book *Man's Quest for Meaning*, Victor Frankl suggests that ultimately the question for mankind is the search for meaning: life must have meaning. God provides us with a meaningful universe and existence; work is central to that process of conveying and receiving meaning.

Work as Experiencing God

We humans are utilitarian; we tend to see things in terms of functions and consequences. But there is a dimension of God which "just is"; where being is all and doing or results are quite secondary. It follows that nothing more can be said about certain aspects of God and His kingdom. So it is with work. Work is a part of experiencing the kingdom of God, as is rest. God said that we should work for six days and rest on the seventh. Thus He instituted a rhythm which defined the nature of His existence and was expressed also in the rhythms of the terrestrial universe: Planetary seasons in which living matter undergoes cycles of growth and decay; and diurnal cycles in which living beings grow, work and rest.

This mutually supportive rhythm of work and cessation of work expresses the very nature of God's creation, including human existence. We cannot say that we work in order to rest. Nor can we say that we rest to work. It would be incorrect to propose that we must work because rest is the goal of existence; but neither can we say the opposite, that we rest in order to achieve the good of work. Each has its own domain, but each is a necessary part of the other; in fact, each supplements and expands the other.[3]

God has created an order in which work and rest are supportive entities for the experience of living. Even if work and rest were not interpreted as helping to build the kingdom of God, they would still extol and explain the nature of human and creaturely life—we work and rest as ends in themselves.

This is a difficult concept for humans to accept and integrate into their living. Because humans tend to be practical and pragmatic, every activity must produce results. They have assumed that everything must be considered in terms of what happens, in terms of result. And although we have affirmed the same principle above with respect to being aware of the consequences of work, there is certainly a sense in which the kingdom of God is not judged by how we *contribute* to it, but whether we *are* the kingdom. In other words, the "achieving society" is *not* in itself the kingdom of God.

The kingdom of God can be understood as that state where God's creation and creatures exist in perfect harmony. Here work and rest could be interpreted as connoting the character of *being and kingdom itself,* not the factors necessary to *achieve* the kingdom. Thus, working and resting *per se,* would be constitutive of the kingdom of God. In metaphorical language, the kingdom would be present and functional when the King, as He moves through the realm, sees His subjects at work or at rest, as appropriate. Whether the barns are being filled then becomes secondary. The kingdom is realized or comes into being when people work and rest to realize or experience the life intended for them by God.

Work as Peoplehood

In chapter 6 we maintained that almost all work is done in organizations. Further, we have said that, in modern society, all work is "collective" in that it implies relationships with all other work. In the kingdom of God work must also be collective, for the laws of that kingdom imply that all of the citizens work for one boss (God) and that all of them work with common purpose, namely, the expression and fulfillment of God's will.

Recognizing that the kingdom of God is only partially realized here on earth, the Christian's work will be oriented to be as noncompetitive as possible. The kingdom citizen will be cooperative in his work, attempting to promote the experience of mutual assistance and concern for others in the work sector, rather than encouraging the "cutthroat" and "him or me" syndrome. The citizen of God's kingdom will avoid work that is destructively competitive; if he is in a position of authority, he will structure the work situation so that it does not become destructive.

Many people reject this approach by saying, "It is not possible to be noncompetitive and survive." As an absolute statement, such a conclusion or position is clearly wrong; often it turns out to be a veiled defense of the free enterprise system. As a relative statement, however, it is fairly correct. There *is* an element of competitiveness in most of human existence, but recognizing that basic reality is a far cry from baptizing the blatant and destructive competition which is present in so much of society today.

Some degree of striving for achievement in the work context is necessary to motivate us to perform at our best level; that factor seems to be inherent in our existence. But Christians are called by Christ to love their neighbors as themselves. We are to feed the hungry, clothe the naked and heal the sick if we want to live in the kingdom.

Thus as employers or employees, we are called to limit and even downgrade the self-interest dimension of work and work instead for the welfare of the community. This does not mean a dismantling of the capitalist free enterprise system any more than it means a dismantling of the socialist system. But it does mean a confrontation of the system in which we live from top to bottom as it were. Instead of simply giving in to the demands of a given system, we hear the call of Christ to serve others and to be compassionate to them; thus, we subordinate the demands of any system—including competition—to the higher purpose of work. What this means specifically in each work position cannot be defined here. Each person must shape his or her application in the workplace.

Work is the tangible means by which human beings recognize their common bond of interdependency, and through which they express their willingness to share in this bond. Western individualism has seriously tested this bond by emphasizing the selfishness of work and by treating it as a commodity which people can buy or sell and from which they can profit. It is not God's will for one person to profit from the use of another person's labor, although he certainly may receive benefit from it. It is this simple but profound conviction that was the basis for Karl Marx's powerful critique of Western Christianity and economics and explains why Marxism has been such a successful movement.

In the kingdom of God, work contributes to Shalom: the condition where everyone will live in peace. Men and women will be at peace with the natural order and thus will have enough to eat. They will have adequate shelter and freedom to move. They will not be restricted by material circumstances so each can realize their full potential as children of God. (See Birch and Rasmussen quote on page 250).

We conclude this section by affirming again the basic conviction that underlies the entire book, namely, that *work is the most fundamental activity of humanity, and that it is the almost total perversion of work that is at the bottom of modern people's alienation from God, from themselves and from their neighbors. Marx was totally correct in his analysis of the predicament: People and their work have become separated and are even in conflict.*

> The more the worker expends himself in work, the more powerful becomes the world of objects which he creates in face of himself, and the poorer he himself becomes in his inner life, the less he belongs to himself (Bottomore, 1956:170).

But man has not been able to save himself. He has not been able to conceive a successful redemptive process or to implement a solution, for his partners are also human. All of his efforts have added up to a bootstrap operation. Mankind needs to recognize that there is hope and help only in God, and only then by submitting to God's will regarding His kingdom, where He is King of Kings, and Lord of Lords.

It is not possible to overemphasize the role of work in human experience. The "splitting off" of work from the rest of human life is the fundamental tragedy. On the fourteenth of September, 1981, the feast of the Triumph of the Cross, Pope John Paul delivered his encyclical *Laborem Exercens*. This document reflects the thesis we have been propounding in this book. In the introduction, section 3 entitled, "The Question of Work, the Key to the Social Question," John Paul says the reason for the encyclical was

> to highlight—perhaps more than has been done before—the fact that human work is a key, probably the essential key, to the whole social question, if we try to see that question really from the point of view of man's good. And if the solution— or rather the gradual solution—of the social question, which keeps coming up and becomes ever more complex, must be sought in the direction of "making life more human," then the key, namely, human work, acquires fundamental and decisive importance (Pope John Paul II:12).

Kingdom Work on Earth

Work is worship of and service to God, but that clear definition still leaves us at a rather abstract level. How can we bring the kingdom of God "down to earth" where we live? We have already provided a sociological perspective on the question. In this section we will derive a "philosophy of work" from the kingdom of God perspective applied to our daily lives and answer the question: What will work look like in the kingdom of God?

In the following remarks, we can only allude to some of the ways in which kingdom ethics can be applied to actual real-life situations. As we seek to practice kingdom ethics, there will be setbacks, but it is our firm conviction that the kingdom can be experienced here and now.

Work as Worship

Many Christian employers have assumed simplistically that if they arrange a fifteen-minute chapel service on company time, that will somehow link work with worship. That may be true for some, but certainly not all. Work as worship cannot be structured by the company or the employer. It is much more the product of an implicit or explicit philosophy of the employers (and employees) about the nature and purpose of the work being performed.

The parable of the three masons at work on a cathedral may be appropriate. If the organization sees work as the first mason saw it, "I am chipping rocks," then work has no worship in it at all. If the corporation or business sees work as the second mason did, "I am earning bread for my family," then worship is possible, but it is indirect: worship as the result of my exertions. But if the viewpoint of the third mason becomes the norm, "I am building a cathedral," then work can become worship in all of its stages from beginning to end.

It is vital that employers and employees work together on this. Only if all participants in the enterprise see work through similar eyes is worship possible. This fact helps to clarify why work as worship may be difficult to achieve today. A monk still can sing and work, but what of the factory workers who cannot hear their own voices over the din of the machines in their work areas?

Work as Service

This theme may be rather easily translated into practical and actual affairs. Most work is service, but first of all, work must be service to the worker. If work does not serve the worker, then it is demonic. Further, work is service to others; if it is not service to others, then it does not fit kingdom goals. Practically speaking, for the citizen in God's kingdom, the crucial matter is being sure to choose work which represents service rather than disservice. This is why certain types of work must be shunned. Working to rob a bank, to deprive a fellow human being or to deceive someone is disservice. But canning tomatoes in a factory in an agricultural community is service. We cannot evade the fact that with all its ills, society still manages to survive because most work is service for the good of all.

Work as Personal Experience

The work experience is intensely personal and therefore subjective. This means, of course, that the authors cannot comment on a reader's particular work setting or on that reader's response to his or her work setting. Nor are the authors able—given the uniqueness of each individual's experience—to make specific suggestions assuredly applicable to every reader's circumstance.

However, throughout Book 2, we do offer the personal testimonies of a number of persons in what may be called *Excursuses* (an excursus is simply a deviation or detour from a main intention). The testimonies we have included in this book about work represent the viewpoints of different persons seen through the grid of their own experience. Each is intensely personal and unique, as they were meant to be. All together they form a collage of work and personal experience—the heading for this brief section.

As we've said, of course, each reader's experience is unique— not improbably, quite beyond the range of any of the work settings or experiences included in the excursuses or personal testimonies.

So, in some sense, the reader must write his own excursus to add appropriate dimension to the individual work experience.

One key element which must be emphasized as a clue to the very personal nature of the work experience is the spirit of an individual. How does the work experience affect who the person really is and who he or she is becoming? Some may feel that external factors in the work setting seem often to be irrelevant to the life of the spirit. But that is not quite true. The spirit is resilient and, with adequate resources, can grow, even where work settings are adverse. However, the spirit of a worker can usually thrive and flourish best when working conditions are conducive to making that person feel like a free person with the capability to choose; happy with a sense of contentment, well-being and fulfillment; productive, that is, making an obvious contribution to the common goal. An individual must be able to sense some relation between his or her work and his or her spirit, or that person dies.

Work as Experiencing God

How can a person, working in a kitchen, or in a mail room or in a laboratory experience God? It is possible, but only if that person is consciously living in the kingdom of God. The person who is aware of the fact that the two realms are intersecting (the present world and the coming kingdom of God) can and will experience God at work. Practically, this means that the working conditions, the interpersonal relations, and the conditions of participation by the powerful and the subordinate are structured so as to allow equal involvement. Fair and adequate wages, consistent work rules, and honest sharing of information are simple but bedrock prerequisites for experiencing God at work.

Work as Peoplehood

There are several specific ways in which the peoplehood aspects of work can be fostered. One such is profit sharing (PS). This option is relevant whether one is an employer or employee. Profit sharing is one expression of the collective nature of work in the kingdom of God because each person in the organization is thereby included in receiving the rewards of the labor performed— not always in a precise or fully equitable way, but in some form.

Profit sharing has been disparaged and resisted by many in the management and labor camps as being unworkable, undesirable and utopian. The facts would seem to indicate that just the opposite is true. It is workable in almost all cases, is desirable for both managers and employees and is definitely not utopian. Of course, there are problems with PS and some programs have failed. Profit sharing works better in some types of industries and businesses than in others; furthermore, the size of a firm is a variable that affects success. But the central issue is not whether this course of action presents difficulties but whether it is right and whether the results are worth the effort.

Evidence is accumulating that profit sharing is definitely worth the effort. Companies that have tried it in *good faith* have found it very helpful in terms of increased quantity and quality of work performed, to say nothing of employee satisfaction. The positive evidence is not universal and many improvements can be made; but from present indications, profit sharing does lead to distinct and measurable advantages. One survey indicated that 89 percent of the companies reported that their profit sharing plans "improved the morale, teamwork, and cooperation" of the employees (Byler:4). In the same survey, 81 percent of the companies reported an increase in productive efficiency.[4]

A word yet about its *rightness:* profit sharing focuses on the humane dimensions of work in an organization because it (1) emphasizes the fact that both employer and employee are working for the same objectives; (2) implies strongly that the success of the cooperation works to the benefit of each person, rather than suggesting that the gains of one party are premised on the losses of another; (3) forces employers and employees to work together in planning work, in the organizing and coordination of effort, and in evaluating the increasing effectiveness of the organization.

It seems almost impossible, logically, to argue that an employee who has "made it happen" should not be allowed to share in the results of his or her own effort. There are many problems in deciding what is equitable, but that ultimately is a technical question answered best in each particular setting. Modern capitalism (if there is such a thing) is clearly not premised on the proposition that all employees should get their fair share of the profits. But then, contrary to what some would have us believe, capitalism and the kingdom of God are certainly not simply different terms for the same entity!

Another program, which is more complex and which has possibly even more both positive and negative consequences is what is commonly called an Employee Stock Option Plan (ESOP). Although there are many variations, the essence of this plan is that employees are given stock as a part of their remuneration for employment at the company. From the viewpoint of the original stockholders, this is a negative plan since it dilutes the value of their stock (money is paid for new stock, which then becomes part of the pool of stock over which profits must be distributed).

From an employee's standpoint, however, ESOPs foster the cooperative relationship even more than profit sharing, since they allow the employee to feel that he is working for "his" company.

That is, his ownership in the company changes his orientation toward the management, toward the company, toward his fellow employees and toward the work. The traditional antagonisms do not apply in the same degree, since employees are also owners and therefore become increasingly unable to polarize their attitudes.

There are many technical and other problems with ESOPs, but such plans do bring the employees into the ownership of the company, and allow them to participate in future earnings of the company. According to some proponents of the program, such plans provide possibly the only way in which the traditional concentration of capital in the "ownership class" can be opened up to allow the common man to have "access to more fair and effective participation in corporate ownership among middle income and low income American workers" (p. 11 ESOPs). Of course, the arguments for PS (Profit Sharing) presented above apply to ESOPs as well, with the added cooperative impulse that comes from changing, over time, the relative status of being a nonparticipant in the ownership of production to becoming, at the least, a minimum participant.

The collective nature of work will not, of course, be fully achieved by either PS or ESOP plans, but they do provide some tangible tools through which to work toward kingdom working conditions. There are many other ways in which work can be made more cooperative but these usually tend to be determined by the specific situation. Structurally, family-owned enterprises or cooperatives, partnerships, and certain other types of organizations do provide amenable structures to foster cooperation and mutuality.[5]

Another major way in which work can be made more cooperative is to consciously structure work in ways which decrease competition. As we have noted earlier, a certain amount of structural competition is inherent in our human existence (for example, the differential reward for disparate work performed creates a certain amount of competition). But it is the challenge of Christians to work at changing the organizations that create competition so that the experience does not become destructive and counterproductive.

The "publish or perish" syndrome of universities is a case in point, illustrating structurally induced competition. It is a complex issue. A certain amount of competition is clearly functional, positive and healthy for college professors. But the best and healthiest resolution of this problem in universities is an ongoing challenge. The same problem applies to the numerous work settings where men and women are related to each other, for good or ill: to themselves and to their peers, to their superiors or to their subordinates.

15

Choosing Work Responsibly

It is not doing the thing which we like to do, but liking to do
the thing which we have to do, that makes life blessed.
(Johann Wolfgang von Goethe)

Man hath his daily work of body or mind appointed,
which declares his Dignitie,
and the regard of Heav'n on all his waies;
While other Animals inactive range.
And of thir doings God takes no account.
Tomorrow ere fresh Morning streak the East
With first approach of light, we must be risn'n
And at our pleasant labour, to reform
Yon flourie Arbors, yonder Allies green.
(John Milton, *Paradise Lost*:166)

We have looked at work from many points of view. In one
sense, all of them point to the past: work as it has been experienced
during decades or centuries; the writings of scholars and others
about work; our analyses of work and the insights some have
offered through writing; even our own involvements with work
positions must, perforce, refer to years gone by—everything has
had a historical flavor. In short, in this book we have considered
how work *has affected* humanity.

But, at every point in our lives, there is also the future: that which is to come. Perhaps it was this underlying orientation toward the future that provided the initial challenge to bring our thoughts together in a form that could be shared more widely. Certainly, the fact that we will always be working and facing the implications of our work and of work in our society has added impetus to the motivation and has provided a significant focus.

Work is part of the social structure which makes us who we are. Work is also the process through which, as individuals, we contribute to our society and its development. So work, society and individuals are tightly bound together; they cannot be separated. The future of one is related to the future of the others.

> The future of work is inherently rooted in the future of
> our society . . . our present culture—the current way of life
> as a whole—is now in transition toward a new cultural
> form, the exact shape of which is still unsettled.[1]

Of course, the future of work is signally important for each of us. And it is precisely because the current way of life is in transition—including long-held views and patterns of work—that many workers are ridden with anxiety, and questions about work and the future of work as we know it abound. If, as we have proposed, we are correct in stating that alienation from work is humankind's deepest problem—and we are not the first to claim this—then the redemption of work is the central problem of the human predicament as a whole and must be related to human salvation.

Simply stated, the thesis of this final chapter is that the Christian gospel constitutes a direct challenge to the so-called "curse" of work and that, in fact, the gospel presents us with a calling to make work part of our salvation, or part of what makes life good and whole. In contrast to certain readings of Paul's writings by persons such as Luther, we maintain that faith and works cannot be separated but rather need to be combined in salvation. Faith without works alienates rather than liberates![2]

According to the Judeo-Christian account of creation, God both worked and instituted work in His acts of creation. His work in creation must be seen in relation to rest as well—the seventh day. Further, His institution of work for His creatures points directly to their responsibility: to exercise dominion. However, God has not ceased working. He continues to work through Christ and the Holy Spirit, through Christian believers and through various other elements in his whole world. He ordained that all creatures, in order to exist, must expend energy—work. Although we know little detail about the work human beings needed to do before the Fall, after the Fall God did command that men should work—"By the sweat of your brow you will eat your food" (Gen. 3:19).

There is no evidence that the fall of mankind introduced the curse of work. On this point, J. H. Oldham writes, "As a result of the fall and of man's sinfulness work ceases to be the free and joyous cooperation of man with God and bears the stamp of hard necessity and burdensome toil. 'In the sweat of thy face shalt thou eat bread.' But this does not alter the fact that work is a mode of man's earthly existence decreed by God" (p. 49). *Work is the means by which God continues to achieve His purpose in all of creation; and it is the means by which human society and human existence are secured. Work is the eternal and comprehensive channel by which creation exists and through which it continues.*

Not all work, but certainly God-ordained work is a way to the salvation of humankind, for as the apostle Paul writes in Philippians 2:12 we are to "work out [our] salvation with fear and trembling." Jesus said, "I must do the work of him who sent me. Night is coming, when no one can work" (John 9:4). By no stretch of the imagination can these statements be limited to "spiritual work," for there can be no spiritual work without energy being expended or without other aspects of work being brought into play. For example, even a verbal witness to God's love takes physical energy and may therefore appropriately be called work.

A Christian understanding of God's will would suggest therefore that work is involved essentially in the salvation of the human race, of the human institutions, and of the created order. This means that we must strive to understand the role that work, jobs, occupations, careers, vocations and callings play in the salvation of the society and its members. This means also that we must participate in a recovery of the Christian role of work in salvation. How can this be done?

A Recovery of the Christian Role of Work in Salvation

1. We must help to free work from its captivity by the job. As Christians, we must return work to its central position in the Christian community where it will serve the needs of the individual, family, congregation (a new variation of the tribe), and the larger society.

For the Christian, work is that expending of energy which serves the well-being of one's self, one's family, one's church or congregation and the world community. A Christian recovery and "re-sacralization" of work will therefore clash head-on with the iron shackles of "job-ism"—a focus on the job which separates individuals from families, families from congregations and all three from their obligations to the larger community.

2. We must challenge the destructive tyranny of the job, career, vocation and calling. In much of contemporary society the job has become the corruption of work. "A major theme of this book is that alienation is a statistically normal condition of modern society" (Rinehart:i).

The tyranny of the job—as it is expressed in the demands for adequate preparation and planning, requisite education and socialization, nurturing the contacts needed to "land that important first job," maintaining the interpersonal relations and "payoffs" needed to assure the planned course of promotion, making sure one does not land in a dead-end position, and above all making sure that the "higher-ups" and one's own colleagues will not be offended—can become in total an incredibly harrowing experience.

Since the Christian has a redeemed concept of work and believes that he experiences some part of his redemption through work, he will not be intimidated by the requirements of the job sequence, the planning for a career, and the fulfillment of all the requirements to find a successful and rewarding vocation. He will work at what the church community considers redemptive in terms of his own psychological and spiritual health, and that of his family. Furthermore, he will consider work as an important aspect of his life in the Christian community, and he will conceive of himself as "working the work of *Him* who sent him."

3. We must be found doing the will of God through promoting God's plan for creation. The *Christian calling* will be the criteria by which each particular job, profession or career is judged. Just as the monastic, communal, and utopian movements have subordinated secular job demands to the Christian vocation, so Christians today must allow the considerations of family, congregation, and community to determine whether one takes a job, and if so, which one and why.

The Christian calling is to serve God and fellow human beings; work is the means through which one carries out that purpose. The Christian calling involves doing the kind of work Jesus did while he, lived on earth.

> The Spirit of the Lord is on me,
> because he has anointed me
> to preach good news to the poor.
> He hath sent me to proclaim freedom for the prisoners
> and recovery of sight for the blind,
> to release the oppressed, to proclaim the year of the
> Lord's favor.
>
> (Luke 4:18)

If our jobs, vocations and careers prohibit or deflect the use of our energies so we do not reflect Jesus' calling, we are in danger of failing to fulfill God's plan. If our own work in any way contributes to the alienation which Marx and others have described and which millions have experienced, then that job is corrupting the very work which should be part of the hope of redemption for humankind.

4. Work must become personalized and debureaucratized. Christian work cannot be inhibited or truncated with distinctions based on tenure, status professionalism or other false barriers.[3] Nor can it be controlled by arbitrary, bureaucratic restrictions which inhibit the free and spontaneous interrelationships between individuals.

The Christian must select work which will allow human reconciliation and salvation to take place. The demonic aspects of professionalism and depersonalized bureaucracies will not simply disappear by themselves, for they serve the selfish individual who enhances himself at the expense of the collective. But for the Christian, who is concerned about the kingdom of heaven, there is no possibility that he can serve in a job that depersonalizes others.

5. Christian work must be made meaningful and significant in its own right. How can a meaningless job allow a person to do the "work of him who sent me"?[4] In this context, Luther's concept of the vocation as calling was correct. But he made the fatal mistake of assuming that any job became meaningful and purposeful, since one worked in a job for the glory of God. That is true, but more than that—and to truly bring glory to God—work must have meaning and make a contribution on the basis of factors which are derived from all of the biblical teachings.

Unfortunately, the "humanization of work" movement has a bitter edge, for if work is not considered meaningful by the person who is to do it, then no amount of engineering can make it otherwise.[5] No amount of clever rationalization should be allowed to convince us that there is little difference in the work done in various jobs, and that what we ultimately do with the consequences of work has no relevance.

6. Preparation for *work* must overshadow preparation for the *job*. In secular society today, preparation for life work is almost entirely focused on preparing for the job. Choosing a college curriculum, attending college and graduate schools, and the choice of a career itself—all are rather heavily premised on the promise each offers for the achievement of more pay or more upward mobility. To suggest that colleges and universities have become midwives for job placement is not an overstatement! Almost invariably, a college education is evaluated on how effectively it assists one in landing a good job and how helpful it will be for promotions.

This is ironic since it is now well-known that the training for many, if not most, jobs can actually be attained on the job, and that a college degree is more of a screen or an arbitrary requirement for employment than anything else. Thus a college degree is now beginning to serve the same function that a high school diploma did some years ago.

From a Christian perspective, therefore, university training should go far beyond mere specific and technical training for a job; it should become relevant for the person's work and planned to provide the basic information, values, and attitudes needed to develop the most effective Christian calling. It is the whole Gestalt of values—that and how they affect one's total approach to the world, that makes an education useful for Christian work.

7. For the Christian, work must be removed from its monetary enslavement. Work has become monetized by the process of the division of labor and measurement in dollars per hour. Women who are protesting the enslavement of their drudgery in the home, in desperation have used the monetary measurement as a lever to achieve some type of recognition for their work. Predictably, in the highest but a most troubling form of one-upmanship, men have countered the claims of women by saying that a housewife or mother's work is too valuable to be monetized.

Selling one's labor, as Marx stressed so strongly, is a dehumanizing fact of life. Considerations of the value of the work to the worker, the conditions of the work with respect to interpersonal relations, and the consequences of the work for the good of society tend to be missing almost totally from the contemporary work scene.

A Christian view of work will not only subordinate the job, occupation, profession and career dimensions to the Christian calling; it will separate the unnatural emphasis on the monetary dimension and in its place emphasize the intrinsic contribution that the work performed in the job makes to the purposes of the kingdom of God. "Well done, good and faithful servant" (Matt. 25:21) should be the ultimate criterion and reward for work.

We have indicated what a Christian redemption of work will look like. But, someone may ask, "Who will pay the rent?" How is any of what has been said possible, given our great dependence on the institutionalized society? The proposals that follow provide at least part of the answer.

The Practical Implications of a Christian Recovery of Work

Various Christian theologians, among them the great Thomas Aquinas, have attempted to provide a Christian perspective on work. Monasteries and other Christian movements, such as the Catholic Worker movement and the Christian Labour Association of Canada, have sought to translate some of these ideas into an active redemption of work. But a much larger revolution must take place if we are to experience our own salvation and aid in the redemption of our society through work. As intimated by Gaskin, it will not happen by attacking Exxon head-on; rather it will come by a quiet but determined change in lifestyle in Christian communities around the globe.[6] What might this mean?

1. Changing the way we choose jobs

We begin the change in lifestyles by deciding to *choose work,* not jobs, professions or careers. If we believe that relieving human hunger is a part of God's kingdom, then we can legitimately choose to work in that arena. Such a choice *may* well result in a *job* in food production and distribution, but the job should not deter our commitment to relieve hunger; instead it should be a vehicle. It *may* require a university degree, *but the education pursued will not be designed for a job—it will be focused on the substantive knowledge necessary to pursue the work of relieving hunger.*

We will choose, secondly, to work in those positions which serve humanity rather than our own advancement or personal advantage. We will choose a job that downgrades the tendency to become a link in the chain of upward mobility, advancement and competitive struggle.

Lastly, we will choose work which is meaningful and purposeful in its own right. A job will be chosen because it provides the context for work that will serve the ends of the kingdom of God. This means that some types of menial work could be more important than certain prestigious jobs.

2. Changing the way we prepare for work

In preparing for Christian work, the first objective is to find out who we are and what contribution we can make in God's economy. The best training for Christian work is not the technical expertise that is offered today in the majority of our institutes of technology—often called universities; rather the training that asks: "Who is man?" "Why does he exist?" "What is God's purpose for him on earth?" This training is not only religious, but also philosophical, ethical and aesthetic.

Secondly, the preparation for Christian work will assess our strengths and weaknesses, particularly what unique assets we possess that will make a difference in God's kingdom. Such preparation will focus on discovering how we influence each other, and what gifts we have so we can work synergystically to achieve God's will in the world.

Finally, preparing for work will also involve an assessment of the relative effectiveness of differing types of jobs in achieving the goals of the kingdom of God. Not all work is equally in line with kingdom objectives. Hence many jobs, professions and careers seen to be minimally useful will be excluded automatically from even the briefest consideration. *"What work, and by implication what jobs make what difference in the world?"* is probably the most important question we can ask as we prepare ourselves for life.

3. Changing work places (jobs, careers and vocations) when the conditions indicate it

Changing jobs, professions, careers, vocations at any point in a life cycle may not indicate failure, incompetence or lack of nerve. Instead, such a change may reflect maturity and wisdom more than anything else. It is entirely possible that work which at one time could be considered useful in the kingdom of God would be less helpful later on. Teaching English to natives in Africa probably was important when missionaries first arrived, but today it may be more important to teach them how to raise food. Building highways may have been an urgent task in North America in times past; now more urgent and useful work could well be the dismantling of many of these roads and the building of mass transit systems.

All this means that the Christian will be flexible in a job, career or profession. The Christian worker will be ready to move, to change locations, positions, and even career tracks if the conditions indicate. The Christian will vote with his feet and hands, often against the majority, for the Christian is working in a city "whose architect is God."

4. Creating work and work positions

There have been historical epochs when Christianity may have made a profound contribution to human society, as for example in the eradication of human slavery in certain parts of the world. But, as has been indicated, the most pervasive revolution must come in the role of work for the Christian; for it is our firm conviction that, in this arena, the Christian church has become more of an accommodating and adapting movement than a challenging, creative and innovating movement. The Christian church must recover its voice with reference to work.

The most significant way, therefore, and possibly the most accessible means available for us to revolutionize the world is to change the nature of work. Because of this, the Christian will not subjectively and selfishly decide which workplace he is going to select from the vast array of jobs, careers, and professions available. Rather, the question will be asked, "What needs to be done, and how will this be achieved in the best way?" In other words, change will be brought about in the world by changing the nature of jobs so that kingdom work gets done.

But, you ask, how can we break down the "creeping institutionalism" that is absorbing almost all of the freedom to create Christian work for individuals? The central issue is security. The basic reason that "creeping institutionalism" has such a strong hold on all of us is that the institutional structures control the allocation of material remuneration and rewards. If we were not so dependent upon our employing institutions for our monthly checks, we would be able to choose to do almost anything, but we are caught!

The security that jobs and professions offer is a fateful disease for the Christian who is seriously concerned about being innovative regarding work in the kingdom. *So it is security, not the lack of opportunity for innovative action, that lies at the heart of the matter.* Here is where we must change the way work and jobs relate to remuneration. Only when we Christians are ready to risk losing security and "suffer" the shame of dependency on others, will we be able to innovate and change the nature of work so that it becomes kingdom work.

This problem can be solved more easily than we think. My grandfather, though a farmer, spent most of his time as a minister and elder shepherding the flock. His sons helped with the farm work; when the work load grew too heavy, the families in his congregation chipped in to help with the chores, planting, plowing or harvesting. Earlier, we pointed out that work has become so separated from the family and community that it *appears* as if a person would lose his right to live if he changed the job situation even slightly. Not at all.

There are almost unlimited ways in which we can return to the *Gemeinschaft* type of situation so that we can free the work from our need to have remuneration. Missionaries for centuries have not paid the rent, yet they have done the work of the church. I know of a partnership of doctors where one of them is able to take a sabbatical every three or four years to serve in a needy part of the world while his rent and salary are being paid. The simple truth is, work can be separated from its monetary prison only by collective action. As Christians return to a collective *Gemeinschaft*-like structure, they can be freed to work for the kingdom of God and still have their needs met.

Can we have our cake and eat it too? We can, if we think hard enough and work at it hard enough. There are untold expressions of the beginnings of redeeming work breaking through all around us. Retiring early to serve on a voluntary basis in some needy areas such as institutions for the mentally retarded is one such example.

Arranging a sabbatical or taking a leave from normal employment duties to work in community development or a service program is another. Christian communities that are freeing some of their members to do kingdom work is one of the most promising present examples of a fuller redemption of work.[7]

We will be redeemed by our work when we are doing what we want to do, and when we know that what we want to do is the work God says we must do. Alienation from work will be solved the day it is no longer fully determined by our need to earn daily bread, the day we feel that the work is what we want to and must do.

Additionally, the Christian revolution in work will come as we choose to change our lifestyles. As we live more simply, we will be less dependent upon the tyrannical job. As we have fewer financial demands and obligations, we will be freer to work at the things that really make a difference. From a Christian work perspective, it is a form of blasphemy for a married couple to lock themselves into a lifetime of struggle and stress to pay for an oversized, overpriced home in suburbia, the two cars needed so each spouse can drive to work, and the budget required for the entertaining and travel necessary to achieve middle-class status! How can this be said to be building the kingdom of God?[8]

We can also begin to revolutionize the larger world of work as we change our own vision and hopes. This will mean not conforming to this world's values, but being "transformed by the renewal" of our minds. Our work will save us and the world if we see it as our response to Christ's call. In his letter to the Philippians written from prison, Paul admonishes his fellow Christians to remember Christ who, though son of God, emptied himself, and became a servant, to the point of death on the cross. Paul then encourages his readers to "Work out your salvation with fear and trembling, for it is God who works in you to will and to act according to his good purpose" (Phil. 2:12–13).

Human work is the way we determine our destiny. It is the activity which shapes our experience and our objectives. Though this is a Christian conceptualization the Christian tradition is still not facing squarely the import of this fact. The answer to godless materialism and communism is not guns and warfare, but redeeming the nature of work so, in turn, a proper understanding of God's purpose for work can help to redeem us. The Christian answer to alienation from work lies not in a sidetracking of the problem through pietistic revival and spiritual opiates, but requires an acceptance of the fact that *I will become what I do*. So the work I do becomes a deeply religious event, for it can either destroy me or redeem me.

In the object which he contemplates, therefore, man becomes acquainted with himself; consciousness of the objective is the self-consciousness of man (Feuerbach:5).

And God said, "By the sweat of your brow you shall eat bread."

But Satan winked and said, "Work is not good."

So he and man invented things to get out of work—like a hoe and a whip.

Thus work became the curse—haunting man.

And Satan had the last word, for Christians agreed . . . "Work closes the gates to heaven."

But the lonely monk's whisper still echoes, "To work is to pray."

—UAB

BOOK FOUR
TO WORK AND SING

16

An Ode to Work

> He, who, having written a bad poem, knows it to be bad, is in his intelligence, and therefore in his nature, not so limited as he who, having written a bad poem, admires it and thinks it good (Feuerbach:8).

> *Ode: 1. In ancient usage, a lyric poem intended to be sung or chanted; in modern usage, any lyric of lofty tone dealing progressively with one dignified theme.*

A poet at work . . .

During the vision transport, all the things that are
Shine with their own inner radiance, their own person.
The colors are suddenly of a different order,
A different brilliant, poignant, a different kind of time ticks.
The sounds each thing that is
Speaks, these sounds articulate themselves as personal voices,
The squeaking of wheels, the leaves' rustle.
How shall I sum it up in a simple,
Sensible way? For I am certain each person experiences
This altered perception frequently.
If it at times increases for me in duration and intensity

Note: This chapter is a collage of letters and poetry by Nick Lindsay.

Until I am knocked down in an ordinary heap on the
    ground, and flow
Into the bright-noon darkness,
Evidently my mystic soul is practical
Enough to take care not to do
Her push-ups and gaudy exercises while I'm on a high
Scaffold, or mincing my way around a twenty-three
    thousand volt
Power line.
This vision transport sometimes speaks words, sometimes
Reveals the angelic host ministering to us, moving vaguely
    in their pastel
Minuet. Usually it contents itself with the spirit-
    intensification
Of all perceptions of the ordinarily visible world
Whenever it comes, it underlines, reveals, and redeems,
Knits into singleness the world, my thought, my "self,"
Redeems the usual complaining voice in this head, the
    justified
Paranoia of my habitual biting of the hand that's
Poisoning me.

(The Vision Transport)

*   *   *

Dear Nick . . . One thing is great news! Zondervan has
accepted our manuscript for publication . . . we are free to include
further what we think is useful and helpful.

Now to your contribution: We think some of the poems you
sent may be part of your contribution. Some prose also on how
poetry, work, faith and life fit together and give you solace would
be wonderful. But how to make it most communicative is a
problem. Your imagery is so powerful and explosive . . . Well, we
will have to get together to see how we can congeal what you have
already sent or ask you to anneal your fertile imagination into
something the more mortal among us can understand.

Sincere greetings,
Cal and Urie

P.S. The editor likes the idea of including your work in our
book. But he wants us also to ask you the big question! *What does it
mean?*

*   *   *

Dear Cal and Urie,
You've given me a tough assignment—or your editor has. I
remember taking a volume to be printed—and the printer, in

refusing to print it, said, " . . . but what does it mean? I understand English, but not that . . . and he sought about in the bins of his mind like groping for potatoes in the dark. *lingo.* Not that *lingo.*
   Alas, I am a no-good writer of straight sentences, so I am told . . . I have already written eleven pages—impossible stuff. Because I'm furious! . . . *What does it mean?* That destructive question hacks at me—a wily antagonist determined to destroy me by treachery rather than joining in the quest of our human delight . . .
   . . . what is the meaning? do you understand? do you want to understand? Here is a sermon, to help you understand! A doggy sermon:

> Let all things praise Him, praise their Creator.
> How does a weed praise God?
> By being as weedy as it can.
> How does a dog praise God?
> By being as doggy as he can.
> How does a man praise God?
> By being as human as he can.
>
> In what does this humanness consist?
> In loving and knowing.
>   Amen.

With best love to you, to all. Nick.
(I will keep trying. Write me back—maybe there's a way.)

*   *   *

Dear Cal and Urie,
Again . . .
   . . . your editor is asking a damaging question: do you understand? Cal, you know Freda. Do you understand her? No! Your relationship to her is described in other and more fruitful terms. . . .
   The literature on left-brain/right-brain specialization almost always must touch on the damaging or quenching relationship between *knowing* and *understanding.* (Left-brain "understanding" quenches right-brain "loving and knowing.") 1. A tennis match of champions—one contestant speaks to the other: "Say, Jack, you really have an unbeatable backhand—tell me just how you keep the right angle between your elbow and the racket?" If Jack is fool enough to turn from his masterly *knowing* to the *understanding* mode, his game is ruined and his wily antagonist with the damaging question wins. 2. An experiment in the teaching of reading, the subjects ranged from 6 to 60 years of age; none knew

how to read. Their learning ability was tested before, during and after they were taught to read. Their ability to learn and know was much dimmed by the analytical override of the reading skill or way of thinking as it took control of their minds. The learning and knowing was of the relationships among objects, as I recall, using things scattered on a table top, a landscape, finding your way back home when you have only once gone a circuitous route. The left-brain left them lost. That question "Do you understand?" is a highwayman that willingly will rob a blind tumbleturd and put him on the wrong way home.

. . . yet . . .

All is well; all will indeed be well.

And with all the grief this question causes us, and much more, yet all manner of rejoicing and happiness tumbles over us—chunks and blocks—we are tumbled in the gross tide of grace . . .

God keep you. Nick.

*   *   *

Dear Cal and Urie,

K. Maybe this touches some of the bases. . . .

The labor of poet is the same as that of carpenter or husband, lover, father and citizen—to articulate praise. It is a matter of discerning the thread of beauty, excellence and of *the holy* as it weaves through. The carpenter's task is to bring the house owner's vision into harmony with the architect's and with that pulse which I know through the study of engineering books and my own sense of wholeness—sense as when I dance with her in close linkage to the music, our gesture is praise, the body's center is the course of authority in house building, in boat building, as in dance.

The sense of wholeness is the same as the certainty of balance and transfer of load when I carry a box of nails for us, for me and my crew. The weight of all those individual hot-dipped galvanized sixteen-penny nails—

(those nails—each is a complete individual, no two alike, for they have been etched by acid, plunged into a searing bath of molten zinc; it's an ordeal by burning—o it's not easy to be a nail, but is worth all the honor and high regard we bestow)—

those nails gathered into their box are like children, like an auditorium full of children, each with a voice, hands, hope, a destiny. Some are stuck together in pairs like young lovers in tight embrace, soldered together by their zinc coatings as are lovers by their naked bodies' grace. I know excellent carpenters who feel it inappropriate to break that bond as if they heard a priest's voice, "Whom God hath so joined, let no man put asunder."

The first strength is the membrane of cardboard around the nails, its yellow plastic bands surrounding in an X. The nails are X-rated, as all the world is. It is charged with erotic beauty and delight when we but have the vitality and discipline to discern it. The sky bent over the earth ages ago, embraced her in the midst of her singing, begot on her time, place, and being, her first-born who show forth the beauty of their progenitors. As we all do also, being a product of that same union.

The nails are banded in their X box, I have it on my shoulder, making sure the fifty pounds aren't resting on my own strength, but are supported, propped on my moving skeleton and sinews to transfer the weight through my toes onto the board here, the block there, into the earth. She is full of supple grace and will withstand these loads which come to her through toes, onto ladder rungs, into herself. Be careful, step on the rung where it joins the side; the ladder's old. As I am myself. If you place your weight onto the middle of the rung, the wood might break. It's oak, yes, but no more than an inch and a quarter square. It's not easy to be a ladder, no. It is a graceful thing though, depending on the theological grace of undeserved bounty, on the earth-grown grace of oak and fir, on the mercy of us who step there, on all the undeserved gifts of ladderhood.

Each rung is reinforced by a steel rod—steel with a tensile strength of twenty thousand pounds per square inch. This rod is so threaded, so washered in its attachment to the fir rails and oak rung as to accommodate and augment the eighteen hundred pounds per square inch extreme fiber stress, the strength of oak.

"What?" you will say, "How does this mathematics obtrude itself into the discourse of a romantic populist poet carpenter?"

Yes, this mathematics, the book-learning of it, the condensed history of it is as essential to my crafty work as the condensed history of tribal myths and the ancient power stories. $M = SI$ over C. The bending moment available as beam strength, the bending moment of a ladder rung of rectangular cross section when the moment of inertia of cross section, the fiber stress, and the depth are known, this is an essential part of the affirmation. The way to know the equation is to know that it says *music:* $M = SI$ over C. Yes, and it's fine music, the engineering interbred with the dear, powerful trees and smelted steel which come from earth. I know my book, study my book in order to be a worthy engineer.

It's not this "I" that does it, but grace moving through, as the weight of a box of nails is transferred through to the dear earth. This "I" is a fiction, does not exist, is a box without dimension, empty in itself, but a fit receptacle for some burdens (not burdens, no, rather radiances, have we but the discerning eye, the ear filled with the desire of hearing).

The book, the sharp, accurate mathematics of history–how beams broke, how kings and governments broke under given stresses, the known limits of language—this is a necessary part of a carpenter's kit, a poet's box of tools.

The ladder's steel rod is threaded through the feminine body of fir and oak as my body is welcomed by hers, and this strength of mine is threaded through and into her own to beget and nurture and carry a corner of the graceful, the grace-filled world—children, grandchildren. Just as this ladder bears upward the weight of men and nails.

Climb the ladder, get out on the roof—it's slippery—the grit off the shingles will roll like ball bearings under-foot and off you zip.

Henry, Jimmy—there are strong hands to catch the nails, the man, pull me up. It's not strength I work with as carpenter, as poet, no. *I'm a transfer point and the real strength is elsewhere.*

I break bones regularly, ribs, a leg now and then. Or cut off pieces—ear, finger, toe. It's called occupational hazard and comes with the territory. Most carpenters depart this life as the result of a fall. There's no defeat in this: to die is a worthwhile act, another transfer of powers and weights in the way of moving—I move as a man in the world—Amen.

The poet's task is three-fold:
To defend the earth,
To terrify tyrants,
To bring courage to the oppressed.

All the work is whole—and sometimes this work is idleness, dreaming, being attentive to the visions and voices of that world which coexists with our own, which interpenetrates our own, the spirit world of the ancestors, the holy beings—yes, I hear their voices, yes, I see them moving here among us, no, it is no metaphor but as real as the rest of this created world.

And sometimes the work includes answering idiot questions by harried editors—What? It's not easy to be an editor. If I break bones and spray the surrounding lumber with blood, I must count on this being included in each working gesture; the editor, he breaks heart and hope against the hard corners of public whim and writer's inadquacies: it's not easy to be an editor.

All the work is whole, is holy, is a sabbath occasion: to terrify tyrants, to bring courage to the oppressed, to defend the earth.
Amen.

*   *   *

The Hounds

I am terrified, I am very much afraid. All who live
As I do are afraid, cranking up their battered Chevy trucks
To get to work, they struggle
Like a strong swimmer against tide and wave, against a tide
of terror—the day breaking loose—they are high heroes and
      mighty
in Manliness.

The day has broken loose—a beast
Of boat, heavy, pounding against pilings
That squirt salty creosote,
Spit shards of crushed shell at each collision—
Broken her moorings and what's to do? We must grab
Each one a line, each his line, run with raw speed to take
      two
Turns of line around pilings, oak trees, buildings—any
Thing—wrap each his line around our dear
Bodies, plant feet and hold
Fast—fast-jerked over
of us are jerked over
Board—o—the heavy hull of day careens down through
      dark
Waters—away, away
Pursued away, the waves pursue her, a pack of hounds, a
      snarl
Of teeth—oh day
Is breaking loose.

Breaking loose: this day is
A runner and is breaking
Away from the pack, is a bright, new athlete among
      Tuesdays
And Thursdays, showing her
Heels to the pack—now singled out, she, alone,
The years—a pack of hounds
Ravening, the years are called
Death baying and ravening, fiery eyes, snarl of teeth
Teeth that snap at her swift heels—oh I
Feel for her, fear for her, the sprinting dancer, fear for
Us all. I am terrified at the breaking loose of the day.

The Breaking Loose of the Day

Hot in the east, the beast, dawn—a snarl of grey;
It's a junk yard dog, ravening and jerking at his chain;

I am terrified at the breaking loose of the day.

This dawn is un-special, ordinary every way—
The tools, the lethargic crew with our yesterdays' wounds,
    and
Hot in the east, the beast, dawn—a snarl of grey.

The boat of beginning, in mad agony tears her mooring
    lines,
                                    spins wild away
In the brutal tide, hot wind, hot storm:
I am terrified at the breaking loose of the day.

Steel beams here: set them by noon; the cable's frayed;
The ten-ton crane booms up with black smoke.
                            Hydraulics hiss and whine;
Hot in the east, the beast, dawn—a snarl of grey.

In peril, Laura and Sue at home in your pregnant labors,
                            the very same way
In peril—breath, life, hope, blood and bone:
I am terrified at the breaking loose of the day.

And she, her hair a darling snarl, presses against
                        then sends me away
Where the man will steal our wage with his fountain pen.
Hot in the east, the beast, dawn—a snarl of grey:
I am terrified at the breaking loose of the day.

*   *   *

Taming the Day

The day.
Do I not know this day?
This day is a horse I have raised from a filly,
Gentled her since she was small and I could carry her in my
    arms,
A squealing bale of
Hay, bale of kicking high spirits.
These hands tamed the mare that bore her, the stallion that
    begot her, she
Is large, she is known to me, she weighs a thousand
    pounds.

Now in the old age of my days
As I lead her in to pasture,
I wrap her lines on this left hand to open the gate. But
    what
Has spooked her to jerk? Jump

Back—o—my hand is gone.
The fingers wrapped in her lines snatched
Away in scraps, bits
Of man scattered on the ground.
The lines of this day are hard, steel whips.
What man can tame the day?

I am going back to church by now
When the day is called "sabbath,"
But I keep that left hand propped on a cushion.
What man can tame the day?

Sabbath, What is That?
Tell That.
Tell Me.

All right. I know, my hand knows
It as a time, a place, a posture, a repose
That includes both me and my work. We both are free
Though the manacles of being hold us fast.
  The hand guides the sharp plane blade;
  The wood grain guides the hand.

Though, yes, chrome tools and many saints fast
Celibate, there is a love talk between me and this work
That makes me call it Sabbath.

It's like lovers standing back to back—
They reach out, touch and embrace not one another
But wind, but climate, earth, time
Past, time future. All this in the driving of three nails.
As though gold, frankincense, myrrh were
Three galvinized nails in this myrrh-pine
Scaffold, work-weary scaffold, these bones, this life.
  The hand guides the sharp plane blade;
  The wood grain guides the hand.

Sabbath:
It's a configuration of turning time's return
Among the stars and busy molecules,
Time to return gifts, time to return
In cadenced flesh and breath,
To forgive desire the debt of ecstasy.

*   *   *

Pilot Boat
(Concerning the poet's work)

Does my work have a face?
Suppose I meet it in some public place,
Outside the church, in the store, does it have hands?
To make things with, or paws? What about its walk?
Does it search avidly for some trace
Of me, whimper, and dig? Like an abandoned dog
With yellow teeth? Beaten away from new tin garbage cans.
O my work's an enemy's gift, an axe wound chopped wide,
Then sewed up by a blind drunk using phone calls
For all his needle stitches, and missed tides.

There is a pilot boat out in the yard
Humped with her keel upward toward the sky.
Thirty years ago a neighbor dumped her there
"Patch her, plank her, put new butt blocks, caulk . . . "
Neither he nor I have bothered to pay for her,
Or haul her away. She's still here, a grey rock
Once stormworthy as a stone. Her strong-framed lines
Flow with the live oaks, palmettos, lofty pines,
Lines ancient, powerful and most ordinary.
Along her crumbling gunwales wild grapes root, down-
        grasp,
Bind her to earth as they climb up to offer
Like a girl her breast their new chaste-wanton blossoms
To the high wild-cherry winds of February.

I may then know my work; this is its sign:
It's an abandoned boat with rotten garboards
Beneath a blossoming tree.
It's hallowed by the signs of humanness:
Signature, wholeness, rootedness, binding.
This rootedness, I set out upon it
As upon the open sea.

*   *   *

A Few Observations Concerning My Birth

A dust and a foretelling
Darkness hung in the high
Heavens—Blessed be the wide
Day I was born. The slack
Sun didn't shine on it, though the loud
Wrens sang out; blessed be the black
Night I came into the world: the swift
Moon didn't shine in it, though the coarse

Mocking birds made three-part songs—Blessed
Be that world:
The little fish winked all about
In Puget Sound
When I was born.

A darkness and a well-fashioned
Trembling, a grace of tremors took the
Mountains; the hills stretched themselves, the valleys
Danced; that strong and sweet-boned woman, the Earth,
    shook,
Danced, the highways uncurled and curled themselves,
The road signs and yellow-stenciled
Margins, like a living coil
Spring of spiral tempered latch
Steel, the chickens laughed, cackled, ran under the clothes
Lines, the jigging shirts snatched themselves
Loose from the clothes pins of the diligent house
Wife, and clapped their empty sleeves.
The cats and maiden aunts gave voice, climbed trees
With self-startled rejoicing
On the day I was born.

It was a big day.

The tides of incandescent
Rock gathered themselves together, they
Splashed against the rib bones
And hip bone cradle of the
Earth, the fissures and fumeroles
Shrieked, they whistled Yankee Doodle o my
Dandy, the Cascade Mountains yielded to my
Time and tune, cracked, opened wide my
Door and the lava poured out—
Me,
The melted magma stepped forth—
Me,
The white-hot rocks tumbling in a tide—
Me.

The birds and fine words flew in their flocks,
They sang tunes and arranged themselves in the Bill of
Rights and the Gettysburg Address
All along the powerlines.

The earth has a fine burning in her wild
Heart: when I was eight years old, my child eyes still
Shot out dangerous drops and specks and sparks so high
Hot the girls and women got pregnant just with long
Looking on me, and went away singing.

I
Have taken sixty years to cool down
Enough so common folk can find and feel me
Without getting burnt. When
I
Went to school the third day
After that darling woman, she,
My Mother, the Earth,
Gave me birth,
They had to invent asbestos for the charred
Chairs, and when I wrote the United States
Dictionary on the fifth day, September Twenty
First, Nineteen Twenty
Seven, they made the pages out of annealed
Copper so I could write the entries with a steel
Pen, and silver solder for ink,
I was so hot.

That was great day, a mighty sabbath.
The day I was born.
                              Nick Lindsay

*   *   *

Dear Cal and Urie,
    Tomorrow is the sabbath and not a bit too soon for me. Grand
to have a day with nothing but dozing during the sermon and
visiting in the afternoon. This is genuinely victorious living . . .
    I much feel for you both, pray for you in your editorial labors.
I have indeed tried my best to respond simply and directly to your
Zondervan question, "How do you translate this stuff? What is the
line of intersection between devotional art and life, as these terms
might be ordinarily defined?"
    . . . I have the feeling this business of including my bits and
pieces in your forthcoming book is a very generous act on your
part, but a needless grief and complication. There is absolutely no
harm done if the whole Lindsay contribution is omitted . . . please
do it this way. I'll never doubt the generosity of your impulse, nor
the wisdom of overriding it.
    God keep you. Love to all. Nick.

    It's raining
    I'm late
    The day is clamoring for my blood
    The crew's assembling in the mud . . .

Authors' Epilogue

God be thanked that the dead have left still
   Good undone for the living to do—
Still some aim for the heart and the will
   And the soul of a man to pursue.
                    (Owen Meredith: Epilogue)

   To think and write about work has been a pleasure and a most
rewarding experience. This book has become my offering of love
to God, who made things good. Indeed, *He said* the world was
good. And so it can be for us. I have always enjoyed physical,
mental, psychic and social work. (The latter is perhaps the most
difficult, for I have always been impatient about working for
"appearances" or working to nurture relationships which I felt
were not genuine.)
   In fact, I have found so much enjoyment in work that some
have given me the label, *workaholic*. If *workaholism* means working
hard and almost mindlessly for certain extrinsic reasons—such as a
doting set of parents who wanted their son to succeed brilliantly, or
a nagging upwardly mobile wife, or a reference group with which I
compared myself and with whom I needed to keep up—I have not
been hooked or seduced. In these terms, I am emphatically not a
workaholic. But if the word means working for the enjoyment it
brings, I am content to let the label apply. In this, I have the
support of my wife, my parents, and the community which I
consider my reference group—my church. They have been most
supportive of my needs to be productive and quite aware of my
fulfillment in work.
   It is possible for the cynic to suggest that regardless of what I
say about the motivations and rewards from work, I have
unconsciously become addicted to the "opium of work," that is, I
have participated fully as a cog in the gigantic engine of industrial
society and have contributed to the materialistic penchant without
knowing it. Thus a subtle form of self-deception has caused me to
give a "religious" sanction to a self-serving activity.
   At times, I must confess, I have been attacked by the virus of
upward mobility, by the germs of prestige and high status, or by
the temptation to internalize the norms of an "achieving society."
But I have been rescued repeatedly by the sage counsel of the Holy
Scriptures, through the many sermons I have heard on Christian

servanthood, as well as by the cautions of many friends and some
of the thinkers whose works I have read. These have inspired me to
live in a governed manner, content to let life bring its own
enjoyments, not measured by the amount of material conquests or
published works.

Work has meant for me all the things I have written about in
the preceding chapters. Work has brought meaning to my life; it
has filled the endless turnings of the world with purpose and joy.
God has been present with me in my work and, along with Brother
Lawrence, I can say truly, "Thus I continued for some years,
applying my mind carefully the rest of the day, and even in the
midst of my business, to the Presence of God, whom I considered
always as with me, often as in me" (p. 35).

Some might conclude that such a life is dull; if an author can
rhapsodize so about work, it must be because he has had no deep
and meaningful relationships with people. Nothing is farther from
the truth. A gratifying life of work does not need to imply that life
is otherwise barren. If human work can be derived in its deepest
nature from God's experience of and pronouncements about work,
then work and human relationships are two parts of a whole. Work
and love are not incompatible, they are reciprocal. Indeed, it is
quite possible that he whose work is not rewarding may also not
have rewarding relationships with people. I can only testify to the
depth of human relationships which I have been privileged to enjoy
in my tribal family, the church and the communities where I have
lived and worked.

One of the burdens of my concern about work is the large
number of people who do not experience work in its full potential.
As Sartre has said, such people go with "one buttock to work." I
am concerned about the *half-life* of people who cannot see work as a
part of the essence of their enjoyment of life, for work is a major
sector of human activity and experience. (A book on sleep, the
other major sector of human life, would have less significance, for
sleep is a necessary and universal reprieve from work; in fact, and
sadly, it is often the only release from the drudgery of work.) Work
is central in most lives; it occupies a large place in our conscious
level of living—that part of our lives that can be shaped by our
own choices and which, in turn, is influential.

But beyond the personal significance of work—either for
good or for evil—my greatest concern relates to the implications of
work for the soul of human civilization itself. Because of the way in
which it fulfills or destroys individuals, work exerts tremendous
influence on the psyche of collective groups including societies,
nations, and even whole civilizations. It is my thoughtful conviction—derived from some of the greatest minds of the ages—that
there is an intimate relationship, probably *the* determinative

relationship, between the satisfaction of and meaning of work and the peace and self-realization of a nation or group of nations. In my view, whether the nations will live in peace or die in mortal combat depends upon the status of work.

If modern civilization succeeds in destroying itself in the next few decades, it could well be because human beings have lost their direction and purpose in terms of personal existence and have transferred their need for purpose to impersonal nationalisms. With the alienation from work and alienation from the consequences of work, man has lost touch with himself and with his creator. If work can measure up to the standards defined in chapters 12–15, then it is probable that we will not get lost in the heavy underbrush of institutional, artificial, technological and structural encrustations, all of which today are destroying the holiness of work.

To suggest that the dehumanizing aspects of work, as we have described them, are the "works" of Satan may be simplistic. But if we acknowledge that Satan, the archangel, was in heaven when the foundations of the world were laid—and that he was one of God's aides—we could assume he was aware of the significance of work. In other words, in terms of human existence, that work was the key to man's salvation or destruction. What greater coup could there be than to separate man from his soul, i.e., from His work! As we know from the biblical account, there developed early an alienation between God and his work (man); a separation took place and a deep gulf was fixed. Indeed, it is possible that the gulf which has been emerging between humans and their work is the Devil's way of trying to win his war with God. However, if we pray that God will help us choose and bless our work, then we can be partners with him in hallowing work and redeeming man's human existence through work. Thus, Satan's destructive intention can be thwarted and instead of tragedy, there can be triumph.   —C.R.

*   *   *

And God called man and woman into being—to be with Him, to be His image, to be His presence in the world He had made.

More than presence, however, He called them into partnership—to work with Him: to have dominion, to name the animals, to dress the garden and keep it. A high privilege! To share with the Creator of the Universe in part of His work: to maintain and name and reign as prince or princess in this earthly kingdom of God.

In this setting and within this relationship work was hallowed. Every effort put forth in the fulfillment of these responsibilities was made holy. Even after the Fall, work remained as a constant reminder of the holy responsibility man and woman were given toward creature and creation.

Throughout the record of God's dealings with His human creation—particularly in the calling of a people to be named after Him—there is threaded the abiding sense that the Almighty One desired the family of man to be in partnership with Himself. The roles of prophet, priest and king pointed to this desire again and again. And finally, in the Messiah, God showed the overwhelming power of that desire to bring His creatures once more into full relationship with Himself, indeed to transform His whole creation into a model of His earlier intention. So Christ came, the prime minister of that intention—the bridge back to divine purpose. In this new economy, Jesus served as cornerstone, foundation to the kingdom of spirit made real on earth among men and women.

But lest we see the image of building as fixed and static, Jesus is spoken of also as Head of the body—the church of Christ to be the presence of God in the world He had made. A presence that lives and breathes and moves about to be with men and women where they are.

More than presence, however, God has given to every redeemed creature a high privilege—to work with Him in creating a spiritual kingdom where men and women live in love doing His will and thus find the joy and peace the human heart desires and which God longs to give to all His creatures.

Thus, the Christian works in two realms. In the natural order of things he exerts effort to provide shelter for, to feed and to clothe himself and his family, as well as to serve his fellows. At the same time, however—and precisely in the same setting of his work and life—the Christian works to build the kingdom of God; he works within the spiritual order of things.

As we view it now, work has been woven throughout the human fabric from the dawn of recorded history. Work is also part of both warp and woof in the tapestry of the divine intention stretched transcendentally across time. It is from within this intention that God calls men and women to be transformed—to enter the realm of faith where all is made new and God's perfect purposes are worked out. This work continues—and shall—until the sun and moon and stars are called out of their orbits and time shall be no more.

When that glorious cataclysm occurs, and God's creatures redeemed stand translated in His presence, work also will be seen in a new light. Stripped of selfishness, injustice, oppression and all the other sweaty stains of sin, work will reflect again its original beauty—a partnership with God as He expended spirit energy and creative power to achieve His desired ends. Then also, at last, we will see clearly a simple definition of human work within the divine context: an activity where expended effort is a gift expressed from the spirit within. Within this setting and perspective, the basic objective is service to each other with glory to God. In that eternal now, we will then also share in God's sabbath. For after He achieved his intended end in earthly creation, He stopped working. He rested.

At the same time, God's redemptive work among men and women by His Spirit has continued, and shall, until that awesome culmination when all the redeemed gather in the presence of God— a new creation made in His image, after His likeness.

Then God shall look upon that new creation and say: "Behold, it is good; it is very good."

Then, He shall rest from His Work.

And we—with Him.

—UAB

Notes

Chapter 1

[1] *Canada's Unemployed: The Crisis of Our Times* (Toronto: Archdiocese of Toronto, 1983), pp. 197ff.

[2] John Farina, "Weaning Society from Work," *Kitchener-Waterloo Record* (November 13, 1982).

[3] The most familiar analysis of this paradox is of course the Marxian one. It is not possible to explicate Marx's theory here but for our purposes we can say that it posits a setting in motion of forces by human action which then "act back" on persons so that they become victims of these forces. It is the development of technology and capital which in the hands of *some* societal members oppresses the rest. But there are other theorists who take a similar position. One such philosopher would be Jacques Ellul. He assumes that technology becomes autonomous and feeds on itself to create oppressive structures.

[4] Sources on alienation are myriad. A popular source is Studs Terkel, *Working* (New York: Avon, 1975). A classic firsthand report is Richard M. Pfeffer's *Working for Capitalism* (New York: Columbia University Press, 1979). One of the most reasoned accounts is James W. Rinehart's *The Tyranny of Work* (Toronto: Harcourt Brace Jovanovich, 1987). Many other sources could be cited, but Marx's discussion on the alienation of work cannot be ignored. One is Karl Marx, "Economic and Philosophic Manuscripts of 1844" in Robert C. Tucker, ed., *The Marx-Engels Reader* (New York: Norton, 1972).

[5] James Lawrence, ed. *The Harrowsmith Sourcebook*. (Camden East, Ontario: Camden House, 1979), page 304.

[6] For a very recent treatment of this argument see Stephen Wood, *The Degradation of Work* (Dover: Hutchinson, 1984), especially chapters 5 and 7.

Chapter 2

[1] Tables 2 and 3 are provided for a general background for reference and we recommend these be carefully studied to provide an overall perspective.

[2] Women and work are discussed in R. Firth, *Human Types: An Introduction to Social Anthropology* (New York: Barnes and Noble, 1956), pp. 73–74.

[3]Karl Marx, *Early Writings* (New York: McGraw Hill, 1963). See especially "First Manuscript," pp. 69–134. The concept of "surplus labor" is one of the foundations of Marx's whole edifice and refers to the excess value a worker produces which the capitalist "exploits."

[4]W. Neff, *Work and Human Behavior* (New York: Atherton Press, 1968), p. 52.

Chapter 3

[1]Felice Battaglia, "Work," in *Dictionary of the History of Ideas,* ed. (New York: Charles Scribners, 1973), p. 530.

[2]"Work, Vocation, Calling," *Encyclopedia of the Lutheran Church* (Minneapolis: Augsburg Publishing House, 1965), p. 2502.

[3]Typical of the new understanding of Jesus' life in the context of the times is John W. Miller, "Jesus' Personality as Reflected in His Parables," in *The New Way of Jesus* , edited by William Klassen (North Newton, Kansas: Faith and Life Press, 1980). The chapter includes an extensive bibliography of related sources.

[4]A brief but very explicit discussion can be found in "The Theology of Work" in the *New Catholic Encyclopedia* (New York: McGraw-Hill, 1967). The bibliography at the end of the article provides sources for the medieval and Catholic position on work.

[5]Ibid., p. 1016. The monastic tradition provides one of the richest incarnations of the relationship of work and piety. Too little attention has been given to this massive phenomenon. Cf. John Paul II encyclical *Laborem Exercens* for a summary view. See also "Work" in *Dictionary of the History of Ideas,* esp. 531 and passim.

[6]Already in the fourteenth century, sociologists were aware of the importance of work for identity. Ibn Khaldun (1332–1406) said regarding occupations, "The differences between different people arise out of the differences in their occupations" (Rollin/Chambliss, *Social Thought from Hammurabi to Comte* (New York: Henry Holt, 1954), p. 305.

[7]See "Work," in *Dictionary of the History of Ideas,* p. 534ff. Hegel says, " . . . work is the absolute law of life . . . ," p. 535.

Chapter 4

[1]The sources are almost endless. See for example an interesting survey conducted by Daniel Yankelovich, "The Search for Self-Fulfillment: Weak and Strong Forms" in *Psychology Today,* April 1981. Yankelovich concludes that "nearly 80 per cent of the population is not engaged in the search for self-fulfillment" (p. 51), and he deduces that work as payoff is changing dramatically (p. 76). See also James W. Rinehart, *The Tyranny of Work,* (Toronto: Harcourt, Brace Jovanovich, 1987).

[2] See Roger Williams, *Tomorrow at Work.* (London: British Broadcasting Corporation, 1973). A national sample in Britain showed that six of 43 important life events pertained to work, also that retirement and being fired from the job ranked among the top ten traumatic events in life (p. 47). See also an excellent study by Rick Luecke, "The Present Unemployment and the Future of Work," unpublished MS, Chicago, 1977).

Chapter 5

[1] Aristotle, *On Man in the Universe* (New York: Walter J. Black, 1943 bk. x, p. 431).

[2] Ibid.

[3] Ibid.

[4] Professionalism is dealt with extensively in chapter 8.

Chapter 6

[1] The role of the informal group has been extensively studied in sociology. Its application to organizations and business organizations in particular is well developed. The power of the informal group in the work setting is very well documented in Pfeffer, op. cit. Group dynamics can both enhance and inhibit individual behavior and goals. See, for example J. Senger, *Individuals, Groups, and the Organization* (Cambridge, Mass.: Winthrop, 1980); also Peter Homans, *The Human Group* (New York: Harcourt, brace, 1950).

[2] This is not to imply extortion, exploitation of business or even an antibusiness stance. Rather it is to recognize that the objectives of the organization and the individual rarely coincide. Marx insisted that the only reason laborers work for employers is the "cash nexus," i.e., cash is what the worker wants, and cash is what the company is willing to pay (an agreed upon amount, that is, and nothing more). When the company exacts requirements which go beyond the "bargain," then it is totally legitimate for the employee to avail himself of all the assistance available to redress the wrongs. See, for example, the section "Business and the Employee: Rights and Obligations" in Thomas Donaldson and Patricia Werhane, *Ethical Issues in Business* (Englewood Cliffs: Prentice-Hall, 1979).

[3] A wealth of new material is appearing which describes and analyzes this new movement. See Charles F. Sabel, *Work and Politics,* (Cambridge: Cambridge University Press, 1982); Hazel Henderson, *The Politics of the Solar Age* (New York: Doubleday-Anchor, 1981).

[4] Most of us have witnessed the rescinding of a democratic decision after the "snowballing effect" of a group decision had dissipated. This is of course the message of the atonement through Jesus Christ. Through one man (Adam) all men were inclined toward death; through one man (Jesus) all men were made alive.

Chapter 7

[1] Alienation is a very general and widely used term, and can refer to many things. We restrict our usage to the more narrowly focused definition used by sociologists. For a brief discussion and bibliography of the classic writings on the subject, see "Alienation" in the *International Encyclopedia of the Social Sciences* (New York: Macmillan and Free Press, 1968), vol. 1, pp. 264–68. One of the most extensive analyses of alienation has been proposed by Melvin Seeman (1972) where six dimensions are given: (1) sense of powerlessness; (2) sense of meaninglessness; (3) sense of normlessness; (4) value isolation; (5) self-estrangement; and (6) social isolation (Zablocki, *Alienation and Charisma* [New York: Free Press, 1980], pp. 8ff.).

[2] This is not the overall impression gained when reading the accounts of work in Terkel's *Working* (New York: Avon, 1975), for the general implication in that volume is that people accept the fact that work may entail monotony, but want to make work meaningful nevertheless. For a close look at the "boring" nature of work, see "What Work is Like" in Richard M. Pfeffer, *Working for Capitalism* (New York: Columbia University Press, 1979). The mechanization and standardization of work assumed monotony and was predicted by Adam Smith and others.

[3] The recession, which has affected North Americans to a great degree in recent years (1983–83) has been extensively reported in the press, especially as it affects family life and tension. It is well known that the divorce rate parallels the unemployment situation and the tension it brings.

[4] Cf. among many other sources the publication of the Profit Sharing Council of America of Chicago, Illinois; this provides extensive evidence that profit sharing and employee stock ownership is profitable for business and employees alike.

[5] The social control mechanisms in work settings, both in terms of union pressures and management coercion is well known. Again, Pfeffer's discussion in part 2 "Workers and the Union" provides illuminating information on the dynamics of individual attempts to "opt out of" or protest against union or company norms.

[6] See the many accounts in Terkel, which point to this fact. In the 1974 national survey by Daniel Yankelovich, among "Very important values," 87 percent stated "fulfilling yourself as a person"; 64 percent stated doing things for others; 52 percent cited work as very important, *The New Morality* (New York: McGraw-Hill, 1974). Most work experts agree that people want to do meaningful work.

[7] Philosophically, the reductionist approach to reality makes the whole seem increasingly less meaningful. Psychologically, we understand as we see wholes which are made up of subparts. The old adage

296 WHO AM I? WHAT AM I?

that scientists know more and more about less and less until they know everything about nothing, expresses this dilemma.

[8] This is the strength of small owner-owned businesses, and indicates why they are so much more adaptable and resilient. Cf. Rein Peterson, *Small Business* (Erin, Ontario: Press Porcepic, Ltd., 1977).

[9] Capitalism is a very vague and imprecise term. We are referring here to the classical way Marx and Smith both referred to work as being downgraded in modern industrial society.

[10] This pertains to the vast activity needed to produce an "economic system as if people mattered," to repeat E. F. Schumacher's famous phrase. For more on the subject, see Schumacher's *Good Work* (New York: Harper and Row, Colophon Books, 1979), p. 34: "Let us ask then: How does work relate to the end and purpose of man's being?" Schumacher asks (p. 30). He answers, to provide necessary and useful goods and services, to enable everyone to use and perfect their gifts, and to liberate ourselves from our inborn egocentricity".

Chapter 8

[1] This may seem harsh and cynical, but the idea of professionals developing their own world of reality has been described in many ways, including literature such as *Catch 22, Brave New World* and many others. In fact, the dystopian literature (the discussion of utopia becoming the opposite) is vast and indicates the need for professionalism to be curbed. One of the most insightful and scathing critiques of the vicious circle of professional life in the social sciences is C. Wright Mill's *The Sociological Imagination* (New York: Grove Press, 1959). Chapter 5, "The Bureaucratic Ethos," is especially germane.

[2] Some parts of this section have been adapted from a chapter entitled "Can I be a Creative Subversive?" which appeared in Don Kraybill and Phyllis Good, *The Perils of Professionalism* (Scottdale: Herald, 1982).

Chapter 9

[1] For one of the best historical overviews, see Elise Boulding, "Preparing the Modern World: The 1800s," in *The Underside of History* (Boulder, Col.: Westview Press, 1976). It describes how women slowly began to emerge from total submission to males, and consequently began to become self-conscious participants in employment.

[2] See for example, Karl Marx, "Private Property and Communism," in *Karl Marx: Early Writings,* T. B. Bottomore, ed. (New York: McGraw Hill, 1963), pp. 152–54, for a statement that women must be released from the category of private property if the revolution is truly to come. The "Communist Manifesto" gets to the center of the issue when it advocates the abolition of the bourgeois family which oppresses the female.

³Cf. Madonna Kolbenschlag, "Cinderella and Women's Work" in *Kiss Sleeping Beauty Goodbye* (Garden City: Doubleday, Anchor, 1979).

⁴Cf. Boulding, above. "Domestic work" however has been quite broad, and includes the positions and roles to which males have assigned her, and does not relate to household duties as such. Hence Boulding suggests that women "worked within the system," to achieve the phenomenal, including the status of queens of powerful states (p. 525).

⁵The history of the relationship of male and female has been presented from various perspectives; no unanimity exists regarding the relative dominance of male and female. Boulding states, "The question of why women are everywhere the 'subordinate sex' has never failed to interest both women and men, and many interpretations have been advanced to explain the phenomenon. . . . " (p. 35).

⁶There is a rapidly growing literature on feminist theological reconstruction. Several can be listed here: Elisabeth Schussler, "The Jesus Movement as Renewal Within Judaism," in *In Memory of Her* (New York: Crossroad, 1983), pp. 105–54. Also Luise Schottroff, "Frauen in der Nachfolge Jesu in neutestamentlicher Zeit," in W. Schottroff and W. Stegemann, eds., *Traditionen der Freiheit*. (Munchen: Kaiser, 1980).

⁷For the most specific research on this issue, see Rosabeth Kanter, *Men and Women of the Corporation* (New York: Basic Books, 1977).

Chapter 10

¹The Declaration of Human Rights, in *Peace on Earth* (New York: Hermitage House, 1949).

²It might be easier to use the term "job," but this would tend to diminish our emphasis on the nature of the activity which is our focus here. Employment work thus excludes voluntary work, work directed toward self-improvement, and many other types which make up the full gamut of work.

³There is a vast amount of literature dealing with the effect that computerization and automation are having on the amount of work and its nature. Representative are Stephen Wood, ed., *The Degradation of Work* (Dover: Hutchinson, 1984); Doreen Massey and Richard Meegan, *The Anatomy of Job Loss* (London: Methuen, 1982); and Clive Jenkins and Barrie Sherman, *The Collapse of Work* (London: Methuen, 1981). Service work is increasing, and some sectors of computerization, but the rest seem to be declining.

⁴Because the changes are so massive, it is difficult to arrive at any reliable estimates or statistics. After emphasizing that modern technology has already created a massive dislocation, Jenkins and Sherman state, "This quantum leap in technology will accelerate the structural changes in the pattern of employment which have been steadily advancing over the past decade and will exert an immensely destructive

impact on both existing jobs and the future supply of work" (*The Collapse of Work*, p. vii).

[5] There are many sources for this claim; one of the most influential is H. Braverman, *Labor and Monopoly Capitalism* (New York: Monthly Review Press, 1974); P. D. Anthony, *The Ideology of Work* (London: Tavistock Publications, 1977) presents the same material from a British point of view. The necessity for a percentage of unemployment to keep the engines of capitalism running has been debated and lamented for a long time. The statement by the Canadian Conference of Catholic Bishops on Canada's unemployed takes strong exception to this "corruption" of economics and calls for a reform of the economic structure which depends upon unemployment for prosperity.

[6] Recent research has shown that the computer is increasingly becoming the "actor" in decision-making, and human reasoning is being pushed into the background. See for example Bryn Jones's discussion of numerical control and its implications in Wood, *The Degradation of Work*.

[7] Cost accounting is difficult; but more and more attention is being paid to this problem. Philip Slater, in *The Pursuit of Loneliness* (Boston: Beacon, 1970), goes so far as to say that "The advantages of all technological 'progress' will after all be totally nullified the moment nuclear war breaks out (an event which, given the number of fanatical fingers close to the trigger, is only a matter of time)" (p. 57).

[8] In the church context, the reference group becomes more than the sociological concept. It also implies moral, ethical and spiritual concern, so that the individual is "ordained" by the spiritual congregation to fill his God-given role.

[9] The "Small is Beautiful" movement that is permeating our society is therefore not a romantic notion, but is based on sound sociological premises—primary type relationships are nurtured in the small group, where each individual is recognized as filling a conscious position in the structure.

[10] Students of industrial organization are discovering that decentralization is the key to a more harmonious and profitable structure. See, for example, Charles F. Sabel, *Work and Politics* (Cambridge: Cambridge University Press, 1982). The case study of the decentralization of Italian industry is most enlightening.

[11] The cooperative movement has two sources, socialism and Christianity. The socialistic trend has been plagued with coercion and oppression. The Christian movement has been plagued with inner dissension and conflict. In fact, the church is often accused of being intensely disruptive and divisive. Herein lies a central challenge to the Christian community.

Chapter 12

[1] A perusal of the literature on work clearly refers to the four dimensions, but we have not found them listed in this fashion in a systematic way. In a sense, the disciplines—the physical sciences, social sciences, theological studies and philosophical disciplines—represent the four types. For the best historical approach to understanding the facets of work, see Adriano Tilgher, *Work: What it has Meant Through the Ages* (New York: Harcourt Brace, 1930).

[2] The concept of psychic energy has not been broadly discussed. One of the most extensive and helpful treatments is found in "Man and His Psychic Equipment" in Mannheim, *Systematic Sociology* (New York: Grove, 1957), pp. 7–40. "Man, besides adapting himself to his natural surroundings, adapts himself also to the psycho-social-institutional environment. . . . " (p. 8). The bibliography at the end of Mannheim's book is useful for further research. In essence, psychic work involves the energy expended to "process" the emotions involved in man's social existence. Georg Simmel alludes to this in "The Nature of the Psychic Process and of Communication" (p. 311) in his *The Sociology of Georg Simmel* (Glencoe: Free Press, 1950). Psychoanalysis and psychotherapy, as well as psychology as such, operate on an understanding of the existence of psychic energy which acts, as it were, as a kind of "hydraulic" principle; thus it seems to express itself in almost physical ways.

[3] As used here, the term *social work* is not to be confused with the professional training for, or the professional field of, social work. Clearly, what we are referring to here is the energy expended to maintain social structures.

[4] One of the most researched sociological factors is stratification. Class, status, prestige and rank are some of the terms which refer to social classes. Occupation continues to be one of the most significant variables in any stratification analysis. A recent survey of class and occupation is presented by Bernard R. Blishen and Hugh A. McRoberts, "A Revised Socioeconomic Index by Occupation in Canada," *Canadian Review of Sociology and Anthropology* 13 (1), 1976, pp. 71–79. University teachers rank 10th and fish canners rank 499th.

[5] Although there are some variations in definitions, the general consensus is presented in "Occupations and Careers," in the *International Encyclopedia of the Social Sciences* (op. cit.).

[6] There is continuing debate as to how rigid the division of labor or specialization is which identifies occupations. It is usually assumed that the more specialized and technical the occupation, the greater is the rigidity of the occupational boundaries ("Occupations and Careers," op. cit., p. 248).

[7]See "Professions," in the *International Encyclopedia of the Social Sciences* by Talcott Parsons (op. cit.) for one of the best discussions of professions.

[8]The origin of morals, according to modern social science, is the evolution of the society itself. This view is best expressed by positivism which emerged from the rationalistic and empiricist philosophy typified by Locke, Hume and Berkeley. The biblical interpretation is that morals were given by God through the revelation to his people.

[9]For a brief account of the significance of Dorothy Day's life, see "End of a Pilgrimage," *Newsweek*, December 15, 1980.

Chapter 13

[1]Work is defined more fully in chapters 4 and 12. Here work is used to refer to the effort needed to do anything, such as getting out of bed in the morning or writing a letter.

[2]The intention here is to indicate that humans are not exempt from the processes of biological existence. Whether the processes of metabolism or the transformation of substances into energy or vice versa can be defined as work is open to debate. From a scientific perspective, it may be seen simply as a chemical or physiological process. From a sociological point of view, it may be defined as "work."

[3]For a classic treatment of social influences see Peter Homans, *The Human Group* (New York: Harcourt, Brace and Co., 1950).

Chapter 14

[1]A considerable amount of material has been written on a theology of work. No ultimately definitive statement can be made since the theology of work depends upon the larger theological and philosophical framework held by a person. For that reason, our presentation grows out of a radical left-wing Reformation point of view. We have tried, however, to remain close to the classical theological formulations in our analysis so we consider both Catholic and Protestant formulations and those from the radical left-wing. The bibliography cites various sources which include theological statements.

[2]The "kingdom of God" term has several levels of meaning here: first, as a metaphor—king and citizens; another is the biblical-theological concept of the purpose or objective of God's plan. Again the definition of the role of the kingdom of God depends upon one's theological orientation. The position indicated in footnote 1 obtains here.

[3]We have resisted opposing leisure and work. They are not mutually exclusive; at the very least they often merge into each other. Some persons' leisure is other people's work and vice versa. Leisure has

never been and is not now an option for many humans in civilization; thus to philosophize about leisure reflects a myopic and ethnocentric perspective. We *can* expatiate about work, however, because *all* societies have had to work. Leisure may be an adjunct to work, but it cannot be its opposite. It has been stated that in the kingdom of God there will be only leisure and no work. Unless the concept of leisure is changed, such a view expresses a blatant case of extrapolation of Western ideas about work.

[4] Ezra Byler, "Some Basics and Basic Questions about Profit Sharing," *Marketplace* (September 1977).

[5] We do not expand upon cooperatives since this involves a substantial restructuring of the consumption and production institutions of a locality or region whereas PS and ESOP are easily instituted. But the cooperative movement is probably one of the most promising solutions to social alienation.

Chapter 15

[1] *Future of Work,* n.a. (Ottawa: Vanier Institute, 1981).

[2] "Faith and Works" is a complex issue. On one level, it is a very specific theological issue, which deals with the problem of how Christian salvation is achieved. Already in the New Testament canon, especially in James, the issue is joined. It is our contention that the biblical record is clear, namely, that both faith and works (i.e., a response to God's grace) are required for salvation. The topic becomes a problem when one aspect is emphasized to the neglect of the other. Hence Luther's *sola fide* was a reaction to the apparent overemphasis of works righteousness—buying righteousness by giving alms, or doing pious acts. Work as a part of salvation in this book must be seen in the sense that Paul and James discuss it, namely, that faith expresses itself in observable behavior, and can be experienced both by the person who expresses those acts, and the person or persons who are the beneficiaries of those acts. It is our contention that the confusion about faith and works on the theological level has tended to denigrate the importance of working in the process of salvation.

[3] It is obvious that from the Christian point of view, a total egalitarianism must prevail. For a specific focus on how professionalism creates inequality, see Donald Kraybill and Phyllis Good, *The Perils of Professionalism* (Scottdale: Herald, 1982).

[4] By meaningless in this context is meant work which does not contribute to the realization of the shalom (peace) which God has in mind for creation.

[5] The human engineering movement, often referred to as "Taylorism," or "Fordism" means the application of scientific knowledge to bring about increases in production. See an excellent discussion on this topic by Charles F. Sabel, "The Rise of Fordism" in *Work and Politics* (Cambridge: Cambridge University Press, 1982).

[6] Changes in lifestyle mean the reduction of materialistic expectations, focusing on nurturing the quality of human relations rather than on competition to consume.

[7] Probably the fullest achievement of what we have in mind are the religious communes, in which sometimes up to half of the employable members are doing volunteer and charitable service work, supported by others who are employed in remunerated work situations. For information on a confederation of religious communes which are attempting to serve the community, see *Coming Together: A Journal About Christian Community*. For information on one specific commune which takes this position, see Dave and Neta Jackson, "Work," in *Living Together in a World Falling Apart* (Carol Stream, Ill.: Creation House, 1974).

[8] By kingdom of God is meant the absolute realization of the rule of God in human history. It might also be defined as "Shalom," the presence of God's peace in all human experience. See Bruce C. Birch and Larry L. Rasmussen, "Shalom and Christ," in *The Predicament of the Prosperous* (Philadelphia: Westminster, 1978). See also Gerald C. Brauer, "Kingdom of God," in *Handbook of Christian Theology* (New York: Meridian, 1958).

Bibliography

Sources for Additional Help in Career Choice

Bolles, Richard N. *What Color Is Your Parachute? A Practical Manual for Job-Hunters and Career Changers.* 2d ed. Berkeley, Calif: Ten Speed Press, 1984.

Bramlett, James, *Finding Work* Grand Rapids: Zondervan Publishing House, 1986

Burt, Jesse C. *Your Vocational Adventure.* Nashville: Abingdon Press, 1969. Discusses clues to occupational choices.

Casewit, Curtis W. *How to Get a Job Overseas.* 3d ed. New York: Arco, 1984.

Clark, Martin E. *Choosing Your Career: The Christian's Decision.* Phillipsburg, N.J.: Presbyterian and Reformed, 1981.

Demos, George D., and Bruce Grant. *Vocational Guidance Readings.* Springfield, Ill.: Charles G. Thomas, 1965. Very extensive treatment from many angles. Dated, but good.

Encyclopedia of Associations. 10th ed. Detroit: Gale Research, 1976.

Farnsworth, Kirk E., and Wendell H. Lawhead. *Life Planning: A Workbook for those beginning to look for a job and those seeking a change in midlife.* Downers Grove: InterVarsity Press, 1981. The title says it all; didactive, but helpful.

Gale, Barry, and Linda Gale. *Discover What You're Best At: The National Career Aptitude System and Career Directory.* New York: Simon and Schuster, 1982.

Kocher, Eric. *International Jobs: Where They Are, How to Get Them.* Menlo Park, Calif.: Addison-Wesley, 1984.

Mattson, Ralph, and Arthur Miller. *Finding a Job You Can Love.* Nashville: Thomas Nelson, 1982.

Pilder, Richard J., and William F. Pilder. *How to Find Your Life's Work: Staying Out of Traps and Taking Control of Your Career.* Englewood Cliffs, N.J.: Prentice-Hall, 1981.

Poutney, Michael. *Getting a Job: A Guide for Choosing a Career.* Downers Grove: InterVarsity Press, 1984.

Rockcastle, Madeline T., ed. *Where to Start: An Annotated Career-Planning Bibliography.* 4th ed. Princeton, N.J.: Peterson's Guides, 1983.

Shelley, Judith Allen. *Not Just a Job: Serving Christ in Your Work.* Downers Grove: InterVarsity Press, 1985.

Staub, Dick. "9 to 5: A New Look at Christian Career Choices." *Eternity Magazine's Doors '82.*
U.S. Department of Labor, Bureau of Labor Statistics. *Exploring Careers* (Pamphlet series). Washington, D.C.: Government Printing Office, 1980.
————. *Occupational Outlook Handbook.* Washington, D.C.: Government Printing Office, 1986.
White, Jerry, and Mary. *Your Job: Survival or Satisfaction.* Grand Rapids: Zondervan Publishing House, 1977.
Zwerdling, Daniel. *Workplace Democracy: A Guide to Workplace Ownership, Participation, and Self-Management Experiments in the United States and Europe.* New York: Harper Colophon Books, 1980.

Suggestions for Further Reading, From a Theological Point of View

There are relatively few full treatments of a Christian view of work. Several of the books listed below are quoted in the text. These are highly recommended.

Bernbaum, John A. and Simon M. Steer. *Why Work? Careers and Employment in Biblical Perspective.* Grand Rapids: Baker Book House, 1986.
Geoghegan, Arthur T. *The Attitude Towards Labor in Early Christianity and Ancient Culture.* Washington: Catholic University Press, 1945.
Kaiser, Edwin G. *Theology of Work.* Westminster, Md.: The Newman Press, 1966.
Nelson, John Oliver. *Work and Vocation: A Christian Discussion.* New York: Harper and Brothers, 1954.
Oldham, J. H. *Work in Modern Society.* Richmond: John Knox Press, 1950.
Richardson, Alan. *The Biblical Doctrine of Work.* London: SCM Press, 1952.

Basic Bibliography

Anderson, G. Lester. *Trends in Education for the Professions.* Washington: American Association for Higher Education, 1974.
Anthony, D. *The Ideology of Work.* London: Tavistock Publications, 1977.
Aristotle. *On Man in the Universe.* New York: Walter J. Black, 1943.
Battaglia, Felice. "Work." in *Dictionary of the History of Ideas.* New York: Charles Scribners, 1973, p. 530.
Berelson, Bernard, and Gary Steiner. *Human Behavior: An Inventory of Scientific Findings.* New York: Harcourt, Brace and World, Inc., 1964.

Birch, Bruce C., and Larry L. Rasmussen. *The Predicament of the Prosperous*. Philadelphia: Westminster Press, 1978.

Blishen, Bernard R., and Hugh A. McRoberts, "A Revised Socioeconomic Index by Occupation in Canada," *Canadian Review of Sociology and Anthropology* 13 (1), 1976, pp. 71–79.

Blood, Robert O., and Donald M. Wolfe. *Husbands and Wives*. Glencoe: Free Press, 1980.

Bolles, Richard N. *What Color Is Your Parachute? A Practical Manual for Job-Hunters and Career Changers*. 2d. ed. Berkeley, Calif.: Ten Speed Press, 1984.

Bottomore, T. B. *Karl Marx: Selected Writings in Sociology and Social Philosophy*. New York: McGraw-Hill, 1956.

_____. *Karl Marx: Early Writings*. New York: McGraw Hill, 1963.

Boulding, Elise. "Preparing the Modern World: The 1980s." in *The Underside of History*. Boulder, Colo.: Westview Press, 1976.

Brauer, Gerard C. "Kingdom of God," in *Handbook of Christian Theology*. Edited by Marvin Halverson. New York: Meridian Books, 1958.

Braverman, H. *Labor and Monopoly Capitalism*. New York: Monthly Review Press, 1974.

Brother Lawrence. *The Practice of the Presence of God*. Westwood, N.J.: Fleming Revell, 1958.

Bugg, Ralph. *Job Power* New York: Pyramid Books, 1965.

Burt, Jesse C. *Your Vocational Adventure*. Nashville: Abingdon Press, 1969.

Byler, Ezra. "Some Basics and Basic Questions about Profit Sharing," *Marketplace* 7,2 (September 1977).

Callahan, Sidney Cornelia. *The Illusion of Eve: Modern Woman's Quest for Identity*. New York: Sheed and Ward, 1965.

Canada's Unemployed: The Crisis of Our Times. Toronto: Archdiocese of Toronto: 1983, pp. 197ff.

Casewit, Curtis W. *How to Get a Job Overseas*. 3d ed. New York: Arco, 1984.

Catherwood, Sir Frederick. *On the Job: The Christian 9-5*. Grand Rapids, Michigan: Zondervan, 1980.

Champion, Dean J. *The Sociology of Organizations*. New York: McGraw-Hill, 1975.

Clark, Martin E. *Choosing Your Career: The Christian's Decision*. Phillipsburg, N.J.: Presbyterian and Reformed, 1981.

Day, Dorothy. "End of a Pilgrimage," *Newsweek*, December 15, 1980.

DeBoer, John. *How to Succeed in the Organization Jungle Without Losing Your Religion*. Philadelphia: Pilgrim, 1972.

The Declaration of Human Rights. *Peace on Earth*. New York: Hermitage House, 1949.

Demos, George D., and Bruce Grant. *Vocational Guidance Readings*. Springfield, Ill.: Charles C. Thomas, 1965.

Dickinson, Emily. "The Wounded Deer."

Dickson, Paul. *The Future of the Workplace*. New York: Waybright and Tally, 1975.

Donaldson, Thomas, and Patricia Werhane. *Ethical Issues in Business*. Englewood Cliffs: Prentice-Hall, 1979.

Durkheim, Emile. *The Division of Labor*. Glencoe: Free Press, 1933.

Ellul, Jacques. *The Technological Society*. New York: Vintage Books, 1967.

Encyclopedia of Associations. 10th ed. Detroit: Gale Research, 1976.

Farina, John. "Weaning Society from Work," *Kitchener-Waterloo Record* (November 13, 1982).

Farnsworth, Kirk E., and Wendell H. Lawhead. *Life Planning: A Workbook for those beginning to look for a job and those seeking a change in midlife*. Downers Grove: InterVarsity Press, 1981.

Feuerbach, Ludwig. *The Essence of Christianity*. New York: Harper and Row, Torchbooks, 1957.

Firth, R. *Human Types: An Introduction to Social Anthropology*. New York: Barnes and Noble, 1956.

Fowke, Edith, and Joe Glazer. *Songs of Work and Protest*. New York: Dover Publications, 1973.

Future of Work, n.a. Ottawa: Vanier Institute, 1981.

Gale, Barry, and Linda Gale. *Discover What You're Best At: The National Career Aptitude System and Career Directory*. New York: Simon and Schuster, 1982.

Geoghegan, Arthur T. *The Attitude Towards Labor in Early Christianity and Ancient Culture*. Washington: Catholic University Press, 1945.

The Harrowsmith Sourcebook. Edited by James Lawrence. Camden East: Camden House Ltd., 1979.

Heller, Joseph. *Catch 22*. New York: Simon and Schuster, 1961.

Henderson, Hazel. *The Politics of the Solar Age*. New York: Doubleday-Anchor, 1981.

Herman, Melvin, Stanley Sadofsky, and Bernard Rosenberg. *Work, Youth and Unemployment*. New York: Crowell, 1968.

Hilliard, Marion. *Women and Fatigue*. New York: Doubleday, 1960.

Hoffer, Eric. *The Temper of Our Times*. New York: Harper & Row, 1967.

Homans, Peter. *The Human Group*. New York: Harcourt, Brace, 1950.

Hughes, Everett C. *Men and Their Work*. Glencoe: Free Press, 1958.

Huxley, Aldous. *Brave New World*. New York: Harper & Row, 1965.

_____. *Brave New World Revisited*. London: Chatto and Windus, Ltd., 1959.

Illich, Ivan. *Shadow Work*. Boston: Marion Boyars, 1981.

International Encyclopedia of the Social Sciences. vol. 1. New York: Macmilland and Free Press, 1968.

Jackson, Dave, and Neta Jackson. "Work," in *Living Together in a World Falling Apart*. Carol Stream, Ill.: Creation House, 1974.

Jasper, Karl. *Man in the Modern Age.* New York: Doubleday-Anchor, 1957.

Jenkins, Clive, and Barrie Sherman, *The Collapse of Work.* London: Methuen, 1979.

Kaiser, Edwin G. *Theology of Work.* Westminster, Md.: The Newman Press, 1966.

Kanter, Rosabeth. *Men and Women of the Corporation.* New York: Basic Books, 1977.

Kocher, Eric. *International Jobs: Where They Are, How to Get Them.* Menlo Park, Calif.: Addison, Wesley, 1984.

Kolbenschlag, Madonna. *Kiss Sleeping Beauty Goodbye.* Garden City: Doubleday Anchor, 1979.

Kraemer, Hendrick. *A Theology of the Laity.* London: Westminster, 1958.

Kraybill, Don, and Phyllis Good. *The Perils of Professionalism.* Scottdale: Herald Press, 1982.

Lee, Robert. *Religion and Leisure in America.* New York: Abingdon, 1964.

Lerner, Max. "Watergating on Main Street," *Saturday Review* (November 1, 1975), p. 12.

Levinson, Daniel J. *The Seasons of a Man's Life.* New York: Ballantine Books, 1978.

Lewellyn, Richard. *How Green Was My Valley.* New York: MacMillan, 1964.

Luecke, Rick. "The Present Unemployment and the Future of Work," unpublished MS, Chicago, 1977.

Maitland, Sara. *A Map of the New Country: Women and Christianity.* London: Routledge & Kegan Paul, 1983.

Mannheim, Karl. *Systematic Sociology: An Introduction to the Study of Society.* New York: Grove Press, 1957.

Marshall, Paul, et. al. *Labour of Love: Essays on Work.* Toronto: Wedge, 1980.

Massey, Doreen, and Richard Meegan, *The Anatomy of Job Loss.* London: Methuen, 1982.

Mattson, Ralph, and Arthur Miller. *Finding a Job You Can Love.* Nashville: Thomas Nelson, 1982.

Meaning of Working International Team. *The Meaning of Working: An International View.* Orlando: Academic, 1987.

Mill, C. Wright. *The Sociological Imagination.* New York: Grove Press, 1959.

Miller, Arthur F., and Ralph T. Mattson. *The Truth About You.* Fleming H. Revell Co., n.d.

Miller, Delbert C., and William H. Form. *Industrial Sociology: The Sociology of Work Organizations.* New York: Harper and Row, 1964.

Miller, John W. "Jesus' Personality as Reflected in His Parables." in *The New Way of Jesus* . edited by William Klassen. North Newton, Kansas: Faith and Life Press, 1980.

Neff, W. *Work and Human Behavior.* New York: Atherton Press, 1968.

Nelson, John Oliver. *Work and Vocation: A Christian Discussion.* New York: Harper and Brothers, 1954.

"Occupations and Careers," in the *International Encyclopedia of the Social Sciences* (op. cit.).

Oldham, Joseph H. *Work in Modern Society.* Richmond: John Knox Press, 1950.

Parsons, Talcott. "Professions." *International Encyclopedia of the Social Sciences.* New York: Macmilland and Free Press, 1968. p. 546–47.

Peterson, Rein. *Small Business: Building a Balanced Economy.* Erin, Ontario: Press Porcepic, Ltd., 1977.

Pfeffer, Richard M. *Working for Capitalism.* New York: Columbia University Press, 1979.

Pieper, Josef. *Leisure: The Basis of Culture.* New York: Pantheon, 1964.

Pilder, Richard J., and William F. Pilder. *How to Find Your Life's Work: Staying Out of Traps and Taking Control of Your Career.* Englewood Cliffs, N.J.: Prentice-Hall, 1981.

Pippert, Wes. "Faith Should Rewrite Your Job Description." *Christianity Today* 26:15 (Sept. 17, 1982): pp.28–30.

Pope John Paul II. *Encyclical Laborem Exercens.* Ottawa: Canadian Conference of Catholic Bishops, 1981.

Poutney, Michael. *Getting a Job: A Guide for Choosing a Career.* Downers Grove: InterVarsity, 1984.

Richardson, Alan. *The Biblical Doctrine of Work.* London· SCM Press, 1952.

Rinehart, James W. *The Tyranny of Work.* New York: Harcourt, Brace, Jovanovich, 1987. Toronto: Longman, 1975.

Rockcastle, Madeline T., ed. *Where to Start: An Annotated Career-Planning Bibliography.* 4th ed. Princeton, N.J.: Peterson's Guides, 1983.

Rollin/Chambliss. *Social Thought from Hammurabi to Comte.* New York: Henry Holt, 1954.

Sabel, Charles F. *Work and Politics.* Cambridge: Cambridge University Press, 1982.

Sayers, Dorothy. *The Mind of the Maker.* New York: Harper & Row 1941.

Schottroff, Luise. "Frauen in der Nachfolge Jesu in neutestamentlicher Zeit," in W. Schottroff and W. Stegemann, eds., *Traditionen der Freiheit.* Munchen: Kaiser, 1980.

Schumacher, E. F. *Good Work.* New York: Harper and Row, Colophon Books, 1979.

Schussler, Elisabeth. "The Jesus Movements as Renewal Movement Within Judaism." in *In Memory of Her*. New York: Crossroad, 1983. pp. 105–154.

Seeman, Melvin in *Alienation and Charisma*. Edited by Benjamin Zablocki New York: Free Press, 1980.

Senger, J. *Individuals, Groups, and the Organization*. Cambridge, Mass.: Winthrop, 1980.

Shelley, Judith Allen. *Not Just a Job: Serving Christ in Your Work*. Downers Grove: InterVarsity Press, 1985.

Simmel, Georg. "The Nature of the Psychic Process and of Communication." in *The Sociology of Georg Simmel*. Glencoe: Free Press, 1950.

Slater, Philip. *The Pursuit of Loneliness*. Boston: Beacon Press, 1970.

Staub, Dick. "9 to 5: A New Look at Christian Career Choices." *Eternity Magazine's Doors '82*.

Temple, William. *Christianity and Social Order*. London: Shepherd-Walwyn, 1976.

Terkel, Studs. *Working*. New York: Avon Books, 1972.

"The Theology of Work" in the *New Catholic Encyclopedia*. New York: McGraw-Hill, 1967.

Toffler, Alvin. *Future Shock*. New York: Bantam Books, 1970.

————. *The Third Wave*. New York: Morrow, 1980.

Tucker, G. H. *It's Your Life, Create a Christian Lifestyle*. Toronto: Anglican Book Centre, 1977.

Tucker, Robert C., ed. *The Marx-Engels Reader*. New York: Norton, 1972.

U.S. Department of Labor, Bureau of Labor Statistics. *Exploring Careers* (pamphlet series). Washington, D.C.: Government Printing Office, 1980.

————. *Occupational Outlook Handbook*. Washington, D.C.: Government Printing Office, 1986.

Weber, Max. *From Max Weber: Essays in Sociology*. New York: Oxford University Press, 1946.

————. *The Protestant Ethic and the Spirit of Capitalism*. New York: Charles Scribner's Sons, 1958.

White, Jerry, and Mary White. *Your Job Survival or Satisfaction*. Grand Rapids, Michigan: Zondervan, 1977.

Williams, Roger. *Tomorrow at Work*. London: British Broadcasting Corporation, 1973.

Wood, Stephen, *The Degradation of Work*. London: Hutchinson, 1982.

"Work, Vocation, Calling," *Encyclopedia of the Lutheran Church*. Minneapolis: Augsburg Publishing House, 1965. p. 2502.

Yankelovich, Daniel. *The New Morality*. New York: McGraw-Hill, 1974.

———— "The Search for Self-Fulfillment: Weak and Strong Forms" in *Psychology Today*, April 1981.

Zwerdling, Daniel. *Workplace Democracy: A Guide to Workplace Owner-ship, Participation, and Self-Management Experiments in the United States and Europe*. New York: Harper Colophon Books, 1980.

Index

Great man 25
Greece 36, 42
Group 87
 and the Christian 87
 informal 87
Growth 123
Guidelines for work 223

Habbegger, Jen 74
Happiness 58-60, 67
Harrassment of women 159
Hegel, George F. 45
Henderson, Hazel 154
Herman, Sadofsky, and Rou-
 berg 177
Hillyard, Marion 101
Hoffer, Eric 99, 102
Hope in God 256
Housework 162
 male 162
Hudson, Margaret 70
Hughes, E. C. 36
Humanity and work 261
Humanization 25, 184
 of work 186-90, 256, 265
Huxley, Aldous 186

Idealism 25
 Hegelian 25
Identity 139
Image, in God's 289
Incompatability of goals 90
Individual 51
 and company goals 89-90
 goals 89
 and group 89
 and work 51, 52, 252
Individualism 255
Institutionalism 269
Integrity, professional 139
Interdependency 255
 through work 255

Jacob 43
Janzen, Pearl 74
Jaspers, Karl 181-82
Jesus 43, 54

 call of 66, 238
 life of 44
 teaching 84, 115, 143
 view of work 44-45, 230
 as worker 44
Jewish tradition 43
Job xii
 defined 221
 deletion 179
 changes 188, 201
 impermanance of 201
 tyranny of the 263
 as work 40
Job choice 267
 changing nature of 267
 security 269
John 43
Journalism 127-28
 Christian 128-29
Judeo-Christian traditional view
 of work 45

Khaldun, Ibn 25
King, Martin Luther 158
Kingdom, earthly 250
Kingdom of God 138
 building 231
 at hand 245
 participants in building 290
 and peoplehood 254-56
 as service 249-50
 and work 246-47
 as work and rest 254
Kingdoms, two 141
Kinship 35
Kornhauser, Arthur 131

Labor 23
 as commodity 112
Labor unions 92
 and the Christian 92-93
 corruption 95
 goals 93
 power-raising 94
Law, Mosaic 43
Lee, Robert 102
Leisure 102-3

Wesley, John 45
Wiebe, Katie 96
Women 34
    ideal Christian 98
    and identity 101–2
    in the labor force 161–62
    and work 97–104, 154
Women's contribution 158
Women's identity, distinction
    of 157
Women's work, denegration of
    155–56
Work 289
    acceptability of 227
    and automation 177
    changing nature of 176
    choosing 58, 109, 195, 244,
        267
    Christian 127–28, 135, 218,
        234
    as commodity 36, 41, 111–
        12
    for community 238–39
    condition of survival 237
    created by God 234
    creating 270
    curses of 262–63
    defines creatureliness 236
    definition of 21, 99, 148–51
    differentiated 34, 35
    and energy 220
    expectations xii
    finding 56, 195
    four types of 218
    future of 262
    glorifying God 239–40
    God's 234, 243, 246
    as human fulfillment 237
    humanizing 256
    as holy 244

    as honorable 235
    as job 35
    in the kingdom of God 252
    loss of 179
    as loving act 235
    man called to 243
    meaningful xii, 20, 27, 265,
        288
    meaningless xiii, 115–17,
        119
    mental 219
    monetary nature of 266
    motives for 287
    in organizations 67
    physical 219
    politics of 103
    preparation for 265–67
    professionalization of 131–33
    psychic 219
    psychological aspect of 252
    qualtity of 22–29, 180
    rationalizing 183
    redeeming quality of 26
    and resting 253–54
    roles 34
    as service to Christ 47
    social 220
    as social structure 240
    sociological analysis of 218
    undifferentiated 30
    as unhealthy 242
    unpredictability of 199, 202
    women's, denigration of
        155–56
    work view 135, 141
Workaholic 287
Worship 247–57
    and work 247–49, 256–57

Xenophon 44